TRACING YOUR ANCESTORS USING DNA

FAMILY HISTORY FROM PEN & SWORD

TRACING YOUR ANCESTORS USING DNA

A Guide for Family and Local Historians

edited by

Graham S. Holton

Contributors

John Cleary, Michelle Leonard,
Iain McDonald, Alasdair F. Macdonald

Pen & Sword
FAMILY HISTORY

First published in Great Britain in 2019
PEN & SWORD FAMILY HISTORY
an imprint of
Pen & Sword Books Ltd
47 Church Street, Barnsley, South Yorkshire, S70 2AS

ISBN 978 1 52673 309 2

Typeset in Palatino and Optima by Chic Graphics

Printed and bound in England by CPI Group (UK), Croydon, CR0 4YY

Pen & Sword Books Ltd incorporates the imprints of Pen & Sword
Airworld, Archaeology, Atlas, Aviation, Battleground, Discovery, Family
History, Fiction, History, Maritime, Military, Military Classics, Politics,
Select, Social History, True Crime, Frontline Books, Leo Cooper,
Remember When, Seaforth Publishing, The Praetorian Press,
Wharncliffe Local History, Wharncliffe Transport,
Wharncliffe True Crime and White Owl.

For a complete list of Pen & Sword titles please contact

PEN & SWORD BOOKS LTD
47 Church Street, Barnsley, South Yorkshire, S70 2AS, England
E-mail: enquiries@pen-and-sword.co.uk
Website: www.pen-and-sword.co.uk
or
PEN & SWORD BOOKS LTD
1950 Lawrence Rd., Havertown, PA 19083, USA
E-mail: Uspen-and-sword@casematepublishers.com
Website: www.penandswordbooks.com

CONTENTS

INTRODUCTION

Graham S. Holton

This is a book on a very new field of study known as genetic genealogy – the application of DNA testing to genealogical research. In less than twenty years, it has grown from a rather speculative interest of a few enthusiasts to a topic with widespread appeal. Mass marketing by testing companies and frequent media coverage has now achieved a high profile for the topic among the general public. The motivation behind an interest in this field may range from those hoping to find answers to questions arising from their genealogical research, to adoptees and other individuals who are seeking to identify their biological parents. This book aims to appeal to the whole range of interest groups and to both those new to the topic and those with some experience.

As you will see, this is a collaborative work, for the simple reason that we believe this will produce the best book possible. There are a number of specific fields of interest within genetic genealogy, some relating to the type of DNA test used, some to the technical aspects of analysing test results and yet others using statistical mathematics to investigate how to date when a common ancestor was living. To these should be added the whole question of the use of ancient DNA, which is now becoming important for its benefits to genealogy. The book draws on the varied expertise of the contributors to give a wide-ranging, but often detailed, view of the topic. If we have succeeded in our aim, it will give both practical guidance on DNA tests and their interpretation and a deeper understanding of the whole field.

Due to the fact that genetic genealogy is such a fast-developing area, producing an up-to-date book on the subject is a challenge, but we have made every effort to do just that, including making some predictions about what developments might be seen in the future.

Making best use of this book

As already indicated, the book contains both practical guidance and broader discussion, and this may affect how you use it. If your priority is to gain a working knowledge of the types of DNA tests available, the results from these and how to interpret them, you can access this in the core chapters of the book, chapters 4–6, dealing with autosomal, Y and mitochondrial DNA testing. Having said this, you will find important pointers on what to look for in choosing companies to test with in Chapter 7 and information on the scientific basis of the tests, which it is helpful to understand, in Chapter 3. If you have particular concerns about questions of ethics and privacy, or are planning to encourage others to take a DNA test, Chapter 2 is the place to go for an informative and thought-provoking look at this important aspect. Since comparison of test results is such an important component of genetic genealogy, DNA projects can be very valuable in helping advance your research. Although newcomers may not realise their significance, we feel some time spent considering this is very worthwhile and is dealt with in Chapter 8. As there will be increasing use of different tests to help answer research questions, Chapter 9 briefly introduces some means of doing this, illustrated with a number of practical case studies. Chapters 10 and 11 look to the future. Although the first of these chapters gives the background to the testing of ancient DNA, its principal purposes are to emphasise the importance of very careful consideration and planning for any projects involving ancient DNA, the significant role that genealogists can play in these and how this type of work can benefit genealogical research in the future. The final chapter discusses the likely increases in the number of test-takers and the level of tests taken, technical developments in the tests being offered and holds out some intriguing possibilities for other future developments.

Challenges

Our subject area has often been seen as challenging – complex and difficult to understand. There has been some justification for this view, but some of the complexity has been caused by particular circumstances and some was perhaps avoidable.

Testing company websites are not always particularly user-friendly and can leave new test-takers confused and bewildered due to a lack of simple explanations. The recent very strong focus on 'ethnicity' estimates (more appropriately called 'admixture estimates') has promoted, very successfully, probably the most unreliable feature of DNA testing for genealogy, in its current state of development. By far the most important feature is the ability to compare how closely test results match in order to predict relationships. It is possible that test-takers disappointed with their admixture estimates may be discouraged from pursuing genetic genealogy and remain unaware of its more useful outcomes.

Currently by far the largest proportion of test-takers are from North America, which in some ways impedes progress in discovering long descents. Immigrant families without any knowledge of, but a great interest in, their earlier origins, find a lack of matches with families in the previous homelands to help them identify these origins. An increase in the number of test-takers from the 'Old World' would be very much welcomed.

Terminology can be rather confusing, partly because of inconsistencies in usage. It is worth being aware that the terms *haplogroup*, *subhaplogroup* and *subclade* can be used rather loosely. There are also different notations used to describe genetic groupings, such as R1b1a1a2, now generally known as R-M269. The general trend now favours the shorthand version. One final point on terminology is that distinct markers called SNPs (usually pronounced 'snips') may have been given two or more different names, because they were identified independently by different labs or analysts. These are alternative names for the same SNP marker. This should not be confused with the concept of equivalent SNPs. These are different markers which are believed to have occurred at the same point in time.

Having highlighted some challenges, we hope that on reading this book, you will overcome these and become competent genetic genealogists. To further develop your knowledge and skills, there are many blogs written by prominent genetic genealogists which deal with specific aspects of the subject and are well worth referring to. In the further reading list we have provided a number of references to books, articles and webpages which you may wish to follow up. There are also various courses and learning opportunities available, but one of the best ways to learn more is by working with actual DNA test results.

Chapter 11 deals with the future. There is much still to be learnt about this subject, but the more test results there are available for study, the greater the opportunities for a deeper understanding. One of the ways to encourage greater participation will be through more user-friendly websites, utilities and tools, which can assist test-takers in analysing and understanding their results. Much analysis can be carried out manually, but is often laborious, so the automation of more of these tasks would be very beneficial in fostering greater activity in the field. A number of such tools are already available and are mentioned later, such as DNApainter, various triangulation tools and Lazarus (from GEDmatch).

Genetics in relation to genetic genealogy – some key milestones
The history of genetics as it impacts on genetic genealogy has seen important contributions from many individuals, particularly from the time of Gregor Mendel (1822–84) onwards. Now recognised as the founder of the science of genetics, Mendel began his experiments with plants – mainly pea plants – in 1856, which resulted in the laws of Mendelian inheritance. These stated that traits were inherited as discrete traits, some being recessive and others dominant. His work was largely ignored for many years and although Charles Darwin possessed a copy of Mendel's paper on inheritance, the pages were found to be uncut and unread!

Early names in the study of surnames and genetics included George Darwin (son of Charles) and, on hereditary genius, Francis Galton. In the first few years of the twentieth century, Mendel's work was rediscovered and shortly after, the concept of genetic linkage was established and then further researched by Thomas Hunt Morgan (1866–1945), after whom the unit of measurement of the probability of genetic recombination, the centiMorgan, was named. You will hear plenty more about this later.

Two of the best-known names are, of course, those of James Watson and Francis Crick, credited with the discovery of the structure of DNA in 1953, although others such as Rosalind Franklin played an important role.

Sanger sequencing, still a much-used technique in DNA sequencing, was developed by Frederick Sanger in 1977, and in around 1984 Alec

Jeffreys introduced DNA fingerprinting. These two processes formed the basis for the basic Y-DNA testing used in genetic genealogy.

Brian Sykes, who did much to popularise the subject of genetic genealogy through his writings, established Oxford Ancestors in England in 2000, while the first company to offer commercial DNA testing for genealogy, Family Tree DNA, was founded by Bennett Greenspan in the USA in the same year. In the meantime, the Human Genome Project, a massive project to map the whole human genome, launched in 1990, was proceeding with its work, which was completed in 2003.

Two further important milestones were reached in 2005 and 2013, when Next Generation Sequencing (NGS) became available, firstly to genomic science in 2005 and then genetic genealogy in 2013. This allowed much larger portions of the human genome to be read than had been possible with earlier technology, proving a major benefit to genetic genealogists.

Undoubtedly there will be more milestones to come. Who knows what might be round the corner?

CONTRIBUTORS

John Cleary
John Cleary is a linguist and lecturer living in Scotland, and author of *So long as the world shall endure* (1991), a history of life in two almshouses. He gives talks across the UK, Ireland and North America on using Y and autosomal DNA to uncover the origins and history of surnames, and is involved in a number of DNA surname projects, including one for the ancient Scottish surname, Cumming.

Graham S. Holton
Graham has a background as a professional librarian, with a lifelong interest in family history. He has been a tutor on the University of Strathclyde's postgraduate programme in Genealogical Studies since it commenced in 2007 and is the author of *Discover your Scottish Ancestry* (2nd ed. 2009). He leads the Battle of Bannockburn and Declaration of Arbroath Family History Projects, focusing on tracing early descents using documentary and genetic evidence.

Michelle Leonard
Michelle Leonard is a professional genealogist, DNA detective, writer and historian. She is an expert in the genealogical use of autosomal DNA and runs her own business, Genes & Genealogy, specializing in solving all manner of unknown ancestor mysteries. She also undertakes traditional research, television research, tutoring, webinars and speaking engagements. Additionally, Michelle is the official genetic genealogist of ancestryhour.co.uk and is known for her work helping to identify First World War soldiers.

Alasdair F. Macdonald
Alasdair is a Teaching Fellow in Genealogical Studies at the University of Strathclyde. With research interests focusing on the use of DNA in genealogical research, he is currently researching the origin and linkage

of male lineages in the British Isles. He also specialises in the history and genealogy of Scottish Clans. Alasdair is a volunteer administrator for a number of projects including the Scottish DNA Project and the Flemish in Scotland DNA Project.

Iain McDonald

Iain McDonald is an astrophysicist and Honorary Fellow in Genealogical, Palaeographic and Heraldic Studies at the University of Strathclyde. His expertise lies in the statistical analysis of Y-DNA tests to identify the relationships between individual test-takers, and the migrations of families over historical and prehistorical time periods. He helps run several independent and company-led projects for the Y-DNA haplogroup R-U106, and assists with Family Tree DNA's Scottish Y-DNA project.

Chapter 1

WHY USE DNA TESTING FOR GENEALOGY?

Michelle Leonard, Alasdair F. Macdonald,
Graham S. Holton

Direct to consumer DNA testing has brought about a revolution in genealogy and is now a very significant resource available for family history. It is a unique new tool in the genealogist's toolbox, but it is important to understand both the benefits and the limitations of each type of test, which we will cover in detail in later chapters.

There are three different types of DNA test available on the market: autosomal DNA (atDNA) (which includes the X-chromosome), Y-chromosome DNA (Y-DNA) and mitochondrial DNA (mtDNA). Autosomal DNA testing has exploded in the last few years and is now the most popular of these tests. Over 30 million people have now taken an autosomal DNA test across all of the different testing companies (over 15 million of these at AncestryDNA alone). All three types of test have their own merits and drawbacks, however, so it is necessary to learn how to work with each of them. This book aims to give you a practical guide to using DNA testing as part of your genealogical research.

Here are some of the top reasons to use DNA testing for genealogy.

Connecting with new cousins
One of the most exciting aspects of using DNA for genealogy is identifying and connecting with new cousins. All of the major testing companies supply you with a cousin match list, which contains people who have also tested on the same platform and share some DNA with

1

you. These lists are organised by closest to most distant, so investigating the top of your match list will be one of the most thrilling moments when you first get your results.

It is important to contact your matches, as sharing information with each other could help you work out your cousin connection. Often you will be connecting with cousins who share your love of family history and may wish to collaborate on your shared lines, so getting to know your new cousins can be really rewarding. You will have many thousands of matches with whom you will never be able to find the link and many will not respond, but those that do may have photographs, documents, family stories and memorabilia they are willing to share with you. More and more people are testing all the time and your match list will grow on a daily basis, with more confirmed cousins who may be able to help with your family history research. Can you imagine how many cousin connections we are all going to have a few years from now? Be proactive and contact your cousins if you want to get the most out of your DNA test.

Adding new branches to your family tree

Adding new branches to your tree goes hand in hand with identifying new cousins via DNA. In general these new branches will be from collateral lines: that is, the descendants of the siblings of your direct ancestors. Collateral line brick walls or gaps are very common – many people only research their direct ancestors or get stuck tracing collateral lines forward, especially if emigration is involved. Your new cousin matches are likely to be able to provide information you are missing on collateral lines since they are the direct descendants of those lines. They can help you flesh out your tree in many different ways and focus your research on the right areas.

Breaking down brick walls

We all have them and we all want to break them down! They are frustrating and challenging but DNA can help. Which test can aid you the most will depend on how far back and on which line your brick wall is located. If you have a brick wall within the last 5–7 generations then autosomal testing is definitely worth trying, but it is imperative to identify and test the most valuable family members available. With atDNA that means testing your older generations if at all possible. For example, if your brick wall is a paternal third great-grandfather and your father is alive and willing, then test your father as he possesses double the DNA from that ancestor. You may have to test a number of different relatives to maximize the amount of the mystery ancestor's DNA you have to work with. Additionally, if the brick wall is on a Y-DNA (paternal) or mtDNA (maternal) line and there is a Y-DNA or mtDNA test-taker available, you could also gain insight from those tests. Cousin matches can aid you in identifying the correct ancestors to break down brick walls and enhance your tree in the process.

Testing hypotheses

If documentation does not exist to provide evidence of a particular relationship, DNA may be able to fill that void. Depending on which line and how far back the relationship falls you could use atDNA, Y-DNA or mtDNA testing to gain insight. If you are looking for evidence for a hypothesis about a sixth great-grandparent, for instance, you will likely need to turn to Y-DNA or mtDNA due to the limited reach of atDNA. If the theory is about a direct paternal line you should look to Y-DNA, and if it is on a direct maternal line then explore mtDNA. Notice I do not say 'your' direct paternal or maternal lines here; that is because there is no reason to limit yourself to these so long as you can find appropriate test-takers on the Y or mt line the mystery is on. If you have a closer mystery (e.g. grandparent or great-grandparent) for which you want to test a hypothesis, you can use atDNA to assess this. For example, you could test yourself then trace forward to living descendants of the potential grandparent to find one who is willing to test. Their results should prove or disprove your hypothesis depending on whether or not and how well they match you.

Surname studies

Surnames continue to be a primary research interest for genealogists and historians due to their linkage to documentary evidence. There may also be an emotional or cultural significance to bearing a particular surname. Unlike our genome, which cannot be replaced as it is who we are, our surname can be changed. If we are female, it may be by marriage. For males, surname inheritance can be more fickle, as the direct line of transmission down the generations can be interrupted due to illegitimacy, unrecorded adoption and personal choice.

Illegitimacy, formal or informal adoption, remarriage of widows causing children to adopt a different name and change of name due to female inheritance are some of the more common reasons for change of surname. Some of these lead to significant problems with genealogical research, resulting in brick walls that until the introduction of DNA testing appeared insurmountable.

Although atDNA tests are advertised as analysing DNA from all your recent ancestors, including your father, they do not test the Y-chromosome if you are a male. This needs a specific test of its own.

In practical terms, a surname mirrors the transmission of the male specific Y-chromosome that is passed from a father to his son (or sons) who pass it to their sons in an unbroken line of descent. Females do not have a Y-chromosome, so to investigate a surname using a Y-DNA test they must rely on a male relative to test on their behalf.

The parallel progression of a surname with a specific Y-chromosome signature down the generations can in theory be used to corroborate the hypothesis that males bearing the same surname, or a variant, share the same patrilineal ancestor. The exact identity of that shared ancestor might be quite recent or in the distant past, but as a rule cannot be identified from a single Y-DNA test. In certain circumstances it may be possible to identify the common shared ancestor, but only if extensive testing of individuals has been undertaken within the framework of a lineage that has well-documented descents. Similarly, combining Y-DNA testing with other types of evidence, such as an autosomal test result, may identify a candidate for the most recent common ancestor.

There are two types of DNA test used for investigating surnames – Short Tandem Repeats (STRs) and Single Nucleotide Polymorphisms (SNPs). It is important to understand the purpose of each type of Y-DNA test as they are quite different from one another. Genetic genealogists use both types of test for investigating surnames. Failure to do so can lead to misinterpretation of STR matching. Not all companies offer both types of Y-DNA test and the main vendors of autosomal tests do not offer any.

Surname research using DNA testing is not an individual pursuit.

You need to test with a company that has a relational database and be willing to share details of your most distant known patrilineal ancestor. To gain the most from such testing it is also advantageous to join a surname project such as those hosted at Family Tree DNA.

Mapping your DNA back to your ancestors

This is a more advanced reason for testing, so it is not advisable to attempt it when you are just starting out on your DNA journey, but it is a really interesting exercise to undertake down the line when you have more experience and additional confirmed cousins in the databases. It is a technique known as chromosome mapping, and it basically consists of assigning segments of your DNA to specific ancestors or ancestral couples. In order to map this DNA you have to be able to identify confirmed relationships between yourself and your DNA matches, because it is the segments you share with them that can be mapped back to your common ancestors. It is interesting and exciting to know which bits of your DNA came from which of your ancestors, but it is not just a curiosity, because it is extremely helpful for DNA matching. Whenever you get new matches that match you on any of the segments that you have been able to map back to particular ancestors, you can narrow down how you match that new person enormously.

Confirming the lines of your tree

You might think verifying your direct ancestors using DNA would just be telling you what you already know and thus not very exciting, but that is not the case at all. It is telling you that what you think you already know is actually accurate! It is priceless verification to add to your paper-trail evidence. DNA is the only record set that does not and cannot make mistakes or lie – human beings can and do both on occasion. No matter how great a researcher you are and how well-sourced your family tree is, it can always be erroneous for reasons beyond your control. For those of us who have spent many years meticulously researching our family trees, or even for those just starting out on that journey, to have confirmation that you genuinely share segments of DNA with the ancestors you have identified on paper is gold-dust supporting evidence. Of course you have to be aware that instead of confirming your tree is correct, DNA could do the opposite and you may end up having to research ancestors you did not know you had. Thankfully this situation is rare, but there is always that risk and you have to go into DNA testing with your eyes wide open. Verifying ancestors is the one thing that most people are likely to be able to do when they get their results and is one of the very best reasons to DNA test for family history.

Adoption and all unknown ancestor mysteries
There are some genealogical puzzles traditional research can never solve, as the documentation simply does not exist. DNA has opened up a whole new world of possibilities for those with adoption, unknown parentage, donor conception, foundling, unknown grandparentage, illegitimacy, and other unknown ancestor mysteries. Adoptees and those with an unknown parent are increasingly using DNA testing to identify their birth parents and connect with close family members. If you were adopted or have a recent unknown ancestor you have to be aware that you may uncover your birth relatives if you test, and anyone who tests has to be aware they may match with an adoptee or previously unknown close relative. If you have a recent unknown ancestor mystery, DNA may be the only way you can solve it. For example, if you have your grandfather's birth certificate and on it there is only the mother's name and a blank space where the father's name should be, there is nobody alive who can tell you who that mystery man was, and there is no documentation that can inform you either. DNA just might help! Using cousin matching it is possible to solve these puzzles and identify your mystery ancestors. There can never be any guarantee of success in these cases, as they are dependent on the relatives who have already tested or will test from the mystery ancestor's family, but with more people testing every day more and more answers are coming to light.

Admixture
Uncovering your admixture percentages is the best known and advertised aspect of DNA testing. All of the main DNA testing companies supply admixture reports as part of their autosomal offerings. These are commonly referred to as 'ethnicity estimates' but

we will be referring to them throughout this book under the more appropriate term of 'admixture'. For some test-takers, this will be their first foray into genealogy and admixture may be the only information they seek; knowing how Irish, Scandinavian or Native American they are forming part of their 'identity'. Admixture results are thought to be generally accurate to the continental level, but should not be taken too literally. They can, however, give you a broad idea of your origins and may provide genealogical clues if you were adopted or have a recent unknown ancestor mystery. You have to be aware that they will vary between companies, because each company has its own reference populations. Admixture is an emerging science, and although it will improve over time as more people test and reference populations increase, it is best not to read too much into the percentages you receive. It is the DNA cousin match list that is also supplied with an atDNA test that is the most useful aspect of your autosomal results when it comes to using DNA testing for genealogy.

Early ancestral origins

While admixture results inform about overall genetic make-up by comparison to company reference populations, research into early ancestral origins uses the two types of DNA that do not randomly recombine at fertilisation but remain intact. These are our mitochondrial DNA (mtDNA), inherited by children, both males and females, from their mothers, and the male specific Y-chromosome. These types of DNA have a direct lineal descent with no interference from other ancestral lines, so their migration over time can be plotted. Associating an ethnic or tribal group to a particular genetic marker such as Viking, Pictish or Celtic became fashionable for a time, partly as a marketing ploy by certain test companies. The problem with this approach is that ethnic groups and tribes in Western Europe were not homogenous. They may have had a shared cultural identity, but would have included individuals with distinctly different genetic origins for both their male and female ancestors. Another issue with inferring early ancestral origins is that until recently most data was from the results of self-selecting individuals alive today, with inherent problems of unrepresentative sampling and the simple problem that our ancestors moved about and left no physical trace. Nevertheless, the wealth of genetic data emanating from Next

Generation Sequencing tests (NGS) is enabling significantly improved and more refined branching of both mtDNA and Y-DNA lineages. Together with the influx of genetic data from ancient remains (aDNA), the dating of branching is slowly improving. Better sampling is leading to a much improved and refined genetic tree. The geographical frequency and distribution of specific DNA markers can be overlaid on the genetic tree, potentially providing evidence of the migration routes of particular lineages.

When genetic testing for genealogy first started, early ancestral origins were traditionally thought of as research into ancient origins thousands of years ago. This is certainly a valid area of research, however today we ought to think about the timeframe before documentary evidence was typically used for genealogy. This means the mediaeval period back to the time of early recorded history. With this as a focus, increasingly test-takers are collaborating to research the interrelationships between lineages bearing different surnames or who carry a specific DNA marker. In the vast majority of cases there is no comparative historical evidence with which to complement the emerging new genetic data.

However, there are exciting areas for research to explore if traditional pedigrees and oral tradition mirror the genetic evidence. Here are some examples. Researchers are investigating the provincial kings of Connacht, Munster, Leinster and Ulster as recorded in the Irish Annals using the Y-DNA of Irish men. Further afield the people of the Levant (Eastern Mediterranean) are being researched. One particular project is focused on the Druze people, using Y-DNA along with historical and oral record sources. The Druze community are composed of those who are descendants strictly in the direct patrilineal line from the clans and families that accepted the Druze faith from 1017–43 CE, after which no new adherents to the faith were allowed.

As there is so much more mitochondrial DNA in our cells than DNA found within our cell nucleus, it survives much better in ancient remains. It has therefore been used for many years in studies focusing on the origins and migration of female family groups. If you have your mtDNA sequenced you will be able to track your maternal origins with a degree of success back to its locus, perhaps in the Middle East or further afield, depending on its type. Early origin research into female lines is hampered for the most part, as communities were patriarchal in nature and females were not recorded in early documents. However, the case of King Richard III of England, whose remains were found in a Leicestershire car park and corroborated with the help of mitochondrial DNA from descendants of his sister, has demonstrated the potential for research into early ancestral origins.

Leaving a legacy

Another reason to DNA test is to leave a legacy for your descendants. The way atDNA inheritance works means that older generations have more of our ancestors' DNA than we do: parents have double, grandparents have triple and so on. The more DNA from our ancestors that we have to work with then the more cousin connections we can identify, the more branches we can add to our trees and the more brick walls we can break down. Test your older generations and, if you are the oldest generation, test yourself to leave a legacy for the generations to come.

Which questions can actually be answered?

Genetic genealogy tests can explore questions that were previously impossible to answer. As we each carry around in us a genetic record of some of our ancestors, the scope of questions that can be answered by testing is limited only by the laws of genetic inheritance and who is available to test.

Having said that, in the majority of cases you may not get a straightforward answer to your question. Firstly, matches, if there are any, will need to be interpreted accurately. If matching is lacking or limited then you may need to be proactive in recruiting others to test to confirm or dismiss your hypothesis.

The type of question that can be answered is largely dependent on whether DNA testing can actually answer it, or provide evidence towards answering it. Start with a hypothesis or statement. Next, identify which test might help towards answering it. Be mindful of the limitations caused by genetic inheritance patterns. Finally, identify which individuals would need to take that test or tests to provide enough genetic evidence to be evaluated and show beyond doubt the hypothesis is right or wrong?

Questions involving use of atDNA will likely need multiple test-takers in order to establish a high degree of probability. Just one mtDNA test might be enough to show that two individuals do not share the same maternal ancestor. Investigation into the early ancestry of a male who matches various other surnames but not his own will likely require investment in further testing. Often the questions that can be answered by DNA testing are not limited by genetics or the tests themselves. Limitations are often to do with the need to recruit and test more individuals, a requirement to increase the resolution of the test or the type of test used.

Can expectations be exceeded?

The answer to this question is always that it depends on your expectations! If you take a DNA test just to see your admixture percentages, then your results may appear to be underwhelming: you need to be prepared to delve into your cousin matches. If you take a DNA test thinking you will suddenly know everything about your family history, without putting a lot of hard work into both building your family tree in the traditional sense and investigating your matches, then you will be disappointed. If, however, you are willing to put that work in, then yes, expectations can be exceeded – many fantastic discoveries and connections can be made, brick walls can be broken down and mysteries can be solved. If you have a mystery and expect to find an answer as soon as you get your results, you may get lucky and find a close enough match to provide that instant answer, but that will not be the case for the majority of people. Again, you will have to be willing to put the work in to solve the mystery.

One area in which expectations may be exceeded is in discovering unknown mediaeval descents. In this context we will define the medieval period as lasting from around 1100 to 1500. Mediaeval genealogy for the masses may become a real possibility through the use of genetic genealogy. The fact is that as a result of downward social mobility from the nobility in England and Scotland, many of the present-day population in the UK and descendants of emigrants from the UK are descended from the mediaeval nobility. It was estimated in 1911 that the living descendants of the English King Edward III probably numbered at least 80 to 100,000. Of course the vast majority of these descents are lying hidden due to lack of documentary evidence. Now, genetic genealogy opens up the prospect of rediscovering these links to mediaeval times with some examples already existing.

Research which formed part of the Battle of Bannockburn Family History Project established genetic links between participants in the battle in 1314 and living individuals who could only document their ancestry back to the late seventeenth or early eighteenth century. Using Y-DNA testing, a McDonald living in Canada was shown to be descended in the male line from Angus 'Og' of the Isles, while a number of Stewarts living in North America are now known to descend from the Stewarts of Bute, whose ancestor Walter Stewart, 6th High Steward of Scotland, also fought in the battle.

The potential to reveal unknown mediaeval descents such as these can be extended by the use of documentary research. A descendant through a female line from a family of Stewarts in Bute was able to prove a genealogical link to one of the Stewarts in North America, using traditional documentary research. Since that family had a genetically established link back to Walter Stewart, the female line descendants now also know that they share the same mediaeval ancestry.

Conclusion
There was suspicion of DNA testing, in the early days at least, that it was somehow in competition with traditional research, but nothing could be further from the truth. The fact is that you cannot get the most out of DNA testing without traditional research, and now that we have the fantastic resource that DNA provides you cannot get the most out of traditional research without also taking DNA evidence into account. Think of DNA as an additional new record set you can use in conjunction with all the regular record sets: it is not a panacea and cannot give you all the answers, but it can add crucial evidence to what you already know, or think you know.

When you get the results of an autosomal DNA test and you first look at your DNA match list, barring any close relatives that may have tested, you are not going to be able to make sense of how the people on your match list relate to you without traditional genealogy. You need to be able to build a robust family tree and use it in reference to the trees of your matches. For instance, 3rd cousins share 2nd great-

11

grandparents, so if a 3rd cousin tests but one or both of you do not know who your 2nd great-grandparents were, then neither of you will be able to recognize the connection! At that point you have to delve back into the records to build both trees out before you can identify the link.

DNA alone will not break down your brick walls or confirm the lines of your tree, but it can if used in conjunction with traditional research. Not only are traditional genealogy and genetic genealogy a great complement to each other, but employing them together is essential for maximizing your research.

Chapter 2

THE ETHICAL AND LEGAL ASPECTS OF GENETIC GENEALOGY

John Cleary

Obtaining DNA samples – ethics and informed consent

When using DNA samples from relatives, new acquaintances or unknown people there are two big principles you should keep in mind. Firstly there is the sensitivity of DNA, which carries delicate information about people – health and disease risks, ancestry or potentially non-ancestry, and ethnic origins. Everyone has the right to *privacy* over their DNA, even when taking part in a hobby that involves sharing and publishing parts of their DNA sequences. If you are organising a family DNA project, you need to act to maintain the levels of privacy that each of your test-takers would feel comfortable with.

The second thing to bear in mind is that you will be leading a research project that involves other people. Your discoveries could in some cases be unexpected, embarrassing or otherwise difficult to accept. Most people will probably enjoy hearing about what you discover, but there will always be a small number of discoveries that conflict with memories or expectations and potentially upset relations between family members. When conducting research involving other people, it is essential to use '*do no harm*' as the basic principle to underpin every decision that you make. Anyone you invite to take part in your research by giving a DNA sample has a right to know in advance why you are taking the sample and exactly how you will use it – before they give that sample.

If fully informed in this way, the people you approach to test their

DNA can give *informed consent*. Respecting their ownership of their own DNA sample and results, and their right to determine the limits for its use and public exposure, is the basis of ethical research in genetic genealogy.

What is privacy (when DNA is concerned)?

Privacy is a concept growing in importance in today's data-driven society; because DNA encodes information about individuals, contemporary beliefs and anxieties about privacy are deeply connected with it. While some years ago the term 'privacy' would be used by most people to refer to their domestic world, separate from the public worlds of work, entertainment or politics, today it captures a tension between the public sharing of data about ourselves via social media, the collection of information about the details of our personalities and lives by public and private organisations, and the anxieties we feel about being drawn into these webs of information.

With genealogical DNA testing, many test-takers keenly feel these tensions, and the people who work with you will have differing degrees of comfort about the public sharing of their results. Their willingness to share results and their comfort in doing so is affected by the *gains* they perceive from it (for their own research and for the general good of helping others with theirs), and the *control* they feel they have over who will see their data and what use they will put it to. How privacy feelings are developing in a data-sharing society has been explored in a recent article by Lee Rainie and Maeve Duggan, 'Privacy and Information Sharing', a thought-provoking follow-up piece on the broader topic.

Considering genetic genealogy and DNA testing, you must first decide your own attitudes towards privacy. You will need to consider that large parts of your DNA are shared by your family members, distant relatives and even complete strangers. If you are testing the Y chromosome or mtDNA, then almost identical Ys will be found in all your patrilineal male relatives, and mtDNA in your matrilineal ones – publishing your data means you are publishing theirs too. There are relatively few sensitive regions in the Y data that you are likely to publish, but there are several significant health-related sites on the mtDNA coding region, which even test-takers with an open attitude to data-sharing lean towards keeping private.

Autosomal DNA is shared in progressively smaller amounts as relatives become more distant from you, but your siblings, parents, children and other close relatives out to second cousins share large amounts of your sequence. Here is the dilemma: it is these shared sequences that allow us to find our unknown relatives – but they are not only ours, they are theirs too, and belong to others who have not tested, or might not want to test and share. Some argue that we are becoming aware of privacy just as we are losing it – and that the world of the near future may expect it less, as we are captured in ever-bigger data.Younger people already seem more comfortable with lower degrees of data privacy, as evidence of social media use may suggest. But there are potential minefields here that need to be navigated if you test other people and share their data – and especially if you begin to run larger projects with multiple test-takers, either informally or as an administrator of an established project (see Chapter 8).

Here are some elements of privacy in respect of managing DNA test results that you may want to build into your practice, when working with other people's DNA, or when permitting others to make use of yours:

- *Control of your information* – which platforms may it be uploaded to?
- *Right to limit (or permit) access to your information* – who may see it under what conditions? Which levels of visibility may it have on public platforms?
- *Freedom from surveillance or being identified (the 'right to be let alone')* – confidentiality, including whether and how your name or identifying information is, or is not, linked to your data.
- *Security from misuse of your data* – it must not be possible to identify information about you that you had not chosen to reveal, or for your personal contact details to be farmed by external agents.
- *Protection against secondary uses of your data you did not consciously permit* – like reselling your data or re-parcelling it for other research purposes, unless you had explicitly given consent for it.

These aspects overlap to a certain extent, but underlying them all are *control* (over who accesses the data, when and how); *confidentiality and security* (of your data when it is in the hands of others); and *use* (what was agreed to and nothing else that was not openly agreed to).

Many countries have legislation in place to regulate data privacy and protect citizens. In May 2018 the General Data Protection Regulation (GDPR) of the European Union took effect, implemented and supported in the UK by the Data Protection Act, 2018. GDPR and DPA 2018 grant strong powers to the Information Commissioner to protect the personal information that organisations hold on individuals resident within the EU and UK, with stringent fines for misuse. While individual genetic genealogists are unlikely to fall foul of GDPR, the Regulation and Act put the onus on 'data processors' to demonstrate they are applying maximum care and confidentiality over the private, personal information of the people they work with – and this is best practice for any genetic genealogist who handles the personal and DNA data of another person.

Ethics and research

Linked to privacy rights over data is ethical conduct of research. In universities and professional research organisations, research proposals are vetted by ethics committees to ensure that people involved in research or impacted by it are protected from risks arising from their involvement. A hobby genealogist working with documents has probably had limited concerns over the ethical impact of their pastime, apart from considering the effect a shocking family story may have on a family member. But with testing relatives' DNA becoming a common activity, the close involvement of other people forces the researcher to think about the ethics of research more in the manner of a professional researcher.

As well as the privacy issues discussed above, a number of risks to the wellbeing of your research partners are created by testing DNA. The 'non-paternity event' (NPE) (discussed in Chapter 5) can be a colourful family story when it is a few centuries back in time, but when it turns out to be someone's grandparent or parent that was the child of an unknown past affair, this can be upsetting to a person and undermine their happiness. If the objective is to investigate a rumoured, suspected NPE in recent generations that directly impacts upon a living person, it should be prepared carefully, with the involvement of the person(s) who will be most affected, so they are not harmed by the discovery. See p20 for a case in which the revelation of a recent NPE by a DNA test had profound consequences for the people involved.

DNA tests bought as presents have revealed unknown children or half-siblings, and such events can tear families apart. There is a substantial cottage industry of adoption searching in the genetic genealogy world, with both professional genetic genealogists and volunteer 'search angels' offering help to adoptees or donor-conceived children to find their birth parents. Even done with sensitivity and accuracy, this can be a traumatic experience for discovered parents who were promised anonymity, and for adopted children who must face parents who gave them up as children; if done incorrectly or insensitively, there is a tremendous prospect for harm. The more people impacted by a study, or the greater the risk of traumatic information being revealed, the more the genetic genealogist should think about adopting ethical procedures used by professional research specialists.

Here are some basic principles in *research ethics*. These are adapted for genetic genealogy from the **Key Ethics Principles** put forward by the Economic and Social Research Council (ESRC) of the UK in its *The Research Ethics Guidebook* (website). Though intended for students and academic researchers, the *Guidebook* is worth exploring for further information on research ethics. 'Study' here refers to any project you may develop using DNA to answer genealogical questions, and 'partners' is meant generally to include anyone who collaborates with you, helps raise funds, carries out interpretation of results, or donates their DNA for you to sequence.

- *Design your study with care to ensure its quality and integrity.* This makes sure it is worth doing, and will not waste the time, resources or money of you or your partners.
- *Inform your partners fully of what you want to do, how their participation will help you, and be upfront about any risks.* This is one component of obtaining informed consent.
- *Guarantee the confidentiality of your partners' data, and preserve the anonymity of your partners' DNA sequences.* Only ever publish their real names if it is necessary to do so and if they have given prior informed consent for you to do so.
- *Participation by your partners must be voluntary and not coerced.* They

have the right to withdraw from your study at any time and to withdraw their data from the study if they do so. This is the second component of obtaining informed consent.

- *Do no harm.* Analyse risks in advance and ensure your partners are aware of them.
- *Do good.* Be independent of, or open and honest about, any conflicts of interest.

Obtaining informed consent

The ethical research principles in the last section are underpinned by the process of obtaining informed consent from research partners. Imagine you have been introduced to a possible distant relative, or someone who has your surname of interest from a line you have not tested before. Maybe this person is not especially interested in genealogy and knows little about it, but wants to help you and agrees to test. You need to explain in full what you are trying to discover, how their DNA may help, and what the process of sampling, testing and analysis involves. Sometimes it can be difficult to cover all this in a conversation – there may be other people or things to do that can distract. Your partner may be generally interested, but not particularly interested in the details. They may be confused by any risks you explain, if suddenly the process starts to sound risky or dangerous. How best to obtain informed consent in this type of situation?

Professional researchers are under the oversight of ethics committees, and will usually need to collect written and signed evidence of consent. Consent forms generally contain two parts:

- *An information statement*: a concise summary of the goals of the research, with key details on how the person will be involved, what they will need to do, and of any risks.
- *A consent statement*: a *pro forma* which the person will sign to signal their agreement to the process as they understand it; and to acknowledge they have been informed of the right of withdrawal.

Professional researchers may also provide a third party, who is not the researcher, who can be contacted in case the research partner feels the need to discuss an issue with someone who is not the investigator.

18

It is arguable that a genetic genealogy project, particularly a small-scale one, would not need to follow all the steps above. Informed consent statements can be long and use complex or legalistic language, which can be off-putting in the world of pastime genealogy research. For genealogists, their partners are often family or possible family, and a bureaucratic process can get in the way of building relationships with them, seeming cold and impersonal – at odds with the personal nature of investigating shared ancestry.

In fact, such misgivings are often felt by professional researchers like anthropologists or sociologists too, as their research with people is built around trust, exploring shared values and the appearance of friendship. Anthropologists accept that informed consent can be given in different ways, including verbal assent in conversation. Genealogists need to develop ways of achieving consent that suit their needs. Receiving a verbal agreement may well be enough, or a short email that confirms the partner has thought about what was said and is happy to agree with it. An informal written information statement to leave with people who have tested, or a short email laying out the key facts, will help to meet the informed component, as well as giving the partners something to refer to if they forget the details. Figure 1 gives an example of how this could look.

Thanks very much for agreeing to take part in my study. I really appreciate it. Here's what I'm trying to do – our surname Squitch is very unusual, and it only seems to be found in Cheshire. Since you live there, you might be from one of the oldest branches of the name to live continuously in the county, and we might be distantly related.

We will ask the testing company to read 37 markers on your Y chromosome, called STRs. We will compare these with the same 37 STRs in my test, and some other Squitches who have Cheshire roots. Our test results have a lot of similarities with some interesting shared differences, or mutations. We will see if you have the same patterns in your STRs which would suggest we could be related.

The testing company will take about 2–3 months to do the sequencing. When it is done, your results will appear in the results table online I showed you. We agreed your results will be on public view, but let me know if you want to change that as we can do it easily and set it for other members only to view. I will help you understand your results and show what they mean for our shared genealogy, and I will answer any questions you have. And don't forget – if you feel uncomfortable about any aspect of this, do remember you can withdraw from our study and stop the test, or withdraw your results, or make them private, at any time. Let me know and I'll show you what to do.

Figure 1: One way an informal and friendly information statement, sent by email after a meeting with a testing partner, could look.

Family members and testing partners introduced as friends could feel uncomfortable signing consent statements, but finding an appropriate way to receive and record that consent is important. You may find an email works well, or if you plan to do any oral history interviewing of people that you test, you can ask a question about consent on the recording. If you do testing of a more formal type, for example associated with a sensitive issue like adoption searching, or for professional work within genealogy, then formal consent forms become more advisable. Often it is a judgement call, but the baseline principle is that anyone who joins your study should receive full information in an appropriate way, and assent freely to what you plan to do. And if you change or add to what you plan to do with that partner's test results, then you should obtain informed consent once again for those new research plans, before commencing. See the next section for a case in which this became deeply relevant.

Ethics and DNA testing Case 1: the Pringle of Stichill baronetcy

An important judgement was made by the Judicial Committee of the Privy Council, which has jurisdiction over titles awarded by the British Crown, in June 2016. On the death of Sir Steuart Pringle of Stichill, 10th baronet, in 2013, two men claimed the heirship to the title – the 10th baronet's son, Simon, and his cousin, Murray. The reason for the disputed succession lay in the discovery that the 10th baronet's father was not the

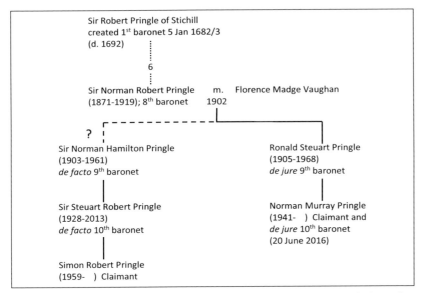

Figure 2: Outline tree for the claimants in the Pringle case, illustrating the line of descent from the 1st Baronet disputed in the case. © John Cleary

biological son of his own father. The 9th baronet was apparently a legitimate son to his father the 8th baronet, as he was born in wedlock (though just over 7 months after his parents' marriage). His legal legitimacy was not challenged in the case, but one of the claimants had something else never used before in a case of this type – DNA evidence.

The baronetcy of Stichill was granted by Charles II in 1683 to Robert Pringle of Stichill and the male heirs of his body (*ac heredibus masculis de suo corpore* in the words of the grant). When a baronet dies, the passage of the title is not automatic, but has to be claimed by an heir whose claim is compatible with the terms of the grant.

Sir Steuart Pringle had donated a Y-DNA sample to a DNA Surname Project for the Pringle surname which had been set up to find relatives of the last Pringle Clan Chief, who died in 1738. This revealed that he did not match the Y chromosomes of other Pringles from the family. This is familiar to genetic genealogists as a common type of NPE (non-paternity event, or 'not the parent expected'), when one child in a family turns out to have had a different biological father, and in most cases it is of no legal consequence.

21

Simon Pringle, son of Steuart, did not contest the implications of the DNA results, but he contested their admissibility as evidence. The defence was put that his father's DNA sample had been given for a particular purpose, researching the Pringle chief's genetic family, but it was a breach of his right to confidentiality to then apply that DNA test result to the different purpose of questioning his right to his title. The court judged that confidentiality had not been breached in this case, since Sir Steuart had voluntarily given his sample to Murray, and that investigating the descent of the Clan Chief and holding a heritable title were both genealogical purposes. Sir Steuart should have been aware that information revealed by Y-DNA on the one subject would do the same on the other, so the court was unwilling to accept there was evidence 'that Murray had obtained Sir Steuart Pringle's DNA on a false premise.'

The court judged that the value of the evidence for resolving the rival claims superseded any concerns over whether confidentiality or data protection law had been breached. As a consequence of the Privy Council's decision the baronetcy was awarded to Murray Pringle.

What does this all mean for you and others like you who may want to collect DNA samples for genealogical testing? There are both specific and general consequences. Specific consequences may be felt by anyone who would like to invite a holder of such a title to take a DNA test.

Approaching a titleholder for a DNA sample is not as unlikely as it may sound: many genealogists researching surnames are interested in the lines with the longest historically verifiable pedigrees and many of these may lead to an invitation to a living titleholder to test to establish the DNA of a 'main line'. It is likely that some clan chiefs or the like may feel that taking a DNA test poses a risk to their interests. A genealogist who wanted to pursue this kind of research would need to offer full explanatory warnings to the potential test-taker of the risks and stringent safeguards for how they would be avoided, and that the data from their test would be used in the most confidential and specific manner.

This is partly an issue of informed consent, as discussed in the first part of this chapter, which is the general consequence arising out of the Pringle case. The court to some extent drew a veil over whether personal data collected for one stated purpose had been applied to another to the disadvantage of the donor. This could be seen as an example of where law and ethics part from each other. While the court took the view that the DNA evidence should be accepted because it existed, because of its quality to resolve the case, and because the way in which it had been obtained broke no law, it is clear that both Sir Steuart and Simon Pringle felt that their DNA data was not being used in the manner they believed it should.

This is an important lesson for all genetic genealogists who are spreading their attention beyond their immediate families towards asking their distant relatives or people they do not know to donate DNA samples. Whatever the legal rights and wrongs of the Pringle case, genealogists running DNA projects must be open and set clear limits around what they will do with the information they obtain from their donors' DNA. If those purposes change, then they must return to their donors to receive clear, informed consent for any additional testing or new forms of analysis. If the donors are actively involved in the project, this is less of a risk, but many people are passive donors giving their DNA to genealogists to help with their research – and their willingness to contribute should be rewarded with the protection of fully committed ethical conduct from the researcher.

Having reviewed this case, now go back and look at the ethical principles for running a DNA project discussed on p16–20. The legal aspects were for the court to decide, but what do you feel about the ethical handling of the DNA sample submitted by Sir Steuart Pringle to the Pringle Surname Project?

DNA test results as legal evidence
Chain of custody
People new to taking ancestral DNA tests are often heard to ask questions like:

- Can my test be used as legal evidence (e.g. of paternity or connection with a crime)?
- Can law enforcement/police use my test results to link me to a crime?

The answer to the first one is a clear no. DNA sequencing undertaken for forensic purposes, such as part of a criminal investigation, is subject to strict *chain of custody* conditions. There are also strict standards governing how DNA is taken from suspects or witnesses to ensure the samples are clean and verifiably given by the person documented as the donor. Chain of custody implies two elements – the process that must be followed to guarantee the integrity of the sample; and the documentation of each stage that validates the evidence to be admissible in a court.

Chain of custody documents all the stages at which a piece of evidence is transferred between persons and places. This may include:

• Seizure of the evidence sample
• Custody of the sample
• Transfers – as few as possible
• Access – authorised and on strict basis of need
• Secure storage
• Analysis at an approved and licensed lab
• Disposition e.g. provision of accurate results to courts and counsel

Now pause to consider that test you administered to your great aunt or uncle in their home one Saturday over tea, biscuits or something stronger. What steps did you take to make sure the sample was theirs, and not contaminated by your DNA or DNA in the general environment? What official forms did you submit to document and witness the taking of the sample according to due process, and to document the legal standing of the agent to whom you turned Aunt Paula's test over, and the legal standing of the lab they passed it on to in turn? Well, I am sure you were careful enough and the test will be perfectly good enough for your goals of comparing her DNA with yours for ancestral research. But what if a canny lawyer was to demand that you prove you did not slip a little kit 'you'd prepared earlier' into Paula's test envelope while she was putting the kettle on, with the DNA of another person entirely inside? Why would you – of course. But in court, in some countries, people are sentenced to death on DNA evidence and miscarriages of justice are too common. So for this reason, your ancestral DNA test can never be used as formal legal evidence that can incriminate you or a family member.

The answer to the second question is also generally no – but the situation may be less clear, especially in jurisdictions with more open regulation over the searching of public databases. As DNA is shared to greater or lesser extents between family members, a technique known as familial searching can attempt to identify a suspect by looking for matches not with the suspect's own DNA, but with the DNA of possible family members who may in turn match with a suspect's sample. This will be discussed in the following Case Study on p26. It is important to remember though that DNA in ancestral databases, whether public or controlled by company Terms and Conditions, will never satisfy chain of custody rules to be admissible in court (the decision in the Pringle case was before a special kind of court, and the DNA results themselves had not been challenged by the defence). They can however provide leads to investigators, which can later be tested by a full legal process. In this way, genealogists need to be aware that chances are growing that family members could be traced from samples that they have put in ancestral databases. Set against this, it is also the case that miscarriages of justice can be set right and wrongly convicted people exonerated by use of the same methods. New technological applications of ancestral DNA databases are appearing fast, and the challenge for current times is to make sure this process is properly regulated and protected against misuse.

Forensic tests and databases

Forensic science has developed its own testing methods for DNA, including specialised testing kits (which in part inspired the kits now used for ancestral testing) and databases. Genealogists are often surprised by how few markers are tested in forensics. The standard test to identify someone uses fifteen autosomal STRs (recently expanded to over twenty), and Y tests use seventeen STRs (expanded in newer tests to twenty-three or twenty-seven, still far fewer than the thirty-seven plus genealogists are used to – and often still find ambiguous). Forensics aims to establish the probability that a DNA sequence in a crime scene sample is DNA left by a particular person, the suspect or accused. To do this, it is not enough to find that a haplotype is identical to the suspect's. The forensic evidence must also be able to quantify the possibility that the two haplotypes could be identical by chance, and to do this, a number of forensic haplotype databases have been built.

We will come back to forensic databases in Chapter 10, but first let's look at a major event in 2018 that may have turned the world of forensic searching upside down.

Ethics and DNA testing Case 2: the Golden State Killer

On 24 April 2018, a seventy-two-year-old man was arrested in Sacramento and charged with being a serial killer and rapist who had been active from 1974–86. Not caught at the time, he was given the label the 'Golden State Killer', or GSK. Californian police revealed he had been identified through a technique that is coming to be known as *familial searching of genetic genealogical databases*. Though this was not actually the first time it had been used, it was the first case of its kind to be made public, creating a media splash, drawing genetic genealogists' attention to the technique and the general public's to the existence of genealogical databases.

To Catch a Killer

There had already been searches made of Y chromosome databases in pursuit of unapprehended violent criminals – though many of these had led to flawed investigations and had been unsuccessful, leaving doubts about the technique. Because Y chromosomes across large kinship groups differ very little from each other, Y-DNA is not a sufficiently powerful discriminator to pinpoint suspects reliably.

However, the new methods used in spring 2018 to crack this landmark case are ground-breaking, and may change forensics and genetic genealogy fundamentally. In early 2018 a sample was found in one of the counties where the GSK had been active, stored in a freezer for thirty-seven years. It was found to be in very good condition and a genome-wide SNP chip test could be carried out successfully.

The autosomal DNA tests discussed in Chapter 4 use *microarrays* that hold a selection of SNPs from the autosomes (often referred to as SNP-chips). The standard chips used today have around 600,000-700,000 SNPs on them, a tiny sample of the full genome, but powerful for comparing genomes on a one-to-one basis for establishing identities and close family relationships. What the investigators did next was to create a profile from the test result that looked like one generated from the standard genetic genealogy companies' SNP-chip tests. This generated DNA profile was then uploaded to the public genealogy sharing database, GEDmatch.com.

This profile matched with numerous distant relatives of the killer. There was no immediate revelation for the investigators, but they found themselves in a position now very familiar to that branch of genetic genealogy that does genealogical research on autosomal matches in unknown parent searches. In this case, they worked up to the great-great-great-grandparents of promising matches, reaching almost back to 1800, before beginning to work forwards again to search for leads among the other descendants of the shared ancestral couple.

Ultimately, a suspect was identified, surveillance was carried out and his DNA was taken from discarded items, which is legal under Californian law, to make a formal legal identification against the crime scene DNA. It is important to stress that the familial searching technique could not provide evidence that would be admissible in court, but is aimed at creating leads that can be tested by legal forensic methods with a full chain of custody. Once the suspect was identified, and his modern DNA taken (surreptitiously in this case), a legal identification could be made using the FBI's forensic markers, and this is what a court eventually will see. It is not known how many suspects had ever been placed under surveillance by Californian law enforcement, though at least one further person is known to have been a suspect up as far as the stage of having his DNA tested.

The GSK, GEDmatch, privacy and informed consent

The apprehension of the GSK suspect came hard on the heels of another celebrated solving of a cold case, the 'Buckskin Girl', an unidentified murder victim (see Chapter 10). In this case, whole genome sequencing (WGS) methods were applied to the sample and then the genealogy companies' file formats were 'spoofed' and uploaded to GEDmatch.

The technical work in identifying the GSK and Buckskin Girl was certainly impressive, and will before long impact on genetic genealogy, where whole genome sequencing is starting to gain traction with test-takers as the prices fall dramatically. But the cases threw up some major ethical issues and at the time of writing they are still being discussed. There has been a visible impact on the availability of databases, with two ageing search platforms, Ysearch and Mitosearch, being closed down, mainly because of GDPR requirements, but also in the shadow of the fallout from the GSK. The biggest impact has been on the Terms and Conditions and Privacy Policies of the platforms used by genealogists to share DNA results.

It is hard to argue that something that led to the apprehension of a violent murderer is not a good thing, and anecdotal evidence from popular forums suggests that the majority of opinions from active users of the GEDmatch site were supportive. However, some voices have pointed to darker ethical issues that users should be aware of, in particular the question of where lines may be drawn. Does searching GEDmatch with criminal samples breach the privacy rights of the members? Is this a secondary use that members have not given informed consent to? It also throws the spotlight onto many activities that have become accepted by the genetic genealogical community, such as unknown parent searching. How can it be judged a breach of privacy to upload a profile that might lead to a serial killer being apprehended, while it is judged not a breach of privacy to confront birth or donor parents with their biological children? There have been cases in which the latter activity breached the 'do no harm' principle. On the other hand, if there should be a serial killer currently active, surely it would be a gross ethical breach *not* to use all means available to catch them, including familial searching of genetic genealogy databases without alerting the public that this was in process.

Set against the privacy and consent issues is the power of DNA testing to 'do good'. The techniques used to find the GSK can also be used to exonerate wrongly accused people and set right miscarriages of justice. In November 2017 a Los Angeles man convicted of multiple murders was exonerated and released after thirty-nine years in jail when DNA evidence proved his innocence – as of spring 2018 the murders were being re-investigated within the GSK case. Statutory governmental databases have strict rules on who may search them and what kinds of searches may be permitted, to protect the individuals within them, largely offenders, who have lost the privacy rights of the wider public not to have their DNA stored. As genetic genealogical databases are non-statutory they can only be protected by the actions of the companies and organisations which created them.

As with other aspects of genetic genealogy discussed in this chapter, you should always read carefully the Terms of Service (ToS) given by any platform you wish to use before uploading your data, and make sure you are comfortable with them. If you are uploading data of family members or other people with their permission, make sure the consent they give is fully informed of the risks as you see them – or let them read the ToS themselves to make their own decision. In May 2018, GEDmatch produced a new set of ToS to address these issues, while still committing themselves to open sharing and to have users take responsibility for their understanding of the risks. (Other testing companies have also been clarifying their ToS under the twin shadows of GDPR and the GSK case). The new ToS or Site Policy includes (with our emphases):

Raw DNA Data Provided to GEDmatch
When you upload Raw Data to GEDmatch, you agree that the Raw Data is one of the following:

- Your DNA;
- DNA of a person for whom you are a legal guardian;
- DNA of a person **who has granted you specific authorization to upload their DNA to GEDmatch**;
- DNA of a person known by you to be deceased;
- **DNA obtained and authorized by law enforcement** to either: (1) **identify a perpetrator of a violent crime** against another individual; or (2) identify remains of a deceased individual;
- An artificial DNA kit (if and only if: (1) it is intended for research purposes; and (2) it is not used to identify anyone in the GEDmatch database); or
- DNA obtained from an artifact (if and only if: (1) you have a reasonable belief that the Raw Data is DNA from a previous owner or user of the artifact rather than from a living individual; and (2) that previous owner or user of the artifact is known to you to be deceased).

'Violent crime' is defined as homicide or sexual assault.
By registering for GEDmatch and using the Site, you agree that you will not upload Raw Data that does not satisfy one of these categories. If you have previously uploaded Raw Data that does not satisfy one of these categories, you hereby agree that you will remove it immediately.

The responsibility remains with the user to obtain the necessary consents to upload, though the requirements are now spelled out more clearly. GEDmatch has also addressed a major ethical conundrum: *if* some law enforcement uses are acceptable, then *which* such uses are they? They have defined this as violent crime and given a definition of that. By definition then, using GEDmatch for solving other crimes such as drug offences, theft or motor offences is not to be permitted. What powers GEDmatch has to enforce this remains to be tested, but as of 2019 an uneasy balance exists between the desire of genetic genealogists to share their data openly and mutually and their need to control who has access to that data and for which purposes.

Ethical standards for genetic genealogy
In 2013 a group of active, mainly American, genetic genealogists self-organised into a committee to draft a set of standards for the field, to answer accusations that it was unregulated and open to poor practice. The group were keen to make clear that they did not represent any company, organisation or interest group linked to the genetic genealogical field, and the Standards were an initial attempt to agree a consensus set of guidelines on good practice. After an open period of consultation the Standards were launched in January 2015 at a colloquium in Salt Lake City, and published online for interested parties to refer to.

The set of twenty-one Standards, which can be viewed at http://www.geneticgenealogystandards.com, addresses many of the concerns dealt with in this chapter, and more. While not official, they are being followed by many practitioners providing professional services and can be consulted by anyone with an interest in ancestral DNA testing, from new test-takers to project administrators and professional genealogists who work with DNA testing, to the companies that sell the testing and analytics. They cover the two broad areas within the activity – eleven standards for the testing process and a further ten for the interpretation process – creating benchmarks to judge best practice.

Several standards cover the areas we have examined in this chapter, including rights to privacy, confidentiality, ownership and for informed consent. The right to anonymity is expressed, but warning is made that this can be curtailed or compromised once results are published, which should be an informed decision of the owner of the DNA test results alone. Genealogists offering testing or interpretation services are expected to be knowledgeable so that information and advice offered is accurate and up to date, and the limits of what can be learnt or proven from DNA testing are understood. There are also useful standards on storage of samples, appointing beneficiaries to guard against kits being orphaned by decease of the test-taker and the use of results in scholarship and educational activities.

Standards will continue to evolve as the tendency for rapid change of the technology creates new uses and situations – and the years 2018 and 2019 delivered a number of shocks to the perceived status quo of ideas within the field. But the twenty-one Standards make the clearest statement so far of an ethical approach to tracing ancestral relations with DNA, and all users are recommended to make use of them.

Chapter 3

UNDERSTANDING THE PRINCIPLES OF DNA TESTING FOR GENEALOGY

Michelle Leonard

In order to effectively make use of DNA testing for genealogy it is essential to understand how DNA is inherited. This chapter will set out the inheritance patterns of the four different types of DNA covered by commercial DNA tests: mitochondrial DNA, Y-chromosome DNA, X-chromosome DNA and autosomal DNA. You do not have to be an expert in genetics to understand these concepts; it is all about grasping the basics and using that information as an aid to your DNA results.

Mitochondrial DNA (mtDNA)

Mitochondrial DNA (mtDNA for short) consists of small circular pieces of DNA present within our cells and is the only type of DNA that does not originate in the nucleus of the cell. It exists in the body in vastly greater quantities and is far more durable than nuclear DNA. We all have hundreds or even thousands of copies of mitochondria per cell as opposed to just forty-six chromosomes per cell as is the case with nuclear DNA.

MtDNA is passed down virtually unchanged for hundreds of years and can reach back around 200,000 years in time, which is a similar reach to Y-DNA and a much longer reach than atDNA. It mutates very slowly, so even exact mtDNA matches can be beyond a genealogically relevant timeframe, meaning it is often not possible to identify a common maternal ancestor. The plentiful nature and longevity of mtDNA is why it has been the preferred testing method for ancient DNA cases e.g. the discovery of Richard III.

The unique inheritance pattern of mtDNA makes it useful for researching the direct maternal line i.e. the mother's, mother's, mother's line. MtDNA is passed down by a mother to *all* of her children (both sons and daughters), but only daughters then pass it on in turn to their children. The same strand of mtDNA, therefore, perpetuates until the interjection of a male breaks the mtDNA line as his children will inherit the mtDNA of their mother.

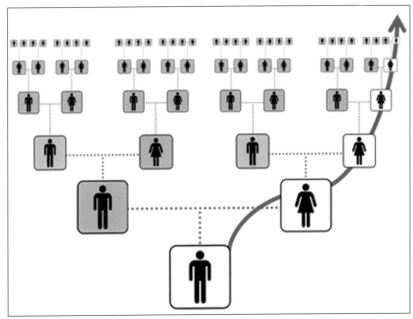

© *unattributed*

To test your mother's mtDNA you can test yourself, but if you wish to test your father's mtDNA you would have to test your father himself or an appropriate relative on your paternal side who shares his mtDNA, e.g. any of his full or maternal half siblings or a niece/nephew descended from a sister.

Mitochondrial DNA is also the only type of DNA for which the standard test is a full-sequence test (offered by FTDNA) – this means that the entire mitochondria (16,569 base pairs) is sequenced and not just select areas on it, as is the case with Y-DNA and atDNA. For a more detailed look at mtDNA testing see Chapter 6.

Y-chromosome DNA (Y-DNA)

There are two sex chromosomes (X and Y) and each person inherits one from their mother and one from their father. Your sex is determined by which one you inherit from your father. The Y-chromosome is the sex chromosome that determines the male gender, so if you inherit a Y-chromosome from your father then you will be male. Only men have a Y-chromosome, so only men can pass it down.

The inheritance pattern of the Y-chromosome is very straightforward: it is passed from father to son down a direct male line and Y-DNA testing, therefore, covers only the father's, father's father's direct paternal line.

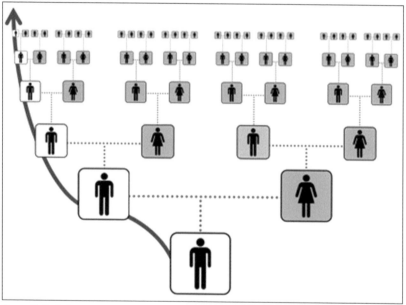

© *unattributed*

Y-DNA is passed down virtually unchanged through many generations and for that reason it can, like mtDNA, reach back over 200,000 years in time.

Only men can take a Y-DNA test, so if a woman wishes to test her father's Y-DNA line she will have to recruit an appropriate male to take

34

the test for her. Due to the nature of Y-DNA it is possible for Y-DNA lines to die out, and this is commonly referred to as 'daughtering out': it occurs when a man only has daughters and, therefore, does not pass on his Y-chromosome to a son. Once he dies his individual Y-DNA line dies with him. That does not mean that his Y-DNA line is untestable, however, until all avenues have been exhausted. Due to the fact Y-DNA is slow-mutating, you could find a suitable Y-DNA donor many generations removed who shares the same Y-chromosome as the man whose line has daughtered out. For example, your father is deceased and you are his only daughter so you cannot test his Y-DNA line. He has no brothers, nephews or paternal first cousins, but by tracing his direct paternal line back to his third great-grandfather and then tracing just the male lines forward you could find a suitable male fourth cousin who shares your father's Y-DNA.

Y-DNA testing is useful for surname studies, testing relationship hypotheses on the direct paternal line, finding cousins, solving paternal mysteries and investigating the ancient origins of your direct paternal line. For a more detailed look at Y-DNA testing, see Chapter 5.

X-chromosome DNA (X-DNA)

The X-chromosome is the other sex chromosome and both men and woman inherit at least one of these. Since women have two X-chromosomes it is only possible for mothers to pass down an X to their children. If you inherit an X-chromosome from your mother and a Y-chromosome from your father you will be male. If, instead, you receive an X-chromosome from both your mother and your father then you will be female.

The unique inheritance pattern of the X-chromosome makes it very helpful when it comes to DNA cousin matching. If you discover a reasonable match with someone on the X-chromosome there are far fewer ancestors you need to look at in order to pinpoint the connection.

Here is a chart showing all of the ancestors from whom a male potentially inherits X-DNA:

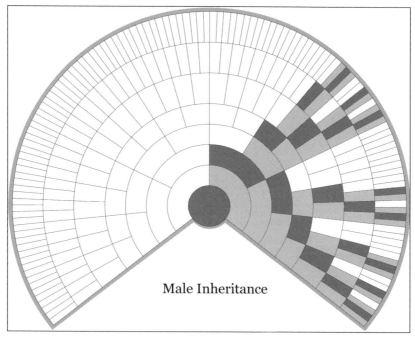

https://thegeneticgenealogist.com/wp-content/uploads/2008/12/MaleChart350dpiVersion2-1.jpg © Blaine Bettinger

Since men do not inherit any X-DNA from their fathers, the entire paternal side of their tree can be discounted when trying to identify common ancestors with an X-DNA match. Any other male-to-male line can also be discounted, as there will never be any X-DNA inheritance between a father and son – e.g. the maternal grandfather's paternal line can always be ruled out. Another key point is that just because you could potentially have received some X-DNA from a certain ancestor, it does not follow that you definitely did. For an X-DNA match a man only has to look at eight out of his thirty-two third great-grandparental lines thus narrowing the connection down significantly.

Here is a chart showing all of the ancestors from whom a female potentially inherits X-DNA:

Female Inheritance

*https://thegeneticgenealogist.com/wp-content/uploads/2008/12/FemaleChart350dpiVersion
2.jpg © Blaine Bettinger*

Women have double the X-DNA men do, so they also tend to have far
more X-DNA matches and more lines that need to be included in any
investigation. It is not possible to narrow a female X-DNA match down
to a side in the way you can with a male X-DNA match, but there are
still many lines that can be ruled out. In particular the paternal
grandfather line can be instantly discounted, thus removing an entire
quarter from the equation and leaving women with only thirteen of
their thirty-two third great-grandparents' lines to investigate.

If you wish to test your X-DNA you cannot purchase a standalone
test like you can for Y-DNA – instead X-DNA is generally incorporated
into autosomal DNA tests. All autosomal testing companies include the
X-chromosome during testing, but not all report on it. 23andMe and
FTDNA do report on it, but Ancestry and MyHeritage currently do not.

For a more detailed look at using X-DNA for genealogy, see Chapter 4.

Autosomal DNA (atDNA)

Autosomal DNA is the all-rounder of the DNA testing world since it covers all of your ancestral lines as opposed to just one like Y-DNA and mtDNA. For instance you have sixteen second great-grandparents, but when you test Y-DNA or mtDNA you are exploring only one of those sixteen lines, whereas autosomal testing covers them all. These tests can be taken by both men and women and matches can be related to you on any of your lines.

You inherit 50% of your autosomal DNA from your mother and 50% from your father. Parent-child, however, is the only relationship that shares such an exact percentage of atDNA; all other percentages are approximate.

Autosomal DNA is structured by chromosomes (chr for short) – these are organized packages of DNA found within the nucleus of every human cell. There are forty-six chromosomes in total: twenty-two *pairs* of autosomal chromosomes (known as autosomes), and one *pair* of sex chromosomes (chr 23/X and Y).

The most important concept to take on board here is the fact that chromosomes come in *pairs* – twenty-three pairs overall. This means you have two copies of chromosome one, two copies of chromosome two and so on. Technically only chromosomes 1 to 22 make up autosomal DNA as the final pair (chromosome 23) are the sex chromosomes. Chromosomes are numbered from largest to smallest with chromosome 1 being the largest and chromosomes 21 and 22 being the smallest. The Y-chromosome is also reasonably small and the X chromosome is three times larger than it.

Why do we have two copies of each chromosome?

The reason for two copies of each chromosome is because one set of twenty-three is passed down by our mother and the other set of twenty-three is passed down by our father. It is best to think of these as your maternal chromosomes and your paternal chromosomes.

Your parents also have two copies of every chromosome passed down to them by their parents, but when they create you, they can only pass half of their chromosomes down. During meiosis (cell division that occurs at the creation of an egg or sperm cell) a process called recombination takes place.

Here is how the process works:

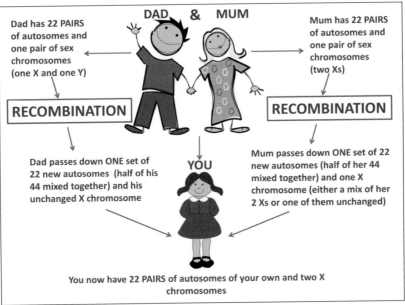

This image depicts a daughter, but the process is exactly the same for a son except for the fact dad passes down a Y-chromosome.

Let's look closer at how it works using just one chromosome (chromosome 1 for argument's sake, but the number is unimportant):

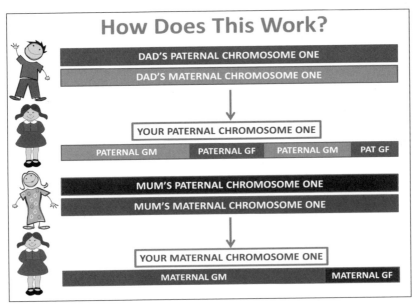

© *Michelle Leonard, above two images*

The daughter inherits a unique pair of chromosome ones:

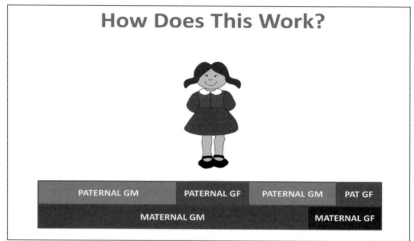

© *Michelle Leonard*

You can see that on her maternal chromosome one she inherited far more from her maternal grandmother than her maternal grandfather, but there's a slightly more even distribution on her paternal copy. This could easily be reversed on some of her other maternal chromosomes – recombination is random so there is no set pattern. This is why while you inherit exactly 50% of your DNA from each parent, you only inherit approximate percentages from more distant ancestors.

You inherit progressively less of your ancestors' DNA with each passing generation and this dropping off of DNA from more distant ancestors highlights the main limitation of atDNA – it can generally only reach back five–seven generations in time.

Sharing atDNA

When you share a piece of atDNA with another person we call that piece of DNA a segment; the segment lies somewhere within the start and end locations of the chromosome in question and can come in all sorts of sizes. The way we measure these segments is via centiMorgans (usually abbreviated to cMs for short). A centiMorgan is a measure of how probable it is that a segment will recombine from one generation to the next. The most important thing to remember about centiMorgans is that the more cMs you share with a match, the closer the relationship. For that reason, it is essential to become familiar with the average number of cMs you should share with different relationship levels. Additionally, it is important to understand that there can be quite a wide range due to the random way autosomal DNA is inherited and that outliers are always possible.

Familiarise yourself with the approximate amounts of DNA you should share with different relationships:

Percentage	Potential Relationships
50% (exact)	Parent/Child
50% (approx.)	Full sibling
25% (approx.)	Half Sibling Grandparent/Grandchild Aunt/Uncle/Niece/Nephew Double First Cousin
12.5% (approx.)	First Cousin Half Aunt/Uncle/Niece/Nephew Great Grandparent/Great Grandchild Grand Aunt/Uncle/Grand Niece/Nephew
6.25% (approx.)	First Cousin Once Removed Half First Cousin Half Grand Aunt/Uncle Half Grand Niece/Nephew
3.125% (approx.)	Second Cousin First Cousin Twice Removed Half First Cousin Once Removed
1.56% (approx.)	Second Cousin Once Removed Half Second Cousin First Cousin Three Times Removed Half First Cousin Twice Removed
0.78% (approx.)	Third Cousin Second Cousin Twice Removed
0.39% (approx.)	Third Cousin Once Removed
0.195% (approx.)	Fourth Cousin (and more distant)

Statistics Courtesy of the ISOGG Wiki

The only absolute is that females inherit exactly 50% and males almost exactly 50% from each parent – males actually inherit 50.8% from their mothers and 49.2% from their fathers, because the paternally inherited Y chromosome is around three times smaller than the maternally inherited X chromosome. All the rest of these percentages are approximate; for example, the 50% you inherit from a parent may be a mix of 22% from your grandmother and 28% from your grandfather. It is all down to how the cards fall during the recombination process.

Then acquaint yourself with the average number of cMs shared by different relationship levels:

Average CentiMorgans Shared

Average Total cMs	Relationship Groups
3,500cM	Parent-Child/Identical Twin*
2,600cM	Full Sibling
1,780cM	Half Sibling, Grandparent/child Aunt/Uncle/Niece/Nephew
875cM	First Cousin, Half Aunt/Uncle/Niece/Nephew Grand Aunt/Uncle/Niece/Nephew
450cM	First Cousin1xrem , Half First Cousin Half Grand Aunt/Uncle/Niece/Nephew
230cM	Second Cousin, Half First Cousin1xrem
120cM	Second Cousin1xrem, Half Second Cousin
75cM	Third Cousin
50cM	Third Cousin1xrem
35cM	Fourth Cousin

Compiled by author based on averages from Shared cM Project

*If one of your ancestors is an identical twin you will share more DNA with the descendants of the other identical twin e.g. the children of identical twins will share double the DNA of regular first cousins and will appear more like half-siblings.

There are two important points to take away from this table:

1. These numbers are just the average amount shared – in many cases the reality will be different and it is best to think in terms of ranges of cMs.

2. There are different groups of relationships that could share exactly the same amount of cMs e.g. a half-sibling is very hard to distinguish from an aunt/uncle/grandparent via the number of cMs shared alone, as all of those relationships should share a similar amount.

For details of a very useful resource to consult for ranges of cMs shared and relationship probabilities, see the description of the Shared cM Project in Chapter 4.

Kinship terminology

Understanding kinship terminology is important for researching DNA matches:

Removed

This simply means you and your cousin are not on the same genetic generation i.e. one or other of you is closer or more distant to your common ancestors. For example, second cousins share a set of great-grandparents and are both exactly three generations away from their common ancestors, so there is no 'removed' involved. A second cousin once removed (2C1R), however, is either one generation closer or one generation further away from the common ancestors – the great-grandparents of one must either be the grandparents or second great-grandparents of the other.

Half

Generally we do not tend to talk about half-cousins or half-aunts/uncles, but it is important to differentiate these relationships for DNA testing, since half relationship relatives will share 50% less DNA with you than their full counterparts. So what do we mean by a half first cousin? This is someone who only shares one grandparent with you as opposed to two and that happens when your parent and theirs are half-siblings. Similarly a half-aunt/uncle is your parent's half-sibling. So when you see a complicated relationship like a half 3C2R this means that person shares one common ancestor with you at the third cousin level, but one of you is two generations closer to that common ancestor than the other. The cousin relationship is always dictated by the cousin who is closest to the common ancestors: for a half 3C2R this means the common ancestor is a second great-grandparent for one cousin and a fourth great-grandparent for the other. Whether you are the person who is closer or more distant makes no difference to the relationship calculation.

Once you know who the common ancestors are with a match, use a chart such as this to identify the actual cousin relationship:

Cousinship Chart

1. Across the top row find what your relationship is to the common ancestor.
2. In the left hand column find what the relationship of the other individual is, to the same common ancestor.
3. The square where the two of you meet [intersect at] out in the middle, is the correct notation of what your relationship is.

Common Ancestor	Grandparent	Great Grandparent	Great 2nd Grandparent	Great 3rd Grandparent	Great 4th Grandparent	Great 5th Grandparent	Great 6th Grandparent	Great 7th Grandparent	Great 8th Grandparent	Great 9th Grandparent	Great 10th Grandparent
Grandparent	1st cousin	1st cousin 1x removed	1st cousin 2x removed	1st cousin 3x removed	1st cousin 4x removed	1st cousin 5x removed	1st cousin 6x removed	1st cousin 7x removed	1st cousin 8x removed	1st cousin 9x removed	1st cousin 10x removed
Great Grandparent	1st cousin 1x removed	2nd cousin	2nd cousin 1x removed	2nd cousin 2x removed	2nd cousin 3x removed	2nd cousin 4x removed	2nd cousin 5x removed	2nd cousin 6x removed	2nd cousin 7x removed	2nd cousin 8x removed	2nd cousin 9x removed
Great 2nd Grandparent	1st cousin 2x removed	2nd cousin 1x removed	3rd cousin	3rd cousin 1x removed	3rd cousin 2x removed	3rd cousin 3x removed	3rd cousin 4x removed	3rd cousin 5x removed	3rd cousin 6x removed	3rd cousin 7x removed	3rd cousin 8x removed
Great 3rd Grandparent	1st cousin 3x removed	2nd cousin 2x removed	3rd cousin 1x removed	4th cousin	4th cousin 1x removed	4th cousin 2x removed	4th cousin 3x removed	4th cousin 4x removed	4th cousin 5x removed	4th cousin 6x removed	4th cousin 7x removed
Great 4th Grandparent	1st cousin 4x removed	2nd cousin 3x removed	3rd cousin 2x removed	4th cousin 1x removed	5th cousin	5th cousin 1x removed	5th cousin 2x removed	5th cousin 3x removed	5th cousin 4x removed	5th cousin 5x removed	5th cousin 6x removed
Great 5th Grandparent	1st cousin 5x removed	2nd cousin 4x removed	3rd cousin 3x removed	4th cousin 2x removed	5th cousin 1x removed	6th cousin	6th cousin 1x removed	6th cousin 2x removed	6th cousin 3x removed	6th cousin 4x removed	6th cousin 5x removed
Great 6th Grandparent	1st cousin 6x removed	2nd cousin 5x removed	3rd cousin 4x removed	4th cousin 3x removed	5th cousin 2x removed	6th cousin 1x removed	7th cousin	7th cousin 1x removed	7th cousin 2x removed	7th cousin 3x removed	7th cousin 4x removed
Great 7th Grandparent	1st cousin 7x removed	2nd cousin 6x removed	3rd cousin 5x removed	4th cousin 4x removed	5th cousin 3x removed	6th cousin 2x removed	7th cousin 1x removed	8th cousin	8th cousin 1x removed	8th cousin 2x removed	8th cousin 3x removed
Great 8th Grandparent	1st cousin 8x removed	2nd cousin 7x removed	3rd cousin 6x removed	4th cousin 5x removed	5th cousin 4x removed	6th cousin 3x removed	7th cousin 2x removed	8th cousin 1x removed	9th cousin	9th cousin 1x removed	9th cousin 2x removed
Great 9th Grandparent	1st cousin 9x removed	2nd cousin 8x removed	3rd cousin 7x removed	4th cousin 6x removed	5th cousin 5x removed	6th cousin 4x removed	7th cousin 3x removed	8th cousin 2x removed	9th cousin 1x removed	10th cousin	10th cousin 1x removed
Great 10th Grandparent	1st cousin 10x removed	2nd cousin 9x removed	3rd cousin 8x removed	4th cousin 7x removed	5th cousin 6x removed	6th cousin 5x removed	7th cousin 4x removed	8th cousin 3x removed	9th cousin 2x removed	10th cousin 1x removed	11th cousin

Overlaps and outliers

Another key concept to understand is that overlap and outlier matches exist and it is always possible that any given match could fall into these categories. An overlap match shares in between two relationship levels, for example 875cM is the average shared between first cousins and 440cM between 1C1R or half first cousins, but what if someone shares 650cM with you? That is in the overlap zone between those two relationship levels and could just as easily be a first cousin as a 1C1R. Matches in the overlap zone are outliers: an outlier is a match that shares either significantly more or less cMs than average. There are a wide range of outliers from small to extreme.

Small outlier

A small outlier could be first cousins sharing 700cM on the low side or 1,000cM on the high side.

Extreme outlier

An extreme outlier could be first cousins sharing 570cM on the very low side or 1200cM on the very high side.

Example

Don is a confirmed 2C1R match sharing 295 cM across fourteen DNA segments.

Mary is another confirmed 2C1R match sharing 13 cM across one DNA segment.

Don and Mary share exactly the same relationship with me, but the difference in the amount of cMs is enormous! These are extreme outliers at both ends of the scale and they demonstrate the need to be careful with relationship predictions.

How can I be so sure my low-sharing with Mary is an outlier, though, and there is not a problem with the relationship? There could be an error such as a misattributed parentage event. Equally perhaps the high-sharing with Don is indicative of a secondary relationship between us. The only reason I can be sure these scenarios are incorrect is because I have tested many other close relatives and the majority of them match both of these test-takers well within the average sharing range for the paper trail relationships.

Relationship to me	Relationship to Mary	cM shared with Mary
Brother	2C1R	37cM over 3 segments
Half Sister	2C1R	15cM over 2 segments
First Cousin	2C1R	182cM over 6 segments
First Cousin	2C1R	139cM over 4 segments
First Cousin	2C1R	128cM over 7 segments
First Cousin	2C1R	123cM over 7 segments
First Cousin	2C1R	40cM over 4 segments
Second Cousin	2C1R	164cM over 7 segments
Second Cousin	2C1R	91cM over 5 segments
Third Cousin	2C1R	141cM over 7 segments

My half-sister and, to a lesser extent, my brother and one first cousin also share far less than normal with Mary, but the majority of my first and second cousins share exactly in the correct range with both me and Mary, so I can classify this as an outlier situation. Being able to determine overlaps and outliers is just one of several excellent reasons for testing as many other family members as you can.

Not all of your cousins will match you

If a close relative (anyone up to second cousin level) does not match you then there is almost certainly a problem that needs to be addressed, as 100% of close relatives up to the second cousin level should match you and there have been, to date, no known instances of genuine second cousin or closer relations not matching each other. From third cousin onwards, however, there is an ever-increasing chance that genuine paper trail cousins may not share any DNA at all:

Relationship	23andMe	AncestryDNA	Family Tree DNA Family Finder
First cousins	100%	100%	100%
Second cousins	100%	100%	>99%
Third cousins	89.7%	98%	>90%
Fourth cousins	45.9%	71%	>50%
Fifth cousins	14.9%	32%	>10%
Sixth cousins	4.1%	11%	Remote (typically less than 2%)[2]
Seventh cousins	1.1%	3.2%	
Eighth cousins	0.24%	0.91%	
Ninth cousins	0.06%		
Tenth cousins	0.002%		

https://isogg.org/wiki/Cousin_statistics

The reason for this takes us back to how autosomal DNA is inherited and the fact that we inherit progressively less from our ancestors the further back in time we go:

Genealogical Relationship	Probability of *No* Detectable DNA Relationship
1 x great grandparent	0.00%
2 x great grandparent	0.00%
3 x great grandparent	0.01%
4 x great grandparent	0.56%
5 x great grandparent	4.95%
6 x great grandparent	17.76%
7 x great grandparent	37.43%
8 x great grandparent	57.53%
9 x great grandparent	73.50%
10 x great grandparent	84.38%
11 x great grandparent	91.12%
12 x great grandparent	95.07%
13 x great grandparent	97.31%
14 x great grandparent	98.54%

https://isogg.org/wiki/Cousin_statistics
Probability of sharing DNA. © Jonathan Hamm

Past the point of fifth great-grandparent level, the probability of no detectable DNA increases exponentially. For example, we each have 128 fifth great-grandparents, and it is almost certain that we will have inherited no DNA from several of these. By the time we reach back to our 1,024 eighth great-grandparents we will have inherited DNA from less than half of them. This means we will have paper trail ancestors that are not genetic ancestors. These more distant ancestors still belong on our family trees – we just did not inherit any segments of DNA from them, so they are not part of our genetic make-up. The further back you can take your tree, the more ancestors who did not contribute to your DNA will be on it. In fact it has been calculated that almost half of our DNA comes from just 200 of our twentieth generation ancestors, the other half coming from around 1,200 ancestors.

Once we get back to the fourth cousin and more distant levels, the regular amount of sharing is one segment of DNA, if that. You are likely to inherit around 1.5% of your DNA from a fifth great-grandfather and a sixth cousin also descended from the same fifth great-grandfather equally will inherit approximately 1.5% of his DNA, and this means the chances that you will both have inherited the same segment are extremely small – your sixth cousin is much more likely to have inherited a piece of the 98.5% of your shared ancestor's DNA that you did not and, therefore, will not match you.

Having said this, you will still have far more distant cousin matches than you will close ones. Here is a study undertaken by AncestryDNA on the number of cousins that the average British person is expected to have. It is unclear which parts of Britain the statistics cover, but the study was put together from information on British birth rates, census data, parliamentary research briefings and other sources on the last 200 years:

Relationship	Number of Cousins
First Cousins	5
Second Cousins	28
Third Cousins	175
Fourth Cousins	1,570
Fifth Cousins	17,300
Sixth Cousins	174,000

*https://isogg.org/wiki/
Cousin_statistics*

While you will only match a small proportion of your sixth cousins, far more of your matches will be sixth or more distant cousins, since there are so many more of them in existence.

Endogamy

Endogamy occurs when groups of people marry within the same ethnic, cultural, social or religious circles. This leads to everyone within that group descending from a much more limited gene pool. Descendants of an endogamous population end up with numerous cousin connections between them because the same ancestors appear on their family trees in a number of different locations.

The more recent the endogamy, the more it affects how you should work with your DNA matches. If you have extensive endogamy within your family tree, *disregard* predicted relationships and ranges of cMs, as distant cousins will share more DNA with you and the closer relationship predictions are likely to be wrong – if someone is your third cousin three times over, they are going to share more DNA with you than someone who is just your third cousin in one way. For those with endogamy, it is often necessary to increase the cM threshold at which they start investigating matches in order to identify connections e.g. a match of 50 cMs for someone from a non-endogamous background is much more likely to be solvable than for someone who has to factor endogamy into the calculation.

If you have substantial endogamy in your tree it is worth running the free 'Are Your Parents Related?' tool on GEDMatch. It checks your DNA for runs of homozygosity (ROHs) which are basically segments of DNA that are identical on both your maternal and paternal chromosome copies, meaning that your parents share those segments of DNA with each other and both passed them down to you.

Pedigree collapse

Pedigree collapse occurs when marriages between cousins take place and some ancestors on your tree occupy more than one slot. We each have thirty-two third great-grandparents, but if your grandparents were second cousins and shared a set of great-grandparents that would mean the great-grandparents they shared belong on your tree twice. This, therefore, reduces or collapses the number of third great-grandparents you have down from thirty-two to thirty.

While there will always be pedigree collapse if endogamy is involved, not all pedigree collapse should be thought of as endogamy. Occasional cousin marriages can also affect DNA matching, but to a much lesser extent than within endogamous communities. The impact will depend on how recently the cousin match falls on your pedigree and the degree of cousin relationship between the cousins who married. For example, if a set of your grandparents were first cousins then that will affect the amount of DNA you share with cousins on that side of your tree much more significantly than if you have a set of second cousins who married at the third great-grandparent level. The latter, in fact, is unlikely to have much impact upon your DNA matches. The key difference between widespread endogamy and pedigree collapse due to occasional cousin marriage is that any effect on DNA matches is localized to the specific line on which the cousin marriage took place, while endogamy can permeate an entire tree.

Test your older generations

Test as many of your older generation relatives as possible; they have more of your ancestors' DNA than you do! Your parents have double and your grandparents have triple. You will share on average around 6.25% with a first cousin once removed (1C1R), but if that 1C1R is your parent's first cousin (I call this the 'magic' generation closer to your common ancestors), then testing them amounts to testing around 25% of your great grandparents' DNA while testing yourself only covers 12.5%.

There are many benefits to testing all older generation relatives, but parents are particularly useful because even if you can only test one parent, you can separate out your matches into either maternal or paternal – just be aware that very small segment matches could be false and match neither of your parents and you may also uncover matches to both.

Your parents will have a lot matches you do not, since many of them will stem from the 50% of their DNA you did not inherit. They will also regularly match people on your match list at a higher level than you do and this can bring a match to your attention that you might otherwise overlook.

cMs Shared with Me	cMs Shared with Mum	Relationship
54.2cM over 3 segments	236cM over 11 segments	2C1R to me/2C to mum
28.9cM over 3 segments	148cM over 9 segments	2C2R to me/ 2C1R to mum
7.6cM over 1 segment	53cM over 5 segments	3C2R to me/3C1R to mum

The 7.6cM match especially would not be one I would be likely to take notice of on my own list, but as soon as I see that they share over 50 cMs with my mum it suddenly becomes worth investigating.

Should I test my siblings?

This is one of the most common questions people ask when starting out on a DNA journey. Many think there is no point testing their siblings if they have tested themselves. The answer to the question, however, is 'it depends!' It can only actually be answered with a question in return: 'do you have parents to test?'

If the answer to that is 'Yes – I have both parents to test' then, if they are willing, test both your parents. Your siblings' DNA will not provide anything extra if you have tested your parents (unless you wish to perform visual phasing with a set of sibling results, but that is an advanced technique and not applicable to the beginner starting out – see Chapter 4). If, on the other hand, the response is 'No' or 'Only one', then the answer is a resounding 'Yes – you should test your siblings!'. To explain why, we need to look back at how autosomal DNA is inherited:

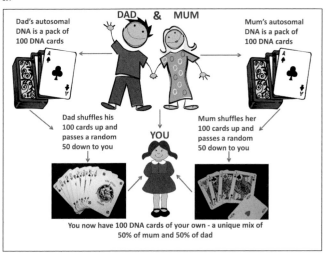

DAD & MUM

Dad's autosomal DNA is a pack of 100 DNA cards

Mum's autosomal DNA is a pack of 100 DNA cards

Dad shuffles his 100 cards up and passes a random 50 down to you

YOU

Mum shuffles her 100 cards up and passes a random 50 down to you

You now have 100 DNA cards of your own - a unique mix of 50% of mum and 50% of dad

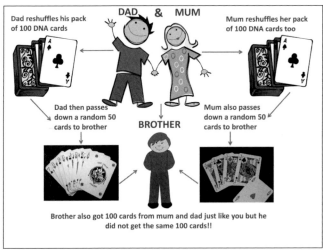

DAD & MUM

Dad reshuffles his pack of 100 DNA cards

Mum reshuffles her pack of 100 DNA cards too

Dad then passes down a random 50 cards to brother

BROTHER

Mum also passes down a random 50 cards to brother

Brother also got 100 cards from mum and dad just like you but he did not get the same 100 cards!!

© *Michelle Leonard*

- ➤ Siblings (including fraternal twins) share approximately 50% of their DNA
- ➤ Identical twins share all of their autosomal DNA so they are the exception to this rule
- ➤ Using my playing card analogy this means the average siblings share around fifty DNA cards with each other
- ➤ It also means they each inherited around fifty DNA cards they *do not* share with each other
- ➤ Two siblings, therefore, should expect to have inherited around 150 of their parents' combined 200 DNA cards between them
- ➤ Thus if you do not have your parents to test then testing just one sibling would get you approximately an extra 25% of your parents' DNA to work with
- ➤ Their results will give you additional matches across all lines since they will match people you do not on segments of DNA from your parents that were not passed down to you personally

Here is a prime example of why testing siblings is so useful: Ben is a 23andMe match at the third to fifth cousin level: he is listed down near the bottom of my second page of matches and, according to 23andMe, we share 0.42% over two segments, which equates to 32 cMs. That is a reasonable match, but it is not going to be top of my investigation list any time soon. I have tested my brother, however, and his highest match after my mum, me and my half-sister is Ben! They share a whopping 159 cMs over seven segments in comparison to the 32 cMs shared with me. Ben now quickly shoots to the top of my investigation list. I immediately messaged him and it turns out he is my 2C1R. He shares a lot less with me than average for a 2C1R, but in the correct range with my brother. Without my brother's test, even if I had contacted Ben and worked out the connection, I would have worried about potential issues in our line since we share so little DNA. Knowing he shares so much with my brother, however, excludes that possibility.

DNA (mainly autosomal) terminology

There are numerous terms associated with genetic genealogy which it is important to become familiar with. The following explanations should give you an understanding of many of these and their significance.

Single Nucleotide Polymorphism (SNP)
A SNP (pronounced 'snip') is a variation on a single DNA building block (nucleotide). Basically when a new cell is replicated and an error is made in the copying process that error is called a SNP – think of it like a spelling mistake. It is a selection of these SNPs across your entire genome that is actually tested when you take an autosomal DNA test. SNPs go hand in hand with cMs and, generally, if you share a large number of cMs with a match, you will share a large number of SNPs too. Just as there is no correlation between start and end locations and cMs, there is also no correlation between cMs and SNP density numbers. It is always best to base your research on the number of cMs.

Base Pairs (bps)
Nucleotide bases are the chemical building blocks of DNA that form the rungs on the double helix. There are four nucleotide bases – adenine (A), thymine (T), cytosine (C) and guanine (G) – and they pair up in specific ways to form base pairs, which are then used in the reporting of DNA results.

  The straight letters (A and T) always pair with each other and the curved letters (C and G) do the same. This means that whenever we know which base is on one side of the helix, we automatically know the corresponding base on the other side. This is why when a sequence of DNA is reported only one side of the helix is presented, e.g. ACTGATG alone instead of ATCGTAGCATTAGC. It is estimated that there are 3.2 billion base pairs in chromosomal DNA, but only between 600,000 and 700,000 of these are covered by current autosomal DNA tests.

Phasing
This is the process of separating out the DNA on your maternal chromosomes from the DNA on your paternal chromosomes so that you can identify which came from mum and which came from dad. Phasing can be used on both autosomes and the X-chromosome. In order to phase your DNA as fully as possible it is necessary to test your parents – testing both parents (known as trio phasing) will achieve the best results, but it is possible to undertake phasing with the results of just one parent (duo phasing). GEDMatch, in particular, offers a phasing

tool that will work if you have just one parent tested. Technically, phasing identifies which values (ATCG) came from your mother and which came from your father and separates them out. Here is a look at a section of unphased DNA:

UNPHASED DNA
AG
CT
CG
AA
TG
AT
GC

One of these values on each line came from the test-taker's mother and the other from their father, but it is not possible to identify which is which from this result alone. Phasing the test-taker's result against the results of their parents, however, can provide the answer:

UNPHASED DNA	MOTHER	FATHER	MATERNAL PHASED	PATERNAL PHASED
AG	AC	GT	A	G
CT	GT	AC	T	C
CG	CA	AG	C	G
AA	AG	AC	A	A
TG	TA	CG	T	G
AT	CT	TA	T	A
GC	GT	CA	G	C

The main benefits of phasing are that it can separate your matches into maternal, paternal or both, identify false matches and aid with chromosome mapping.

Identical By Descent (IBD)
IBD segments are segments of DNA that have been passed down by a common ancestor. Research suggests 100% of segments that are 15 cMs or larger in size are IBD and the point at which 50% of segments are IBD

is reached between 7 and 8 cMs. The smaller the segment, the higher the chance it is not IBD. Just the fact a segment is IBD, however, does not mean it will be easy to work out the common ancestors – for many smaller segments the connection will still be too far back to identify.

Identical by State (IBS)

IBS segments are either population segments or false segments. Since this term refers to two distinct types of segments it is problematic and can cause confusion. For this reason it is actually being phased out of genetic genealogy parlance. Two newer terms (IBP and IBC) have been created to combat this issue and it is best to use whichever of those is most appropriate for the particular segment you are investigating.

Identical by Population (IBP)

IBP segments are genuine segments that are common to a group of people from the same area. They are usually older segments that stretch beyond a genealogical timeframe, making it impossible to identify the common ancestors. Endogamous populations will also have many more of these segments.

Identical by Chance (IBC)

IBC segments are small segments that develop due to the chance mixing up of DNA values (alleles) and are, therefore, not real. In addition to IBC segments, there are a number of different terms for this phenomenon: false segments, false positives, pseudosegments, phantom segments and even frankensegments. The reason we end up with false segments is because the data is not phased. It is not possible to phase or separate out your maternal and paternal DNA segments without testing at least one parent, so in a number of your small segment matches the alleles will have been reported as a single sequence, but will actually be a mixture of alleles, some from your mother and some from your father. You, therefore, have to be alert to the fact that not all of your matches will be real cousins, as small segment matches could be IBC.

The easiest way to be 100% sure if a match is IBC or not is to test both your parents. If you are lucky enough to be able to do that and you find a match of yours does not match either of them, that raises a red flag. Many people sadly do not have that option, but it may be possible to find out that a segment is IBC by testing enough other close relatives. For example, while a match could just as easily be matching a full sibling in the same chance way they are matching you, a half-sibling could be extremely helpful. Since you only share DNA from one parent with a half-sibling, a match that you both share cannot be zigzagging back and forth between the DNA on your maternal and paternal chromosomes. This would also work with any other confirmed relatives with whom you only share one side of your tree – if the match also matches them on the same segment then you can eliminate the possibility of it being IBC.

Your Maternal Chromosome	Your Paternal Chromosome	IBD Match (Maternal)
A	G	A
G	T	G
C	A	C
C	T	C
G	C	G
G	A	G

Your Maternal Chromosome	Your Paternal Chromosome	IBC Match (Not Real)
A	G	A
G	T	G
C	A	A
C	T	C
G	C	C
G	A	G

Equally, just working with larger matches generally precludes this from being a concern since the vast majority of IBC segments will be smaller than 7cMs. As a result, FTDNA's use of small segments as small as 1cM is problematic (see Chapter 4 for how to deal with this). It is also why it is not advisable to lower the threshold below 7cMs on GEDMatch: you will share tiny segments with almost anybody if you lower the threshold far enough. This does not mean that we should completely ignore small matches (especially if common surnames/locations are present), but most people will have enough larger matches they can focus on before it is worth spending time on very small matches that could be IBC wild goose chases.

False Negatives

These are IBD segments of DNA that do not show up as a match due to an error in the testing process e.g. miscalls or no calls. If you have parents tested and a test-taker matches you but neither of your parents, the most likely explanation is that it is a false segment, but it is always possible there could have been an error on that particular segment during the running of the parent's DNA and it is a genuine match after all. Only by seeing if this person also matches other close relatives who share the same segment with you and your parent can you distinguish between these likelihoods. False negatives, like false positives, will occur with smaller segments.

No Calls

These occur during the testing process when a particular allele cannot be read and instead a blank value is recorded (usually as a dash or a zero).

Miscalls

These occur during the testing process when the wrong value is recorded for a particular allele.

Pile-ups

A pile-up region (also known as excess IBD sharing) is an area of a chromosome where a large number of test-takers all match each other on the same segment of DNA but no common ancestors can be identified between them. Pile-ups are generally smaller in cM size and could be population-based segments. If you have access to segment data and find you are matching a large number of people on a particular segment, but you cannot identify common ancestors for any of the matches, then it is quite likely you are dealing with a pile-up.

An important point in relation to pile-ups and population segments is that AncestryDNA tries to exclude them from your matches. The company developed a proprietary algorithm called Timber, which attempts to eliminate segments that match large numbers of people. There has been a lot of debate since Timber's introduction in 2014 as to how effective it is and it has been known to strip out some valid segments as well as pile-ups. If you test at different companies and find some of your Ancestry matches have also tested elsewhere, you will often notice that you appear to share more cMs with the same match on the different platform. Generally the reason for this will be that Timber has removed some segments on Ancestry.

Consult the ISOGG Wiki (https://isogg.org/wiki/Identical_by_descent) for a list of known excess IBD regions.

Number of Segments

The more segments you share with someone, the closer your relationship in general, since if you share more segments then you share more DNA overall. In the case of parents you share exactly twenty-three segments because you inherit entire chromosomes from them, whereas you may share significantly more than twenty-three segments with a sibling or aunt/uncle as segments are more broken up across the chromosomes. There is no pattern to the number of segments you share with a match, but the general rule is that if you share more than one significant segment you have a better chance of identifying a common ancestor. Be careful with the number of segments given on Ancestry, as the Timber algorithm has a tendency to break segments up and incorrectly inflate the number. When you see that you share 15 cMs over four segments with someone on Ancestry it could well be that it is actually just one segment broken up in this way.

One Segment Matches

Matches with whom you share just one segment of DNA are much more difficult to predict. For instance, a 20 cM one segment match has such a wide gamut of relationship possibilities – it could be an extreme outlier such as a 2C1R (as we have seen), but equally it could be anything from a third to a tenth or even more distant cousin, especially if a population or sticky segment is involved.

Sticky Segments

These are segments of DNA that pass down through a number of generations without recombination decreasing their size. Often you will find you and your parent share just the one segment with a match and it is the same size for you as it is for them; while many of these will not be sticky segments some of them certainly will be. These segments reach much further back in time since they have passed through several generations intact so it is extremely difficult to identify common ancestors.

Fuzzy Ends

Occasionally you will come across matches that share slightly more or less DNA with a parent than they do with a child. If the difference is only a few cMs then generally this can be attributed to a margin of error in the testing process, or what we call 'fuzzy ends'. Every segment of DNA has a start and end location, but these can vary slightly from parent to child as reported in test results.

Non Identical Region (NIR)

This is a non-match – an area of DNA where you match someone on neither copy of your chromosomes.

Half Identical Region (HIR)

This is a segment of DNA shared on just one of your two copies of a chromosome. For instance the DNA I share with my mother is half identical, since I inherited all of my maternal chromosomes from her but none of my paternal chromosomes.

Fully Identical Region (FIR)

This is a segment of DNA that is shared on both copies of a chromosome. Outside of identical twins, who are fully identical across all chromosomes, the relatives with whom you will share the most FIRs are full siblings, since you each inherit significant amounts of DNA on both your maternal and paternal chromosomes. Double cousins and those with an endogamous background may also share more FIRs. You can view HIRs and FIRs on GEDMatch and 23andMe.

Now we are well-versed in how autosomal DNA works, Chapter 4 will explain how best to use it for genealogy.

Chapter 4

atDNA TESTS

Michelle Leonard

Now that we have covered the inheritance patterns of autosomal DNA, it is time to delve into how to work with autosomal DNA test results. This chapter will provide a practical guide on how to get the most out of these results for genealogy purposes.

Before we begin it is important to understand that you may discover something unexpected about your ancestry when you take an atDNA test. DNA is the one record set that does not and cannot lie or make mistakes, whereas human beings can and sometimes do. While those who receive surprising results are exceptions, you have to be aware of and prepared for this possibility when you choose to test. Additionally, while DNA cannot deliberately mislead, it can be misinterpreted and occasionally false conclusions are drawn from it. Look upon DNA as an additional evidence source that requires understanding, interpretation and most of all amalgamation with other research-based evidence.

Here is a summary of what you can use autosomal DNA testing for:

➤ Confirming and supporting your family tree research
➤ Breaking down brick walls (both direct and collateral)
➤ Adding new branches to your tree
➤ Discovering and connecting with new cousins
➤ Testing hypotheses about relationships and ancestors
➤ Solving adoption, unknown parentage and other unknown ancestor mysteries
➤ Mapping your DNA back to your ancestors
➤ Learning about your ethnic make-up

There are two distinct aspects to the results that you receive with an autosomal DNA test:

1. DNA match lists
2. Admixture estimates

DNA match lists
When you take an autosomal test at AncestryDNA, Family Tree DNA (FTDNA), 23andMe, MyHeritage or Living DNA you are provided with a DNA match list that displays the names of others who have tested at the same company and share segments of DNA with you in accordance with the thresholds used by that specific company.

The DNA match list is by far the most important and genealogically useful part of an autosomal DNA test. Admixture information is initially interesting and exciting to look at, but it is via working with your DNA matches that you will get the most out of your autosomal DNA test results. You can continue to work with your DNA match lists indefinitely as they grow over time, while you will probably only look at your admixture estimates a handful of times.

No matter which company you have chosen to test with, the best way to begin working with your DNA match list is to start at the top, where your closest matches are located, and work down towards your more distant matches. Your closest matches share the most DNA with you, so theoretically they should be the easiest to work out and in general they will be, but there is always a chance either you or your match has an error on your tree or within your known ancestry that increases the difficulty level e.g. a research error or an NPE in a recent generation (NPE stands for non-paternity event, but I prefer 'not the parent expected', which is a phrase coined by genetic genealogist Emily Aulicino.)

Most of us will have so many distant matches that it is impossible to ever look at them all, and with databases expanding so rapidly more and more new matches are being added to our lists on a daily basis. In order to get the most out of the new matches, it is imperative to direct your efforts in the right areas and, in general, that means working with the highest matches possible.

After checking out your DNA homepage, the next thing you want to look at is your DNA match list page, but what does a DNA match list look like? The answer is that it depends on the company you have tested with as they all have different features, tools and ways of displaying similar information.

Here is the top of my 23andMe match list as an example:

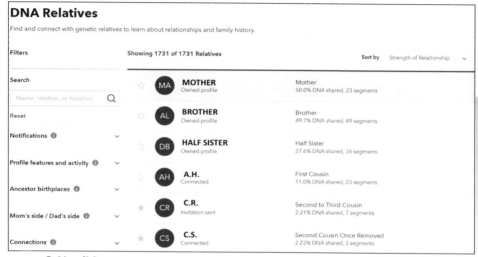

© 23andMe

The following table gives a summary of the basic data which the various companies report on:

	Predicted Relationship	Shared atDNA (cMs)	Shared atDNA (%)	Largest segment	Number of segments	X-matches
Ancestry	Yes	Yes	No	No	Yes	No
23andMe	Yes	No*	Yes	No*	Yes	Yes
FTDNA	Yes	Yes	No	Yes	Yes	Yes
MyHeritage	Yes	Yes	Yes	Yes	Yes	No

*available if open or individually sharing.

Relationship Predictions

Each of the testing companies has their own relationship prediction categories and ranges e.g. first–second cousin, fourth–sixth cousin, fifth–eighth cousin. These are a rough guide to the expected level of relationship between the test-taker and the match. No matter where you have tested, however, I would recommend consulting the extremely useful DNA Painter Shared cM Project Tool to get the most accurate picture of possible relationships and probabilities.

The Shared cM Project is one of the best resources available for understanding ranges of shared cMs and relationship probabilities. It is a collaborative project, run by American genetic genealogist Dr Blaine Bettinger, which collates data from real matches and displays the averages and ranges for a wide variety of relationships. There have been over 25,000 submissions to the project so far. I recommend submitting your own data from confirmed relationships using the data submission portal here: https://docs.google.com/forms/d/e/1FAIpQLSc5a0SIH IeiwLl5Wxn4sLqgnRV-su2klK2W_YzIJc9xq2i4zw/viewform

The most exciting tool to emerge out of the Shared cM Project in recent years is 'The Shared cM Project 3.0 tool' created by DNA Painter developer Jonny Perl. This automates the investigation process for you and can help enormously with relationship predictions and probabilities. When you look at the number of cMs you share with a DNA match and want to identify the possible and probable relationships for that level of sharing, go to the tool, either key in the cM or percentage total (percentage is the default at 23andMe) and it will generate a full list of probabilities, percentages and relationships. It is incredibly helpful and simple to use.

My first cousin Ann shares 634cM with me and is predicted to be a second cousin at Ancestry, but if she shared just 6cM more the prediction would be first cousin. It is best to investigate the number of cMs as opposed to the relationship estimate, so take the cM number and plug it into the Shared cM Project Tool.

The result shows that there is only a 0.9% probability that Ann is a second cousin, but there are many possible relationships at higher probabilities. Always look at the highest probability relationships first, but do not dismiss the lower probabilities and beware of confirmation bias: try to disprove a preferred outcome as opposed to trying to prove it. In this case probability suggests my known 1C (first cousin) is more likely to be a half 1C or 1C1R, so I had to consider that possibility. Due to the much higher amounts of DNA she and I both share with many other close relatives, however, it is certain she is a slightly low-sharing

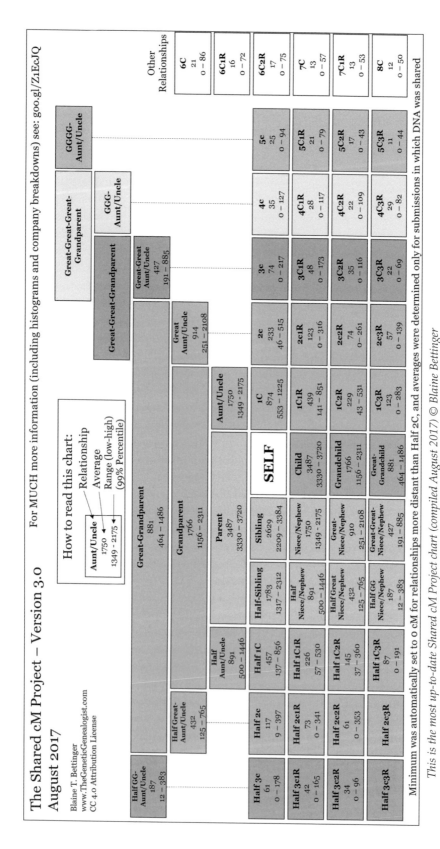

The Shared cM Project – Version 3.0
August 2017

Blaine T. Bettinger
www.TheGeneticGenealogist.com
CC 4.0 Attribution License

For MUCH more information (including histograms and company breakdowns) see: goo.gl/Z1EcJQ

How to read this chart:

Aunt/Uncle	← Relationship
1750	← Average
1349 - 2175	← Range (low-high)
	← (99% Percentile)

Other Relationships

6C
21
0 – 86

6C1R
16
0 – 72

6C2R
17
0 – 75

7C
13
0 – 57

7C1R
13
0 – 53

8C
12
0 – 50

GGGG-Aunt/Uncle

5C
25
0 – 94

5C1R
21
0 – 79

5C2R
17
0 – 43

5C3R
11
0 – 44

Great-Great-Great-Grandparent / **GGG-Aunt/Uncle**

4C
35
0 – 127

4C1R
28
0 – 117

4C2R
22
0 – 109

4C3R
29
0 – 82

Great-Great-Grandparent / **Great-Great Aunt/Uncle** 427 / 191 – 885

3C
74
0 – 217

3C1R
48
0 – 173

3C2R
35
0 – 116

3C3R
22
0 – 69

Great Aunt/Uncle 914 / 251 – 2108

2C
233
46 – 515

2C1R
123
0 – 316

2C2R
74
0 – 261

2C3R
57
0 – 139

Aunt/Uncle 1750 / 1349 - 2175

1C
874
553 – 1225

1C1R
439
141 – 851

1C2R
229
43 – 531

1C3R
123
0 – 283

Great-Grandparent 881 / 464 – 1486

Grandparent 1766 / 1156 – 2311

Parent 3487 / 3330 – 3720

SELF

Child
3487
3330 – 3720

Grandchild
1766
1156 – 2311

Great-Grandchild
881
464 – 1486

Sibling
2629
2209 – 3384

Niece/Nephew
1750
1349 – 2175

Great-Niece/Nephew
910
251 – 2108

Great-Great-Niece/Nephew
427
191 – 885

Half-Sibling
1783
1317 – 2312

Half Niece/Nephew
891
500 – 1446

Half Great Niece/Nephew
432
125 – 765

Half GG Niece/Nephew
187
12 – 383

Half Aunt/Uncle
891
500 – 1446

Half 1C
457
137 – 856

Half 1C1R
226
57 – 530

Half 1C2R
145
37 – 360

Half 1C3R
87
0 – 191

Half Great-Aunt/Uncle
432
125 – 765

Half 2C
117
9 – 397

Half 2C1R
73
0 – 341

Half 2C2R
61
0 – 353

Half 2C3R

Half GG-Aunt/Uncle
187
12 – 383

Half 3C
61
0 – 178

Half 3C1R
42
0 – 165

Half 3C2R
34
0 – 96

Half 3C3R

Minimum was automatically set to 0 cM for relationships more distant than Half 2C, and averages were determined only for submissions in which DNA was shared

This is the most up-to-date Shared cM Project chart (compiled August 2017) © Blaine Bettinger
https://thegeneticgenealogist.com/2017/08/26/august-2017-update-to-the-shared-cm-project.

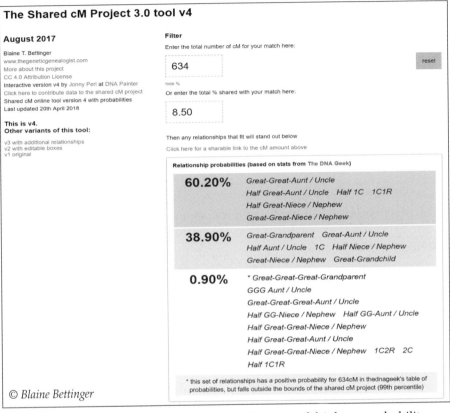

The Shared cM Project 3.0 tool v4

August 2017

Blaine T. Bettinger
www.thegeneticgenealogist.com
More about this project
CC 4.0 Attribution License
Interactive version v4 by Jonny Perl at DNA Painter
Click here to contribute data to the shared cM project
Shared cM online tool version 4 with probabilities
Last updated 20th April 2018

This is v4.
Other variants of this tool:

v3 with additional relationships
v2 with editable boxes
v1 original

Filter

Enter the total number of cM for your match here:

634

reset

hide %

Or enter the total % shared with your match here:

8.50

Then any relationships that fit will stand out below
Click here for a sharable link to the cM amount above

Relationship probabilities (based on stats from The DNA Geek)

60.20% Great-Great-Aunt / Uncle
Half Great-Aunt / Uncle   Half 1C   1C1R
Half Great-Niece / Nephew
Great-Great-Niece / Nephew

38.90% Great-Grandparent   Great-Aunt / Uncle
Half Aunt / Uncle   1C   Half Niece / Nephew
Great-Niece / Nephew   Great-Grandchild

0.90% * Great-Great-Great-Grandparent
GGG Aunt / Uncle
Great-Great-Great-Aunt / Uncle
Half GG-Niece / Nephew   Half GG-Aunt / Uncle
Half Great-Great-Niece / Nephew
Half Great-Great-Aunt / Uncle
Half Great-Great-Niece / Nephew   1C2R   2C
Half 1C1R

* this set of relationships has a positive probability for 634cM in thednageek's table of probabilities, but falls outside the bounds of the shared cM project (99th percentile)

© Blaine Bettinger

1C and the relationship falls within the second highest probability grouping at 38.9%.

Never take relationship predictions too literally, especially for more distant relationships, and always remember that multiple relationships could fit the same number of cMs and outliers are possible.

Bookmark this tool and use it whenever you need some help working out the potential relationships and ranges: https://dnapainter. com/tools/sharedcmv4

Shared atDNA

The total amount of shared atDNA is reported either as a percentage figure or as a number of cMs, generally on the main match page. On Ancestry this information is both on the main match page and the individual match page under the 'i' button. It is important to get into the habit of checking cM information when looking at new matches.

Largest Segment/Longest Block

This refers to the largest segment of DNA you share with your match. FTDNA and MyHeritage report on it and it can be seen on the DNA Comparison page on 23andMe. It is not available on Ancestry. It is often useful to filter your list by longest block on FTDNA, as opposed to shared cMs, due to the fact that segments as small as 1 cM are included in that total. As illustrated in Chapter 3, very small segments are problematic and more often than not will be false. I prefer not to count these segments so I calculate my own total, adding up just the segments over 7 cMs via the chromosome browser table view (see p76-7).

Number of Segments

The larger the number of shared segments, the closer the relationship is likely to be, but the overall amount of shared atDNA and the size of the largest segments are much more important indicators of relationship level.

X-Matches

This indicates that you share a segment on an X-chromosome with that particular match. You should note that Ancestry and MyHeritage do not report X-matches. Since X-matches can only occur on a number of specific ancestral lines, it is easier to narrow down the genealogical link to particular lines. For example, the most obvious benefit for male test-takers is that all their X-matches must be on their maternal side. FTDNA report tiny segments of X-DNA, so it is best to check the actual size of the segment on the X-chromosome via the chromosome browser tool before accepting any match highlighted as an X-match on the main match page as real.

Other features and tools

The companies all provide differing features and tools; the following are perhaps the most useful.

Ancestral Surnames/Family Trees and Search Options

All of the companies have the facility for test-takers to list ancestral surnames and, in some cases, locations. Additionally all, except 23andMe, allow family trees to be created or uploaded, although a link to an externally hosted tree can be added to the latter. All offer surname search options, but only Ancestry and 23andMe provide location searching. It is helpful to search your entire match lists for matches with common *surnames* and common *locations*; if a match has both you have a better chance of identifying the link. Work through all of your ancestral surnames and filter by birth locations every so often in case you get any interesting hits. Keep in mind, however, that this type of filtering works better for less common surnames and locations. There are obvious benefits to uploading a tree, making it much easier to spot possible genealogical links with matches. Once you find clear indications of a link via surnames, locations or trees, you may wish to make contact with those matches. For advice on how to go about this, see p82-4.

Shared Matches/In Common With (ICW) Tools

These tools, described differently by the various companies, list people who match both you and another match you have selected. In the majority of cases the use of shared matches will be key to working out how you and your matches relate to each other. Additionally the more confirmed relatives you have in the databases, the more useful shared matches will become.

On Ancestry the 'Shared Matches' list is limited to test-takers who match both you and the comparison match at the fourth to sixth cousin or closer level i.e. sharing over 20 cM. You cannot, however, see how many cMs they share with each other, unless they share their results with you. FTDNA's 'In Common With' list is similar in that it allows you to see which of your matches also match one specific match, but not how well they match each other. 23andMe's 'Relatives In Common' and MyHeritage's 'Shared DNA Matches' tools are more detailed, as they include both the amount of DNA you share with the shared match and the amount shared between them and the comparison match.

It is important to be aware that it is always possible a match could connect to you in one way and the shared match in another. Don't assume that matches only relate to you in one way – even without endogamy it is always possible that you could have more than one connection with a given match.

Predicted Phasing
This process has already been described in Chapter 3, and although none of the companies provide full phased segment data, there are some tools for narrowing your matches to the maternal or paternal side of your family.

Ancestry adds 'Mother' and 'Father' filters if parents test, but be aware only matches in the fourth to sixth cousin or closer categories will appear on these lists.

The Family matching feature on FTDNA offers 'Maternal', 'Paternal', and 'Both' buckets that populate if you attach a family tree and link entries of known relatives on that tree to their test results via the complimentary Linked Relationship tool. This tool uses uploaded results for relatives from parents to third cousins. The 'Both' bucket will only contain full siblings and cousins who match on both sides of your tree.

If you have a parent tested at 23andMe it is automatically noted on your match list if matches are on that side, e.g. 'Mother's side'. If the other parent is not tested a very useful 'Not Mother's/Father's Side' tool is also available to separate out paternal or maternal matches.

Shared Ancestor Hints (SAHs)/Smart Matches
These hints, provided by Ancestry and MyHeritage respectively, are generated when the same ancestor or ancestral couple is found in both your linked family tree and that of a match. Remember that, although often accurate, errors are always possible and these are only 'hints' – they do not prove that you and your match inherited the DNA you share from the common ancestors identified.

Sharing Results
Some companies facilitate the sharing of results with your matches – sharing match lists in particular and having them share theirs with you can be very beneficial. Sharing is currently possible at Ancestry and FTDNA (via projects).

Get in all the databases
There are pros and cons to testing at each of the major testing companies, but it is important to get into as many of the different databases as you can in order to maximise your chances of detecting

your best matches. I have many more matches at Ancestry than elsewhere. That will be a standard experience for many since Ancestry has the largest database, but it does not mean your best matches will also be at Ancestry, as you simply do not know where they may choose to test. The only way to be confident you are not missing out on any important matches is to get into all the databases. DNA testing has significantly reduced in price over the past few years and frequent sales make this a more affordable goal. Additionally several of the companies (FTDNA, MyHeritage and LivingDNA) accept free transfers, as does GEDMatch (Ancestry and 23andMe do not) so it is possible to get into all of the databases without buying standalone tests for each of them.

Build your family tree wide and deep
It is absolutely vital to pair traditional research with DNA analysis if you want to get the most out of DNA testing for genealogy. One of the most important things to consider both before and after you test is the building of your own family tree. The more robust and extensive your tree, the more you will be able to achieve with your DNA results and the more cousin matches you will be able to identify. Try to work as many lines forward to the present as you can, including collateral lines, since it is your distant living cousins who will show up on your DNA match lists. If one or both of you do not have your tree developed enough then neither of you will be able to identify the connection.

For example, my match Mary has a tree that only goes back to her grandparents, one of whom was Alfred Kerr from Lanarkshire, Scotland. My great-grandmother was a Kerr from Lanarkshire so I checked my extensive tree for Mary's grandfather Alfred and he was already on it. It took very little effort to identify this connection as all the required research had been completed previously and this DNA match enabled me to make contact with a new cousin, add a recent branch to my tree and confirm a line. Verifying the accuracy of your tree via DNA evidence is one of the most important reasons to DNA test for genealogy and your goal should be to confirm as many lines as possible.

Extensive tree-building, however, is not possible for everyone, including adoptees and those with recent unknown ancestor mysteries or brick walls. While building a personal tree if you possibly can is extremely helpful, it is not essential to success as DNA is also the best tool for uncovering unknown ancestry. For those who do not have a recent unknown ancestor mystery, however, spending time building out a tree should be a top priority.

Narrowing down your matches

As covered in Chapter 3, it is very important to test your older generations if at all possible, starting with parents and grandparents. This will not only give you more of your ancestors' DNA to work with, but will also help you enormously with narrowing down your results; testing just one parent can narrow your matches by 50%.

If you do not have older generations to test then test your peers (half-siblings, first cousins, second cousins etc). Full siblings are not included for narrowing purposes, but are also very important test-takers if you do not have parents to test, as they received DNA from them that you did not.

Note that half relationships are incredibly helpful for narrowing purposes: while you share less DNA with a half-relative than a full one, all of the DNA you do share can be effectively narrowed a further generation since the common ancestor is one parent, one grandparent etc.

Let's look at how this works in practice. Since I have many close relatives tested I can significantly narrow down my connection to this match, D.H., via researching our shared match list:

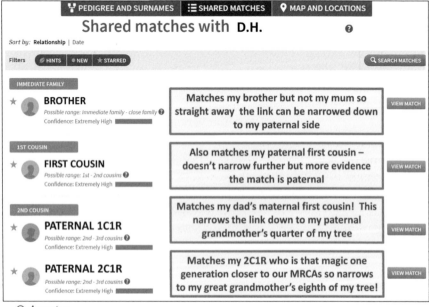

© Ancestry

Via this analysis I have eliminated 87.5% of my tree and can focus on my great-grandmother's eighth to find the connection. My great-grandmother, Janet Cullen, was the daughter of John Cullen and Janet Nicol, so it must lie on one of those lines. Investigating D.H.'s tree one name stood out – her grandmother Christina was a Nicol. I now have a common surname that matches with the small part of my tree D.H. narrows to, so it is worth investigating further.

Fact-check and build out the trees of your matches

Tree investigation is a vital component of successful DNA matching and many matches can be solved if you spend time building out their trees yourself. Many will only have small trees comprising of a few names or maybe even just parents' names, but do not dismiss these matches or trees. Do not accept the tree is too small to find the link – be proactive and build your own versions of the match's tree to see if you can pinpoint the connection. Before deciding to spend time on this, however, you have to evaluate whether the match is worth the effort: would a 12 cM one-segment match with no clues be worth it? Probably not. Would a 90 cM six-segment match be worth it? Almost certainly.

Let's return to D.H. as an example: her tree only reaches back to her grandparents, so traditional research was required to see if her grandmother Christina connects to my Nicol line. This research broke a collateral line brick wall for me as I found Christina's father, William Nicol, was my second great-grandmother Janet's brother, whom I had not been able to trace past the 1841 census. When exploring trees it is essential to remember that many contain errors. Always pursue sources and, if matches have large but unsourced trees, it is wise to build your own sourced versions. You may, in the process, uncover mistakes that help identify common ancestors.

Genetic generations v age

Knowing the age of your match can be very helpful when it comes to determining how they may relate to you. The general starting point is that people of a similar age are most likely to be of the same genetic generation, but do not assume that will always be the case as there will be exceptions to the rule. Be aware that only 23andMe and MyHeritage display the ages of matches, and only if they have consented to share this information.

The most telling aspect to look out for when it comes to genetic generational anomalies is an older father skewing the generations. A perfect example of this is my mother and her 2C2R Rob who is two generations closer to their common ancestors despite being three years younger. The reason for this anomaly is that Rob's grandfather was in his sixties when his father was born.

In order to be confident there are no generational anomalies, look closely at the trees of your matches going back several generations and if your and their parents, grandparents and great-grandparents all fit within regular generation spans (20–35 years) then the likelihood that you and your similarly aged match are part of the same genetic generation is much higher. If, however, you find a much older father or very long generations then you have to factor that into relationship prediction calculations.

Chromosome browsers

A chromosome browser is a tool that provides a visual representation of the exact segments of DNA shared between a test-taker and one or more (in the case of one-to-many chromosome browsers) of their DNA matches. They provide information on the start and end locations of matching segments and the amount of cMs in those segments. FTDNA, 23andMe and MyHeritage all provide Chromosome browsers, but Ancestry does not.

All chromosome browsers display twenty-three lines to represent the twenty-three Chromosomes (twenty-two autosomes plus the X-chromosome). Remember that there are twenty-three *pairs* of chromosomes though, so why is there only one line on the chromosome browser to represent each pair? The reason is that it is not possible to automatically differentiate between the maternal and paternal chromosomes so they are basically merged together. Never lose sight of the fact that both exist, however, and two people matching you on the same segment on the same chromosome could be matching on either your maternal or paternal copy. It is possible they match each other but equally likely they do not, so you have to find out if they do through comparing them to each other if possible.

Here is my comparison with my brother on 23andMe:

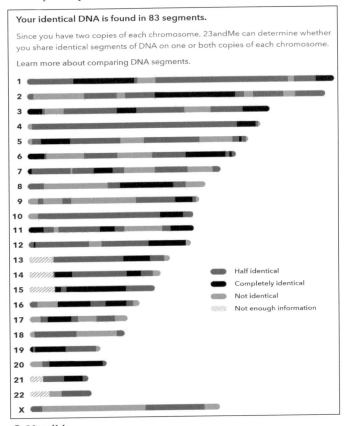

© 23andMe

An interesting additional feature of 23andMe's chromosome browser is that it supplies information on whether shared segments are half or completely identical (often referred to as fully identical). If a segment is half-identical this means you share it on just one of your two copies of that particular chromosome and if it is completely identical you share it on both copies. 23andMe also makes it possible for you to compare not only yourself to a number of your matches, but also your matches to each other via their DNA comparison tool. Knowing how your matches match each other can be extremely helpful when trying to work out a connection.

FTDNA and MyHeritage also provide one-to-many chromosome browsers, but it's important to note MyHeritage does not report on the X-chromosome. You will notice some criss-crossed greyed out areas on chromosome browsers; these indicate SNP poor regions that have not been tested, because there is not enough data available to sample them.

Chromosome mapping

Chromosome mapping is fun, but it is more than just a fascinating DNA jigsaw puzzle you might be interested in working on, as it can bring real benefits to your family history research. The more DNA you can map back to your ancestors, the easier it becomes to narrow matches down and successfully pinpoint cousin connections. This is a process you can begin working on as soon as you have test result data from known relatives, and is likely to remain a work in progress while you encourage more relatives to test and attempt to identify connections with matches.

So what exactly is 'chromosome mapping' and how do you do it? Chromosome mapping is the process of assigning specific segments of DNA to specific ancestors with the use of confirmed cousin matches. If you share a segment of DNA with a known second cousin, it is extremely likely that piece of DNA was passed down to you and your second cousin by your shared great-grandparents (your most recent common ancestors) and therefore you can map this shared DNA back to them. You do not have to only practise chromosome mapping on your own chromosomes either – if you have parents and other relatives tested you can also map their DNA.

It is only possible to undertake chromosome mapping if you have segment information to work with, so this means it cannot be done with Ancestry matches unless they transfer their raw data somewhere that provides segment information. You can currently map matches from FTDNA, 23andMe, MyHeritage and GEDMatch.

GenomeMatePro (GMP) has an excellent chromosome mapping section and in 2017 a new tool named DNA Painter, created by developer Jonny Perl, was released. It has fast become the go-to tool for chromosome mapping. Different colours are used to represent particular ancestors and the segments that have been mapped back to them.

Chromosome mapping can also be carried out independently by recording specific segments of DNA and which ancestor they have been assigned to on, for example, a spreadsheet, but DNA Painter undoubtedly facilitates the process and produces a clear visual representation of what otherwise might seem a dry collection of numbers.

It is exciting to see your map develop and chromosomes start to fill up, but it is also extremely useful. The advantage of starting your chromosome mapping early is that whenever you get new matches, you can check the segment data for them in case they match up on any of the segments you have already mapped. Whenever they do, you can instantly narrow them down to the ancestors the DNA is already mapped to.

I would advise first spending time getting to grips with the tools at the testing sites and working your way through your top matches, but once you have a bit more experience, chromosome mapping is an excellent way to advance your DNA adventure. It can be quite addictive trying to map as much as you possibly can and see exactly which pieces of your DNA came from which of your ancestors.

Not In Common With

As we have seen, FTDNA's shared match list is called 'In Common With' but they also provide a 'Not In Common With' tool which can be equally useful.

It is important not to assume too much from 'Not In Common With' lists, as the only relationship for which you can run a 'not in common with' search and narrow to a side is parent/child. For all other relationships there is a chance the test-takers on the list still match you on the same side. For example, a list generated between my mum and her maternal first cousin Isobel only tells me that these test-takers match my mum but do NOT match Isobel. I cannot assume that they are paternal matches, however, as mum and Isobel only share approximately 25% of their maternal DNA, meaning there is 75% they do not share and these test-takers could match my mum on segments within that 75%. There is a way I can potentially narrow some of them down to paternal, however, and that is by comparing segment data in the chromosome browser. Let's focus on a match named 'Kate' and analyse the exact segments she and Isobel share with my mum.

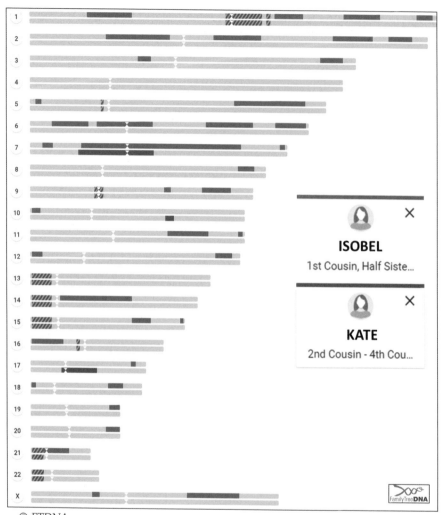

© FTDNA

While my mum shares a large number of segments with her first cousin, there is only one significant segment with Kate. The interesting thing to note, though, is the fact that this segment is on chromosome 9 and clearly overlaps with a segment my mum also shares with Isobel.

The best way to investigate start and end locations is to view the data in a table, using the Detailed Segment Data link near the top of the screen.

Match Name	Chromosome	Start Location	End Location	Centimorgans(cM)	Matching SNPs
ISOBEL	9	108,966,384	127,196,340	25.88	5,389
KATE	9	93,452,361	124,646,012	42.24	8,666

FamilyTreeDNA

FTDNA

The numbers confirm that part of the segment of DNA on chromosome 9 my mum and Kate share does indeed correspond with the same segment that my mum and Isobel share (from start location 108,966,384 to end location 124,646,012 – since these numbers are large it is generally easier to shorten them to 108.9 – 124.6). The 'Not In Common With' list, however, reported that Isobel and Kate do not match each other. Since Isobel matches my mum on her *maternal* copy of chromosome 9, we can therefore deduce that Kate must match my mum on her *paternal* copy of chromosome 9. Kate's match can be narrowed down to the paternal half of my mum's tree since it is not possible for two people to match you on the same segment but not match each other, unless they are matching you on opposite copies of the chromosome. After further research into Kate's family tree this was proven correct as she is a 4C2R via a paternal line. While FTDNA is the only site that provides a 'Not In Common With' tool, this kind of inferred segment analysis can be undertaken on any of the sites that provide segment data so long as your starting point is two matches who do not match each other.

Moving a step beyond identifying 'in common with' matches is the process of triangulation.

Triangulation

Triangulation is another major term that you will often hear in the genetic genealogy community. It occurs when three or more DNA test-takers all match each other on the exact same segment of DNA. When this transpires it indicates that these people all have a common ancestor from whom they inherited their shared DNA segment.

True triangulation is not possible at Ancestry as it requires segment data which is not supplied, but it can be partially completed at FTDNA (partially as it requires the co-operation of the match to complete a full comparison) and can be fully realised at 23andMe, MyHeritage and GEDMatch.

Let's look at an example of triangulating a segment of DNA using the chromosome browser at FTDNA. When looking at my mum's account and comparing her to her maternal first cousin Isobel and another match named Kim, one chromosome immediately stands out – Isobel and Kim both match my mum on a segment of DNA on chromosome 7. This only tells us that they both match my mum, however, and the key to triangulation is that all three must match each other. In order to determine whether they triangulate or not we need to know if Isobel and Kim also match each other on the same segment on chr 7. Unfortunately this is not something the chromosome browser on my mum's account can tell us, as I cannot compare Isobel to Kim. There are, however, two ways I can find out whether Kim and Isobel match each other. I can look at the 'In Common With' list for one of them to see if the other is on it, or I can use the matrix tool which can be accessed from the FTDNA dashboard.

The matrix confirms that Isobel and Kim do match each other, making it more likely that the segment they both share with my mum is on the same copy of chromosome 7, but it does not prove that it is, since Isobel and Kim could conceivably match each other in a different way.

In order to obtain proof I would either need to have access to one of their match lists, or they would have to do the comparison on their own accounts. Thankfully, in this case, I manage Isobel's test so I have the required access to compare them:

HOW MUM MATCHES KIM ON CHR 7				
Chromosome	Start Location	End Location	Centimorgans(cM)	Matching SN
7	31,485,492	76,908,131	38.75	8,7

HOW MUM MATCHES ISOBEL ON CHR 7				
Chromosome	Start Location	End Location	Centimorgans(cM)	Matching SN
7	31,796,620	130,536,623	84.08	20,5

MILLION DOLLAR QUESTION: DO THEY MATCH EACH OTHER ON CHR 7?

HOW ISOBEL MATCHES KIM ON CHR 7				
Chromosome	Start Location	End Location	Centimorgans(cM)	Matching SN
7	28,047,018	76,908,131	44.26	9,9

© FTDNA

We have triangulated! Mum, Isobel and Kim all match each other on the same segment of DNA on the same copy of chromosome 7, so they inherited this piece of DNA from the same common ancestor. In this case it is my mother's maternal chromosome 7 as Isobel is her known maternal first cousin. We cannot say that the full segments they share with each other are triangulated though – we have to count the triangulated segment from the highest start location between the three of them to the lowest end location since that is the exact segment they all share. In this case that would be 31.7 – 76.9.

The chromosome browser at MyHeritage automates this process for you.

If triangulated segments have been detected between you, your comparison match and the shared match, a triangulation symbol is displayed. In order to see the details in the one-to-many chromosome browser, click on this symbol.

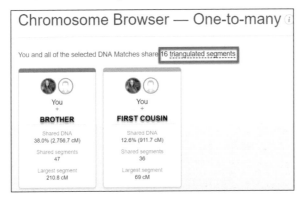

© MyHeritage

The site highlights all of the triangulated segments and provides tables with full details of the triangulated and regular segments.

23andMe also provide automated triangulation information if a match is open or individually sharing with you. Any match with a 'Yes' in the 'Shared DNA' column on the 'Relatives In Common' list shares a triangulated segment and any with a 'No' shares DNA with both you and your match but not on the same segment.

Triangulation can be useful for narrowing down matches and identifying groups of people who all share common ancestors, but it also has to be remembered that triangulation between cousins at more

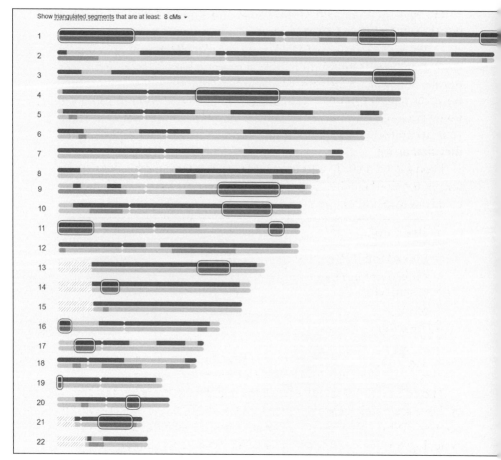

© MyHeritage

distant levels is a rare occurrence and attempting to triangulate small segments is not generally useful. Triangulation is a helpful technique, but the majority of DNA puzzles can be solved without it.

The dreaded no tree situation

There is a great deal of frustration in the genetic genealogy community about lack of trees hampering success. Many feel discouraged by the fact that a large number of test-takers do not upload trees and often ignore these matches. While this frustration is understandable, and it would be ideal if every test-taker uploaded a robust, well-documented tree, it is unrealistic to expect this.

While there are many matches who do not have a tree, there are many others who do but just have not linked their tree to their DNA results. Ancestry highlights when matches have unlinked trees, however, so you can investigate them, but always bear in mind that the home person of the tree will not necessarily be the test-taker. Linking your tree to your results is one of the most important steps to take when they first arrive.

I conducted a study into how many trees are available on Ancestry for my top 200 matches (excluding those I have tested myself as they could skew the data):

Tree Designation	Number	Percentage
Linked Public Tree	79	39.5
Linked Private Tree	15	7.5
Unlinked Tree	47	23.5
No Tree	59	29.5
Total Public Trees	126	63.0
Total Trees	141	71.0

The fact that 71% of my top 200 have a tree of some kind and 63% of those are public belies the idea that the majority of test-takers have no tree. While this is an individual study, several other genetic genealogists have conducted similar ones and ended up with comparable results. Additionally, out of the fifty-nine test-takers with no trees, many provided family history information upon contact that helped me work out the common ancestors in eighteen cases, so do not bypass those without a tree. We also have to take into account the quality of the trees and many will not be helpful, but even a tiny tree can often be enough to solve a match if you are prepared to work with it.

Also never forget that some people will have no tree or private speculative trees because they are adopted or have unknown parentage. What if there really is no tree though? The obvious step is to attempt to make contact.

Contacting DNA matches

Once you have familiarised yourself with the various processes and tools described above, you may feel it is time to take the plunge and contact some selected matches. One of the keys to successfully using your DNA test results for genealogy purposes is contacting matches and eliciting successful responses. Connecting with your matches can provide the breakthroughs needed to identify common ancestors.

At Ancestry, 23andMe and MyHeritage you can only contact matches via their proprietary messaging systems. This can be hit and miss at times, but do not be discouraged from trying. FTDNA and GEDmatch supply email addresses, which are often a more fruitful contact method. Also, do not avoid messaging those with no tree or private trees – some of my most helpful contacts have emerged from those circumstances.

Personalise your profiles to let people see you are friendly and interested in contact and they may be more willing to reply.

Before sending an opening message to a match do some preliminary research. Investigate their tree (if they have one) and shared matches to try to work out the connection. Can you pinpoint any shared surnames or locations? Can you narrow the link down via matches to other confirmed cousins?

In the subject title and first line of your message always state who matches whom. Never write 'I match you' or 'you match me'. You have to make it as easy as possible for your contact to find and evaluate the match. Many people manage multiple tests, so if you do not identify the match properly they will not know which test to check. Write something along these lines: 'My test under the name ML matches the test you manage under the name JS'. If the match is at GEDmatch include the kit numbers involved. If the match is at FTDNA, however, it is not useful to provide FTDNA kit numbers because it is not possible to search the FTDNA database by kit number.

Your initial message should be short, friendly, informative and non-technical. It should aim to grab your match's attention and, if possible, offer an incentive to reply: I call this 'carrot dangling' or, more aptly, 'record and photo dangling'! If you do not have such an incentive to offer, try to find one by doing some research.

Tailor contact to the match and situation. Tell matches you would love to work with them to figure out your common ancestors. Do not be vague, but also do not give everything you know away at once either, as too much information can overwhelm or be a disincentive to replying. Give them the chance to be involved in the discovery process and ask you questions too.

Offer family history information and ask for some in return. Include a simple question or two but no more than that – you do not want to bombard them or make replying anything other than quick and easy. I would caution against asking for invites to private trees; private tree owners may offer invites themselves but, equally, they may be reticent to reply if you ask for one outright. Instead ask for basic information which they may feel more comfortable providing. If your match does not have a tree, ask if they could supply some simple details about their four grandparents.

Do not assume that your match understands genealogy. DNA testing has become the new gateway to genealogy, so it is very possible the reason there is no tree is because your match has never compiled one. Asking for a tree, therefore, may not be the best idea as they could feel daunted if they do not have one to share. Additionally, try not to befuddle them with genealogical or DNA terminology like pedigree chart, MRCA, centiMorgans (cMs), segments, chromosome mapping etc. This can come later once you have established a dialogue.

It is also important not to assume your matches can see everything you can on subscription sites. On Ancestry, for instance, those without a subscription cannot see your tree, so you have to offer them an alternative viewing method; you could send an invite or – my personal preference – offer to email a copy. I recommend sending a pdf pedigree chart for the pertinent side or line of your tree as this focuses the match's attention on the correct ancestors and is easier for them to assess.

Always try to migrate the contact from the testing company's messaging platform to email as that is better for long-term communication and you can attach images and photographs, which is currently not possible on most of the messaging platforms.

One of the most common things many want to ask Ancestry matches to do is to transfer their results into FTDNA, MyHeritage or GEDMatch for access to segment data. This is not something I advise broaching in a first message. New contacts will generally be more receptive to transfer requests once you have built up a good rapport with them, so leave this for several messages down the correspondence line.

It is important to keep on top of your match lists and contact any new high matches as soon as you can after they appear – there is a better chance of replies when people have just received their results as they are more likely to log in at that time. That does not mean rush the contact, but have basic templates ready that can be tweaked depending on the match and situation.

Finally try to be patient! Do not send several messages in a flurry. At the end of the day many will not reply no matter how well-written your message is, but a thoughtful missive will elicit more replies than a poor one. Focus on the goal of getting any initial reply and then try to make progress from there.

Match organisation

Putting a system in place to organise your DNA matches is crucial and one of the most important organisational aspects is note-taking. Each of the major companies has a notes facility and it is a good idea to familiarise yourself with where they are located and get in the habit of writing notes on each match you examine. Work out what the most important information to you is and add it in the order you feel is most helpful.

My notes system:

1. cMs/segments in shorthand so 305 cMs over 9 segments written as 305x9
2. Paternal or Maternal (if it can be narrowed that far)
3. Confirmed relationship in shorthand if known e.g. second cousin once removed = 2C1R
4. Names of the most recent common ancestors (MRCAs) if known or the line I believe the match to be on if not known – failing those any shared surnames/locations
5. Date match appeared
6. Whether I have contacted the match and if so when and where I sent the message
7. If the match has responded and we are in contact (also when this occurred)
8. If the match has an unlinked or private tree

9. If the match is on any other testing sites or GEDMatch (if on GEDMatch I add the kit number)

Another way you can organise information and notes on your matches is via a custom master spreadsheet and many prefer to do this instead of or in addition to writing notes on the different websites. The advantage of having an external system is that people can delete tests from the sites and you could lose information and notes.

Genome Mate Pro (GMP), a free third-party utility, is another excellent tool for match organisation. You can add your matches from all of the different companies and combine them together, although Ancestry matches are of less use as GMP is based around the use of segment data. Matches are grouped by chromosome, which makes it easy to quickly assess things. Within each chromosome all matches are listed from the lowest to highest start location by default, but there is a great deal of filtering choice in how you wish to view your lists. Each match has a profile page on which you can write notes, so if you prefer you can use GMP as your master spreadsheet and add all the information you have gleaned about a match there. Setting up GMP is a fairly time-consuming task with a steep learning curve, but it is an extremely useful tool once you get the hang of it. There is a comprehensive set-up guide and dedicated Facebook group.

Adoption and unknown ancestor mysteries
Before affordable DNA testing for genealogical purposes burst onto the scene in recent years, many family history mysteries were simply filed away in the unsolvable drawer. DNA testing has opened up a whole new world of possibility for adoptees and those with unknown parentage mysteries, and by unknown parentage mysteries I am not only referring to an unknown parent, but also perhaps an unknown grandparent or great-grandparent. DNA testing has become the logical next step for those faced with brick walls such as a grandfather's birth certificate with a blank next to the father's name. It is a very powerful tool that can be used to help reconnect biological family members in the here and now, as well as unlock secrets from the past, which we thought had died with those who kept them.

An important recommendation for those with an adoption or

unknown parentage mystery is to get into all of the major autosomal databases. It is like going on a fishing trip and not knowing which pond your big fish might be swimming in. If you are fishing in them all then you will not miss out on landing your personal big fish.

The starting point is the same as it is for those with known ancestry – investigate your top matches and examine or compile family trees for them. I recommend building the trees of matches on one 'Master' tree as opposed to many separate trees; this can make it easier to spot connections between matches and, if everything is on the same tree, when links have been identified it is a simple task to merge common ancestor entries and trees.

Many cases will require contacting matches and hoping they will be willing to provide information. This can be daunting and there may well be disappointments and frustrations if close matches do not respond. Try not to get discouraged. Screenshot close match information, including trees, in case they decide to delete or go private and you lose that information.

When you do not have a tree of your own to compare to the trees of your matches, it is essential to investigate the shared matches of your highest matches and try to work out how they match each other! If you can narrow their connection down to a particular ancestor or ancestral couple it is likely they, or a set of their ancestors, are also your ancestors. Once you have identified a likely common ancestor or ancestral couple you need to build their lines forward to identify potential grandparents and ultimately birth parents via age and location. Who was in the right place at the right time? There may, at this point, be several birth parent candidates that only further targeted DNA testing can separate out. If you end up with different hypotheses to consider I recommend using the 'What Are The Odds?' DNA probability tool: https://dnapainter.com/tools/probability.

Target testing will involve the tricky task of contacting people on the line you have identified and asking them to test.

You need to think carefully about how to initiate this contact and have a support network on hand. It is worth reading the contact advice at www.dnaadoption.com.

Be aware that how successful you will be is totally dependent on whether or not close enough relatives test. By close enough I mean second to fourth cousins as opposed to extremely close matches such as parent, half-sibling or first cousin, which would fall under what I call 'jackpot matches' for unknown parentage mysteries. Some will find they do not have close enough matches to begin with, but more and more people are testing on a daily basis and match lists are constantly updating, so closer matches can come along at any point.

DNA match quick guide
1. Whichever platform you test at find the shared cM/segment numbers and familiarize yourself with the relationship probabilities using the DNA Painter Shared cM Project Tool
2. Study shared matches as they may help you narrow the connection down
3. Check for shared surnames and locations
4. Investigate the match's tree if there is one and build it out if it's too small to be useful
5. If no tree search online in case there is one elsewhere or the match can be identified via their web presence
6. Contact the match once you have fully investigated the potential connection
7. Work with segment data if available using phasing (when possible), chromosome mapping, inferred segment matching and triangulation

Case study (Breaking down a brick wall)
This case study centres on the breaking down of a brick wall via DNA matches.

My third great-grandfather Robert Cullen represented a long-standing brick wall on my tree (see p88).

Robert died in the 1820s and there is no existing documentation containing the names of his parents. I have searched births and baptisms and there is one possibility:

Robert Cullen, born 7 June 1802, Barony, Lanark, Scotland, son of John Cullen and Elizabeth Morton.

Robert was born long before statutory registration began in Scotland in 1855 – up until this point there was no legal requirement to register a birth in Scotland so, while his baptism may have been registered, it is perfectly possible no record exists. Additionally,

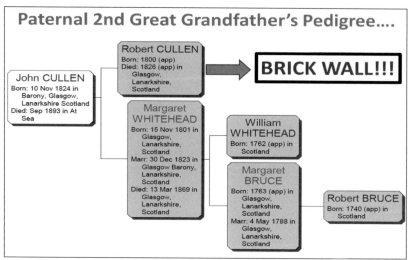

Paternal 2nd Great Grandfather's Pedigree....

John CULLEN
Born: 10 Nov 1824 in Barony, Glasgow, Lanarkshire Scotland
Died: Sep 1893 in At Sea

Robert CULLEN
Born: 1800 (app)
Died: 1826 (app) in Glasgow, Lanarkshire, Scotland

→ **BRICK WALL!!!**

Margaret WHITEHEAD
Born: 15 Nov 1801 in Glasgow, Lanarkshire, Scotland
Marr: 30 Dec 1823 in Glasgow Barony, Lanarkshire, Scotland
Died: 13 Mar 1869 in Glasgow, Lanarkshire, Scotland

William WHITEHEAD
Born: 1762 (app) in Scotland

Margaret BRUCE
Born: 1763 (app) in Glasgow, Lanarkshire, Scotland
Marr: 4 May 1788 in Glasgow, Lanarkshire, Scotland

Robert BRUCE
Born: 1740 (app) in Scotland

© *Michelle Leonard*

although he married and died in Glasgow I have no proof that he was actually born there. For these reasons there is simply no way for me to be sure whether the Robert born in Glasgow in 1802 to John Cullen and Elizabeth Morton was my Robert and, thus, it is far too speculative to add to my tree.

One of the first matches I ever confirmed a connection with was a paternal fourth cousin and upon comparing notes on our common ancestors, Robert Cullen and Margaret Whitehead, I discovered her great-grandmother (Robert's granddaughter) was named Elizabeth Morton Johnston. I found corroboration that she called herself this on the Australian birth record of one of her children.

It is quite a coincidence that the name Elizabeth Morton was given to a potential great-granddaughter of an Elizabeth Morton so I filed this away as a decent piece of documentary evidence in support of John and Elizabeth being my Robert's parents, but with the caveat that it is still circumstantial. The DNA match with my fourth cousin could only confirm this line as far back as our common Cullen ancestor (Robert himself) and not his parents.

Then another DNA match came along:

S.J. predicted as a fourth-sixth cousin.

Let's look at a selection of my shared matches with S.J.:

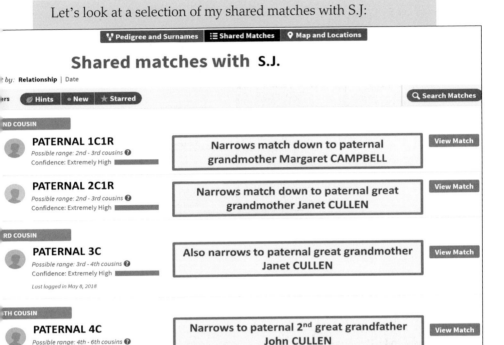

by: **Relationship** | Date

Shared matches with S.J.

ND COUSIN

PATERNAL 1C1R
Possible range: 2nd - 3rd cousins ?
Confidence: Extremely High

Narrows match down to paternal grandmother Margaret CAMPBELL — View Match

PATERNAL 2C1R
Possible range: 2nd - 3rd cousins ?
Confidence: Extremely High

Narrows match down to paternal great grandmother Janet CULLEN — View Match

RD COUSIN

PATERNAL 3C
Possible range: 3rd - 4th cousins ?
Confidence: Extremely High
Last logged in May 8, 2018

Also narrows to paternal great grandmother Janet CULLEN — View Match

TH COUSIN

PATERNAL 4C
Possible range: 4th - 6th cousins ?
Confidence: High
Last logged in Jul 24, 2018

Narrows to paternal 2nd great grandfather John CULLEN — View Match

© *Ancestry*

Investigating the shared matches strongly suggested that the connection is on my Cullen line and most likely at least as far back as my third great-grandparents Robert Cullen and Margaret Whitehead, since S.J. also matches the fourth cousin with whom I share those common ancestors.

Next I studied S.J.'s tree – a small, unlinked seven-person tree. It is a very interesting small tree as we have a surname in common! S.J.'s grandfather was a man named Thomas Cullen who died in Glasgow. My Cullens were also from Glasgow, so I now have a common surname and location as well as confirmed cousins on my Cullen line who also match S.J. Since S.J.'s tree was not developed any further back than her grandfather I had to be proactive and build it back myself. I started by getting the 1905 marriage record for S.J.'s grandfather Thomas Cullen. The most important pieces of information I required in order to work the Cullen line backwards were the names of Thomas' parents:

Robert CULLEN Carpet Weaver (deceased) and Margaret CULLEN M.S. GRAY

I proceeded to get Robert and Margaret's 1881 marriage record which confirmed Robert's parents as follows:

Thomas CULLEN Carpet Weaver and Martha CULLEN M.S. MCLEAN (deceased)

Thomas and Martha married in Glasgow in 1853, but as this was prior to statutory registration their marriage record did not contain the names of their parents. Thomas's 1893 Glasgow death record, however, did list his parents:

William CULLEN Yarn Dresser (deceased) and Sarah CULLEN M.S. MORRISON (deceased)

I then sourced the 1879 Glasgow death record for William Cullen, which listed his parents:

John CULLEN Mason (deceased) and Elizabeth CULLEN M.S. MORTON (deceased)

The exact couple I had always thought may have been my Robert's parents! This one match alone doesn't prove they were his parents, but it is an excellent piece of evidence in favour of the hypothesis and I have since identified five more DNA matches that all descend from different children of John and Elizabeth and match confirmed cousins on my Cullen line. I believe the weight of evidence is now substantial enough that I can add John and Elizabeth to my tree as Robert's parents. Every piece of extra evidence you can add to a theory via different matches gives it additional credence.

John and Elizabeth had a number of other children, so I was also able to add many new collateral lines to my tree. One of the new matches, descended from their daughter Christian, was even able to provide me with amazing early photographs from the 1850s.

Without DNA evidence I would never have been confident in John and Elizabeth being my Robert's parents and would never have added them or their other children to my tree. I have broken down this brick wall, made new cousin connections, acquired copies of priceless family photographs and added hundreds of new collateral relatives to my tree thanks to DNA, in combination with traditional research. DNA provided the clues, but it took both DNA and traditional research to crack the case.

Remember that brick walls do not only exist on direct ancestor lines but also on collateral lines.

No tree case study (names anonymised)

Many matches are difficult to solve due to lack of information, and this next case study will cover that kind of situation. The starting point is a male fourth-sixth cousin match with initials D.R., whose test is managed by a Jolene Roddin, but there is no tree, no useful shared matches and no additional information on the manager's profile.

When a match offers such minimal information, the first thing to do is attempt contact, but unfortunately there was no reply in this case. So should I just give up and chalk it up as unsolvable? I did not and it paid dividends.

Since the manager is female and her surname starts with the same letter as the surname of the match it is likely they share that surname. This makes it probable that the match is the manager's father, husband, brother or son. In most cases when someone manages another person's DNA they are a close relative; I say in most cases because there are always exceptions. I manage many kits for clients and friends who are completely unrelated to me personally, for example. I am not representative of the database as a whole, however, and in this case I began by exploring the most likely option, which is that the test-taker and manager are close relatives who share a surname.

Online searching is your friend! It is always worth searching to see if you can identify the test-taker or results manager. Of course you need a bit of luck with this: if the manager was 'Jane Smith' as opposed to 'Jolene Roddin' then my chances of turning anything up via an online search would be negligible. A search for Jolene Roddin, however, led me to a US-based woman with a husband named David Roddin. This matches the initials on the test, so he quickly became the most likely candidate. Via online obituaries and traditional research methods I traced his ancestry back several generations. The majority of his lines yielded nothing until I hit upon a set of my own fourth great-grandparents! David descends from their eldest daughter, who was hitherto missing from my tree as her birth had not been registered and she was already living away from the family by the time of the first genealogically useful Scottish census (1841). Without this match I may never have known of her existence and emigration as a young woman. From nothing more than a set of initials, a manager's name, some online sleuthing and a little work building a tree I was able to identify the most likely connection with this match and enhance my own tree even if I never receive a reply or they never upload a tree of their own.

X-DNA case studies

As set out in Chapter 3, the inheritance properties of the X-chromosome are such that a match on the X can be narrowed down more extensively than a match on an autosome.

It is essential to take the gender of the test-takers being compared into account when it comes to X matches:

➤ An X-DNA match between two men means the connection can be narrowed down to the maternal side for both
➤ An X-DNA match between a man and a woman means the connection can be narrowed down to the man's maternal side, but cannot be narrowed to a particular side for the woman (many lines can be discounted though, particularly her paternal grandfather's entire quarter)
➤ An X-DNA match between two women is the scenario that can be narrowed the least but again there are still lines that can be discounted

When working with X-DNA matches make sure you fill out an X-DNA table for the ancestors you could have inherited X-DNA from and consult this as it can aid you in working out the connection and will focus your search on the correct lines.

An example from FTDNA identifies Ruth as an X-match, but you have to be careful with this designation due to the fact FTDNA take into account very small segments – a match could be listed as an X-match even if only one 1 cM segment has been detected. I have outlined that small segments are problematic already, but it has been reported that there is an even higher rate of false positives on the X-chromosome, so it is best not to spend too much time on very small X-matches. A common recommendation is that in most cases only matches of 10 cMs or more should be investigated for males and 20 cMs for females.

The first thing you must do when 'X-Match' is listed on FTDNA is look at the match in the chromosome browser to check if the X-DNA segment is a reasonable size or should be discounted as too small. Be aware that the cMs you share on the X are not counted in the 'Shared Centimorgans' total on the main match page.

Even if an X-DNA segment appears to be of a reasonable size on a chromosome browser, it is always worth checking the actual numbers via the Detailed Segment Data view:

Chromosome	Start Location	End Location	Centimorgans(cM)	Matching SNPs
2	157,113,214	159,347,591	2.44	500
3	113,264,489	115,065,234	1.91	500
3	137,224,255	140,842,100	2.30	600
4	154,783,347	157,914,101	4.26	800
6	32,186,351	32,977,023	1.06	1,200
6	33,928,037	35,542,251	1.64	500
7	99,118,577	100,851,748	1.94	500
8	52,879,721	55,080,776	1.56	500
10	34,666,119	54,535,327	13.52	3,445
11	84,433,193	86,712,858	1.78	600
X	22,245,322	42,592,114	35.16	3,125
X	54,224,837	68,235,478	4.00	550

FamilyTreeDNA

Ruth and I share a 13 cMs autosomal segment on chromosome 10, but it is clear that the largest segment shared between us is on the X-chromosome. At 35 cMs this is certainly a significant enough segment to warrant analysis.

The next step is to look at shared matches via the 'In Common With' tool, where Ruth matches confirmed paternal relatives. One curious detail is that my paternal half-sister, with whom I share my entire paternal X-chromosome, is not on the list. The reason for that is because my sister and Ruth do not share any autosomal DNA and you have to share a segment on an autosome at FTDNA to be considered a match, even if you share a significant X segment.

Knowing that my match with Ruth is on my paternal X-chromosome immediately narrows things a further generation to just one quarter of my tree, because my paternal X-chromosome was inherited in its entirety from my paternal grandmother. Additionally I can discount even more lines using my previously compiled paternal X-DNA inheritance table:

Michelle LEONARD[1]	Patrick LEONARD[2] Contributed 100% of the X-DNA to the focus person	Margaret McPherson CAMPBELL[5] (100%)			
			John McPherson CAMPBELL[10] (50%)	Margaret MCPHERSON[21] (50%)	John MCPHERSON[42] (25%)
					Catherine MCKENZIE[43] (25%)
			Janet Kerr Stevenson CULLEN[11] (50%)	John CULLEN[22] (25%)	Margaret WHITEHEAD[45] (25%)
				Janet NICOL[23] (25%)	William NICOL[46] (12.5%)
					Elizabeth KERR[47] (12.5%)

© Michelle Leonard

All of the white boxes represent lines I can discount since I could not have received X-DNA from those ancestors. Out of my eight paternal second great-grandparents I can only have inherited X-DNA from three of them (Margaret McPherson, John Cullen and Janet Nicol, with Margaret McPherson being statistically more likely due to the fact I may well have inherited a larger amount of X-DNA from her). Apart from the fact that 100% of my paternal X-chromosome came from my paternal grandmother, the rest of the percentages here are approximate. They are interesting as a guide and also show one of the most important differences between the X and autosomes. On an autosome the average you would inherit from a grandparent would be 25%, whereas here you could inherit 100% and the average you would inherit from a second great-grandparent is 6.25%, whereas on the X it could be 50% or even higher for a particular line. I call this the disproportionate X-DNA line: it lies on the paternal X and is the line in which a male interjects every other generation. Additionally the X-chromosome does not recombine quite as often as autosomes, so it is actually plausible that my paternal X-chromosome could be inherited entirely from my second great-grandmother Margaret McPherson: if she passed an X to my great-grandfather, who passed it whole to my grandmother, who may have passed it unrecombined to my father, who would then pass it whole to me.

Since this is an X-DNA match I only need to investigate the lines of Ruth's tree she could have inherited X-DNA from, so I can discount a number of them and narrow things down to just a few. One in particular stands out: that of her second great-grandmother Ann McPherson.

We already know that my second great-grandmother, Margaret McPherson, could have contributed a significant proportion of my X-chromosome, so the fact Ruth also has a McPherson ancestor on an X-DNA line is a good lead to follow. It turned out that my Margaret and Ruth's Ann were sisters. This X-DNA match gave me information on Ann's line and enabled me to add a number of new branches stemming from her to my tree, as well as mapping a 35 cMs segment of my X-chromosome directly back to my second great-grandmother.

Let's look at another X-DNA match, this time on 23andMe:

Comparison	Chrom.	Start Position	End Position	Genetic Distance (cM)	Number of SNPs	Identity
Michelle Leonard / Linda	X	23063857	40177459	27.61	2340	Half
Michelle Leonard / Linda	X	90535101	139887091	55.32	4470	Half

© 23andMe

Linda and I do not share any autosomal DNA, but we share a whopping 43% of one of our X-chromosomes (83 cMs). Linda also matches on the same X segment as Ruth, so it seems very likely the whole 83 cMs can be mapped back to Margaret McPherson. The trouble here is that the actual connection is further back than either of us can take our trees. It would be virtually impossible, barring endogamy, to share 83 cMs with someone on an autosome and not be able to pinpoint a fairly recent common ancestor. The way the X-chromosome is inherited and the fact whole generations can be skipped, however, means matches on the X can end up being further back in time than matches on autosomes.

One thing it is important to be aware of is that Ancestry and MyHeritage do not report on the X-chromosome, so if you want to see X-Matches from those companies you have to transfer your raw data to GEDmatch or FTDNA.

The most important point to take away from these case studies is that it is essential to combine traditional genealogical research with DNA know-how in order to make the most of your results and successfully identify cousin connections.

GEDmatch

There are a number of third-party tools that can aid you with your DNA results (we have already covered DNA Painter and GenomeMatePro), but the best known is GEDmatch.

GEDmatch is a free volunteer-run website that gives people a chance to match with those who have tested across all of the major companies and provides a suite of extremely helpful DNA analysis tools. There is also a subscription level, known as Tier 1, which provides several advanced tools for a small monthly fee.

In order to use GEDmatch you must download your raw data from your testing company and then upload it to the GEDmatch Genesis website. Instructions on how to do this are available on the website.

The most important tools you will want to get to grips with are 'one-to-many', 'one-to-one' and 'people who match both, or one of two kits'. 'One-to- many' is GEDmatch's equivalent of the match list and should be your first port of call:

	Kit	Name (* => alias)	Email		GEDO WikiTree	Age(days)	Type	Sex	Haplogroup Mt	Haplogroup Y	Autosomal Total cM	Autosomal Largest	Autosomal Gen	X-DNA Total cM	X-DNA Largest
	A	Allan	@gmail.com		GED	1284	2	F	H1C1		3587.1	281.5	1.00	196.1	196.1
	A	Leonard	@gmail.com		GED	571	2	M	H1C1	R-BY20934	2773.8	211.0	1.19	82.1	62.6
	A		@gmail.com			341	2	F			1935.0	162.5	1.45	195.8	195.8
	A	Leonard	@gmail.com		GED	571	2	M			959.8	131.3	1.95	63.2	34.9
	A		@gmail.com		GED	588	2	F			890.1	68.0	2.01	26.8	26.8
	A		@gmail.com		GED	571	2	F			832.4	69.9	2.05	35.6	35.6
	A		@gmail.com		GED	602	2	F			787.5	77.8	2.09	70.3	45.4
	A		@gmail.com			447	2	M		R-BY20934	772.6	99.5	2.11	0.0	0.0
	A	Leonard Black	@gmail.com		GED	1023	2	F			452.2	37.0	2.49	9.5	9.5

© GEDmatch

The layout is set up in such a way that it imparts a lot of information on one page – do not be daunted by all of the numbers. GEDmatch comparisons are based on kit numbers, which are generated when you upload your DNA. Each kit number migrated from the earlier classic GEDmatch website begins with a particular letter and which letter depends on the company your raw data originates from e.g. A for Ancestry or M for 23andMe. On Genesis, however, there is a new column entitled 'Source', which lists the company name or initial.

If you click on a kit number, a new window will open to show the full match list for that kit – this is something you cannot easily access on the other platforms. You can also upload a Gedcom of your family tree. GEDmatch supplies full segment information (total centiMorgans/largest segment) for both autosomes and X-chromosomes. If you click on the highlighted largest cM numbers under their respective 'Largest' columns this will display an autosomal or X one-to-one comparison with the chosen match. A one-to-one comparison imparts even more detail as follows:

GEDmatch® Genesis Autosomal One-to-one Comparison - V1.

Software Version Jan 16 2019 01:57:49
Comparing Kit A_____ (Michelle Leonard) [Migration - F2 - A] and A_____ (*C.D.) [Migration - F2 - A]

Segment threshold size will be adjusted dynamically between 200 and 400 SNPs
Minimum segment cM to be included in total = 7.0 cM
Mismatch-bunching Limit will be adjusted dynamically to 60 percent of the segment threshold size for any given segment.

Chr	B37 Start Pos'n	B37 End Pos'n	Centimorgans (cM)	SNPs
2	150,858,540	169,701,054	15.1	2,146
13	110,397,022	115,090,019	12.8	901
22	23,253,893	28,015,322	14.8	1,131

Largest segment = 15.1 cM

Total Half-Match segments (HIR) = 42.7 cM (1.190 Pct)
Estimated number of generations to MRCA = 4.2

3 shared segments found for this comparison.

400341 SNPs used for this comparison.

© GEDmatch

The one-to-one comparison provides the actual segment information with start/end locations and cM/SNP numbers. This is especially helpful for Ancestry matches since segment data is not reported on the testing site.

As opposed to relationship predictions, GEDmatch supplies an estimated number of generations to the MRCA under the column entitled 'Gen'. Like other relationship prediction tools it is best not to take this number too literally and to once again use the Shared cM Project Tool instead.

GEDMatch's equivalent of a shared match list is 'People who match both kits or one of two kits' (see p99).

This is very detailed and tells you exactly how much DNA the shared matches share with the two comparison kits.

It is also possible to complete full triangulation on GEDmatch both manually (via 'one-to-one' comparisons of three or more matches) or search via the Tier 1 'Segment Search' and 'Triangulation' tools which automate the process.

eople who match both kits, or 1 of 2 kits

t 1: A▨▨▨ (Michelle Leonard)
t 2: A▨▨▨ (*Jan)

atches both kits
ubmit Select 3 or more from '√' column, and click this button for additional display and processing options.

Match	√	Name	A232978			A358208			Generations Difference	Email
			Shared	Largest	Gen	Shared	Largest	Gen		
A▨	☐		2773.8	211.0	1.2	40.5	30.6	4.2	3.0	▨▨▨@gmail.com
A▨	☐		1935.0	162.5	1.4	56.6	47.2	4.0	2.5	▨▨▨@gmail.com
A▨	☐		959.8	131.3	2.0	83.6	30.7	3.7	1.8	▨▨▨@gmail.com
A▨	☐		890.1	68.0	2.0	53.7	24.7	4.0	2.0	▨▨▨@gmail.com
A▨	☐		832.4	69.9	2.1	34.4	24.7	4.4	2.3	▨▨▨@gmail.com
A▨	☐		772.6	99.5	2.1	58.8	41.0	4.0	1.9	▨▨▨@gmail.com
A▨	☐		396.6	56.7	2.6	63.3	30.8	3.9	1.3	▨▨▨@gmail.com

© GEDmatch

For a comprehensive list of other third-party tools (e.g. DNAGedcom, Rootsfinder and clustering tools such as Genetic Affairs) consult the ISOGG Autosomal DNA Tools page.

Visual phasing (advanced)

Visual phasing is an advanced methodology, developed by Kathy Johnston, which can be a great aid in narrowing down matches to ancestral lines. Ideally three full siblings are required in order to undertake a visual phasing project, but it is possible with just two full and one half-sibling (as I have done) or two siblings and a number of other close relatives. When you practise visual phasing what you are doing is looking at the points on the chromosomes at which crossovers occur between siblings and using the crossover information to determine which of your four grandparents contributed which pieces of your DNA. The goal is to be able to map your DNA to your four grandparents using this method. It can be time-consuming and complex, but it is well worth the time invested.

I have developed a full visually phased reference chart for my chromosomes, which I can now use whenever I have access to segment data for a match. All I have to do is look at where we match, then consult my VP reference chart for that chromosome and I will know which of my four grandparents contributed that segment of DNA. This means I can narrow all matches down to at least one quarter of my tree. I also, however, still consult my regular chromosome map (e.g. on DNA Painter) since I have mapped many segments further back than my grandparents.

It is important to learn the technique properly before trying out visual phasing: there is a visual phasing Facebook group that provides excellent information on how to go about the learning process as well as courses and articles. Additionally, developer Steven Fox has created an incredible spreadsheet tool for visual phasing that automates much of the set-up process and is a great time saver (only available via the Facebook group).

Admixture estimates

Admixture is the most recognisable and eye-catching aspect of an autosomal DNA test. It is the feature companies highlight the most when advertising their products. For that reason many people test solely for the admixture portion of the results but, in reality, it is far less useful for genealogy than DNA match lists.

When creating admixture estimates all of the different companies use their own proprietary reference population sets and computerised algorithms. A reference population is a DNA dataset comprised of samples from individuals whose ancestry is believed to trace back to specific areas. To build these reference sets companies test people with four grandparents who all came from the same area or use academic project data along the same lines. These results are then used as a reference for the specific area concerned. There are always going to be some errors with this process, as admixture aims to predict ancestry from 500–1,000 years back in time and there is no way to know for sure that the ancestry of those tested for the reference panels genuinely does stem from the correct areas. The larger the reference populations become, however, the more accurate they should be. When a new customer takes a test, their DNA is compared to all of the reference samples and an estimate is generated via computerised comparisons. There is no universal reference set or method of calculating admixture and, therefore, results can and will differ across platforms. If you examine estimates for the same person at more than one company you will see that there are different categories, interpretations and percentages.

It is widely believed admixture results are accurate to the continental level, but more problematic and changeable when drilling down to country and regional levels. It is important not to put too much stock in very small percentages reported by any of the companies as they could be considered background 'noise'. As DNA segments become smaller there is a greater chance of matching random and inaccurate ethnicity patterns. The science behind admixture is evolving all the time, so admixture estimates will occasionally be updated as companies improve their reference sets and algorithms.

Ancestry calls the admixture portion of their test 'DNA Story' and another major facet of this is the 'Genetic Communities' feature. Rolled out in March 2017, this has now been fully integrated into the 'Ethnicity Estimate' area of the results and the term 'Genetic Communities' has been replaced by 'Regions' and 'Migrations'. The 'Ethnicity Estimates' are based on reference populations, but Regions do not stem from DNA analysis and are actually determined by the family trees of your matches. For example I match a large number of test-takers who have ancestors from Ulster on their tree, so the system determined that I am also likely to have ancestors from Ulster, which I do, and placed me in the Ulster Region as well as the more detailed Tyrone, Londonderry and Antrim sub-region. This is, of course, dependent upon the accuracy of the trees of your matches and will not always be correct, but it has proven very accurate for many, especially for regions with a high number of matches.

23andMe is the only company that provides a chromosome map which breaks down segments via admixture group and, if you have one or both parents tested, they also split your ethnicity by parent. This is not particularly helpful if all of your ancestry comes from similar areas, but it can become valuable when you have markedly different ancestral components. LivingDNA currently provides the most detailed regional breakdown for British and Irish ancestry.

My cousin Marion's results are an example of how admixture analysis can generate clues to help solve unknown ancestor mysteries. Three-quarters of Marion's ancestry is documented, but she has an unknown grandfather. In the three identified quarters there are no known Jewish ancestors, so the fact that around 25% Ashkenazi Jewish is reported in her estimates is a good clue as to the origins of her unknown grandfather.

GEDmatch also has a number of admixture calculators (mainly developed for academic purposes) that you can explore if you are interested in yet another perspective.

Admixture key points:

➤ Admixture estimates will vary between companies because they each use different reference populations
➤ They are accurate to the continental level but cannot be taken too literally at the country and regional levels
➤ Be especially cautious with tiny percentages as these could be erroneous
➤ Estimates can only cover DNA you have personally inherited from your ancestors and you do not possess all of the same DNA they did
➤ Estimates can give you a broad idea of your origins and may provide genealogical clues if you were adopted or have a recent unknown ancestor mystery

This is an emerging science that will improve over time as more people test and reference populations increase, but be careful in reading too much into estimates for now – they are called 'estimates' for a reason.

Summing up

➤ Use DNA in conjunction with traditional research as that is how to get the most out of it
➤ Start with your largest matches and work your way down your first page
➤ Test close relatives especially older generations to narrow your matches down and gain more of your ancestors' DNA
➤ Upload your family tree no matter how small and make sure you link it to your results
➤ Build your tree as extensively as you can and build the trees of your matches to find links
➤ Study shared matches as they may hold vital clues, especially if you have no tree of your own

➤ Be proactive – contact your matches! Many will not respond but keep trying and you will find new cousins to collaborate with
➤ Organise your data and take advantage of all the help out there
➤ Explore third party tools and techniques such as chromosome mapping, autosomal clusters and visual phasing
➤ Remember there will be many matches you cannot work out, but each one you do adds to or confirms your tree

Have fun with it!

Keep in mind that genetic genealogy evolves rapidly and all of the companies will change aspects of the way they display things, so the images and exact directions given in this chapter may become out of date, but the basic premises and techniques should endure.

Chapter 5

Y-DNA TESTS

Alasdair F. Macdonald, John Cleary

Using Y-STRs in genealogical research
STRs – a short introduction
The development of commercial genetic testing for surnames emerged on both sides of the Atlantic in May 2000 through the work of Dr Bryan Sykes at Oxford University, England (founder of Oxford Ancestors) and Bennett Greenspan, who founded Family Tree DNA in Houston, Texas in the United States.

They both realised that in patrilineal societies genealogical questions about surnames could be addressed using the male specific Y-chromosome. This is because surnames and the Y-chromosome descend down the generations in parallel as they are inherited by boys from their father. Women do not have a Y-chromosome, therefore cannot take a DNA test for surname research. However, they can ask a male relative such as a father, brother, uncle or nephew to take a test to enable them to investigate the male line in question using genetics.

Traditional genealogical research techniques and practice typically at some point come up against problems when using documentary sources such as incorrect data, contradictory evidence, damaged or destroyed records or simply lack of enough corroborating evidence. Such factors may cause research to stop in its tracks, though there are other, often less obvious, scenarios that may limit research such as illegitimacy, informal adoption, fosterage, formal change of name due to inheritance and one that is often overlooked, researcher error. A particular strength of DNA testing is that it links an individual to an immediate ancestor using evidence that is objective and unambiguous.

For example, Alexander George Macdonald was born according to his civil birth certificate illegitimate in 1895 at Watten in Caithness. Although his father Alexander Macdonald acknowledged that he was the 'father' by allowing his name to be recorded on the registration of birth, his identity beyond that was unknown. There were fourteen men aged between fifteen and forty-five in the 1891 census in the area, anyone of whom might have been the father. How can men descended from Alexander George Macdonald identify which Macdonald line they descend from?

Through traditional research several candidate Macdonald men whose ancestors had lived in the same area in which Alexander George was born were encouraged to take a Y-STR test. When their results came back, A and S both matched F, a descendant of Alexander George Macdonald who had previously taken a Y test.

Investigation of their genealogies revealed that 'S' was the descendant of an Alexander Macdonald who was twenty-two years of age in 1895 and born on a farm very close to where Alexander George was born. The other test-taker (A) was a descendant of a Macdonald who had emigrated from Halkirk in Caithness to Suriname in South America in the 1820s. When the genealogy of 'S' was researched further it was found that his Macdonald family had lived at the township half a mile from that of 'A'. Comparison of their results demonstrated that 'S' was more closely connected to 'F' than to 'A' as they had more similar DNA results.

Now knowing that there was indeed a connection to 'S', the descendants of Alexander George Macdonald looked for corroborating evidence to firm up the link, but also sought evidence to eliminate other candidate men who may have been the father. Matching on a Y-DNA test does not necessarily confirm parentage, but may certainly point to a lineage for further investigation.

Y-STR tests ought to be seen as an introduction to testing for surname research. They may in certain circumstances confirm a hypothesis both positively or negatively. However, they have limitations, so ought to be complemented by the use of strategic testing strategies and techniques to enable the meaningful comparison of results.

For many test-takers the expectation is that the test company will do the filtering and evaluation of test results. They may certainly do the former, but not the latter, which really needs to be learned by the test-taker, which is why you are reading this book. To that end, choose a testing company such as Family Tree DNA that has a large relational database along with surname and lineage projects. The type of test taken is also important and may vary depending on your research goals. As there are different levels of test available, understanding their pros and cons is also important so that you use the best test for your research question.

What is an STR?

The earliest DNA tests for surname research were low resolution Y-STRs (Short Tandem Repeats) and in retrospect had limited application except for specific research questions. As the resolution of tests improved by increasing the number of locations on the Y-chromosome analysed, and as the number of individuals tested also increased, their usefulness for addressing genealogical questions expanded exponentially. A location on the Y-chromosome is technically known as an allele, but more commonly in genetic genealogy as a genetic 'marker'. When commercial testing started in 2000 only twelve markers were tested. Today an individual would test at least thirty-seven markers or even sixty-seven when entering the market.

An STR records the number of times a short sequence of genetic code has been repeated at a given location. For example, the STR value at marker DYS393 is the number of times the sequence AGAT has been repeated. The number of repeats of this motif may range from nine to seventeen repeats, but is more likely to be in the range of twelve to fifteen. An individual who has a value at DYS393 of thirteen has thirteen repeats of the motif AGAT.

A typical 37-marker Y-STR test would return the number of repeats at thirty-seven individual locations on the Y-chromosome. When these are all listed together it is called a Y-STR haplotype. When the haplotypes of two or more individuals are aligned and compared, differences in the number of 'repeats' can be observed. As a rule of thumb, the more differences, the greater the time to a shared common ancestor. The fewer differences, the closer the time to when the men shared the same common male ancestor.

In the simplified table below, the twelve-marker Y-STR haplotypes of three men are presented who all carry the same surname. Males 1 and 2 only have one difference on multi-copy marker DYS385. This marker is highlighted, which indicates it is less stable and more likely to mutate when copied and passed from father to son.

Such a match would be would be written as an 11/12 marker match. However, more markers would need to be compared to confirm a genealogical connection. Using the infinite allele mutation model (see later), Male 3 has six differences to Male 2 and seven differences when compared to Male 1, indicating he is unrelated to either man. Testing more markers in this case would just reveal more differences.

	DYS393	DYS390	DYS19	DYS391	DYS385	DYS426	DYS388	DYS439	DYS389i	DYS392	DYS389ii
Male 1	12	25	15	10	12-13	12	12	12	12	13	28
Male 2	12	25	15	10	11-13	12	12	12	12	13	28
Male 3	13	25	14	11	11-14	12	12	12	14	13	30

The Y-STR markers selected for genealogical testing are a mixture of slow and faster mutating markers. Markers have different rates of mutation that can vary between lineages that belong to different genetic male lines. Over extended periods of many thousands of years, small fluctuations in mutation rates noticeable within genealogical time are balanced out. However, within the last 5,000 years different rates are still apparent when comparing Y-STR haplotypes within different male lineages and between haplogroups. We use STRs because they mutate often enough, but not too often, to enable the genetic distance between individuals to be calculated. This indicates a likely timespan within which the common ancestor of two test-takers lived. However, these mutations are random, so paradoxically this causes a problem. Some markers will back-mutate to their original value and make the genetic distance appear much closer. Others will mutate in parallel on different lineages at the same time and cause lack of divergence, also making individuals appear closer than is actually the case. The nature of mutation means that they can occur anytime: yesterday, last week or

100 years ago. Over shorter periods, there might be no mutations or several mutations may occur on different markers in two individuals. If the latter occurs, it may cause two individuals to appear not connected, as they are outwith the matching threshold.

What is a SNP?

Related haplotypes belong to the same genetic family, which we call a haplogroup. There are eighteen male haplogroups, each defined by at least one mutation called a SNP (pronounced 'snip') at a known location on the Y-chromosome. Each SNP is itself located within the context of a chronological series of older nested mutations that identify its descent from a shared ancestor.

As we saw earlier, the base molecules that make up our genome are called adenine, cytosine, guanine and thymine. They are known simply by the initial letters of their names. Whereas Y-STRs report how many times a small motif sequence is repeated, a SNP is the value reported for the base molecule at one known location.

In the example below, three men have the ancestral base value of 'C', while the fourth male has a value of 'T', indicating that he carries the mutation. He would be said to be 'derived' for the mutation. He passes on the 'T' mutation to all his male descendants, so identifying them as belonging to his genetic family.

Test-taker	DNA sequence
Male 1	TGCAGTGCTTGAAACCGAG
Male 2	TGCAGTGCTTGAAACCGAG
Male 3	TGCAGTGCTTGAAACCGAG
Male 4	TGTAGTGCTTGAAACCGAG

SNP mutations rarely if ever back mutate to their original value, therefore they can be used to indicate branching and sub-division within lineages. Haplogroups and smaller subdivisions within them are known by SNP names, for example G-P303. G stands for haplogroup 'G', while P303 is the alphanumeric identifier given to the mutation. There is no significance to the prefix letter or number – they simply indicate the name of the individual or laboratory that discovered the marker. In this case 'P' indicates Michael Hammer, PhD, of the University of Arizona and it was the 303rd marker to be discovered by him.

The term haplogroup is not restricted to Y-DNA populations and is also used for mitochondrial populations. Within genetic genealogy, haplogroups are divided into smaller subgroups that we call subclades. Haplogroups are distributed throughout the world according to how they have developed and evolved over many thousands of years. Subclades, each defined by a SNP marker, break up haplogroups into much smaller subfamilies. The various subclades and haplogroups all coalesce back to a single trunk and ultimately back to our ancestral origins in Africa. When they are all joined together they form a haplotree, which to all intents and purposes can be understood as a genetic version of a descendant tree.

Y-STR testing strategy
Before setting out to order a Y-STR test it is important to have a testing strategy. You ought to consider: what is the best level of test to meet your research goals; what is the best company from whom to order that test; and if you are female, who is the right person to take the test?

There are few companies that offer Y-STR tests and tests offered by other companies are in fact SNP tests, not necessarily useful for all genealogical questions. The reason for this is that unless you pay for more advanced testing of SNPs the age when they were created will be long before the timeframe of genealogical research, i.e the last 400–500 years.

There is a chart comparing different test companies available at the ISOGG wiki: https://isogg.org/wiki/Y-DNA_STR_testing_comparison_chart

The genetic distances calculated by comparing Y-STR test results allow predictions to be made of the time to the most recent common ancestor. We call this TMRCA. There are, however, limitations with Y-STRs that we will come onto later in this chapter.

Y-STRs will not on their own identify the name of the individual from whom two or more men descend, or the exact date – rather, they may confirm that men belong to the same lineage within a certain timeframe. That timeframe can be narrowed by the testing of extra STR markers, other related individuals or testing of specific SNP markers, along with evaluation techniques such as triangulation and the use of an inbetweener.

We saw with the Macdonald illegitimacy scenario how Y-STR matching in combination with traditional genealogical research enabled a possible genealogical brick wall to be overcome. Here are several other scenarios.

a. Robert Smith was born in the parish of Scunthorpe. His marriage certificate indicates his parents were called George Smith and Jean Bell, but there are two couples in the parish called these names living at the same time. There is no corroborating evidence that might indicate which is the correct couple. Testing male descendants of both couples may reveal the correct parentage for Robert.

b. Archibald Robertson died in South Carolina in 1840 and was believed to have been born in Perthshire in Scotland. Nothing else is known about his origins other than the name of his father, Duncan. If a male descendant took a Y-STR test he might match an individual who does know the origin of his ancestor. This might lead to documentary clues that can be followed up.

c. John Auchterlonie lives in Australia. He knows that his ancestor lived in Fife, Scotland, before he emigrated. He wishes to explore the medieval origins of his lineage, which took its name from the lands of the same name in Angus.

d. John Malcolm and Harry Malcolm both believe they descend from the same great-great-great-grandfather. They are taking a DNA test to corroborate their documentary research.

Out of these four scenarios, the 37-marker STR test might be sufficient to answer d) as there is already corroborating evidence: same surname and documentary evidence. The other three require a higher degree of certainty. The further back in time the anticipated connection, the more likelihood there is that matching can be over-.interpreted due to false-positive matching (caused by convergence). Alternatively, no match might be reported, the genetic distance being outside the matching threshold used by the test company. For example, a 32/37 match is not reported by Family Tree DNA, while a 33/37 would be reported. Therefore, the 67-marker test would be recommended for the first three scenarios.

Even with exact or near-exact matching at the 37-marker level, we would urge caution when interpreting. Do not assume that close matches are as close as predicted. Matching could be the result of the convergence of marker values between yourself and your match, but you do share the same distant ancestor. If a different surname predominates in your matches, do not assume there has been an illegitimacy in your line. There might have been over-sampling of the other name and under-sampling of your own lineage.

Often upgrading to 67-markers or 111-markers can weed out false positive matching, but even then, if your line belongs to a lineage that has experienced significant growth in a short period of time, you may match many dozens of individuals bearing different surnames, all apparently within the last few hundred years. In such a scenario only SNP testing can help.

Not everyone will find themselves with lots of matches. It might be that you have few or no matches at all. Although under-sampling might be the cause, we also have to bear in mind that not all lines survive in perpetuity. Rolls of the evolutionary dice mean that although twenty-two individuals may exist at a point in time in the past (see Figure 1), some will produce no sons, others one son and some several sons. In each generation the same dynamic will affect each lineage.

If there were a constant population size throughout time, on average only one of the twenty-two men would have descendants alive today. So, at any point in time your lineage might be somewhere on the spectrum as illustrated below and on the verge of dying out.

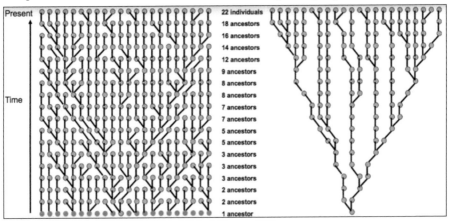

Figure 1: coalescence of male lines. ©Mark Thomas UCL.

How to evaluate matches
Your test results will be presented in two ways: a list of the marker values for each allele and a list of the men that you match. Staring at your marker values will generally not do you much good; it is in the comparison process that real value comes from an STR test. The estimated time-frame to the most recently shared common ancestor (TMRCA –Time to Most Recent Common Ancestor), is dictated by the number of markers tested, the genetic distance between the two individuals and the probability desired.

Genetic distance is a term used to describe the count of the number of mutational steps between different haplotypes and often shortened to GD. Mutations are sometimes called mismatches. Genetic distance can be calculated using two different mutation models: the infinite allele mutation model and the stepwise mutation model.

For the most part you might not be concerned with counting differences and rely on various tools to help establish TMRCA. If you are seeking to tie down the timeframe when two individuals shared a common ancestor, it may make a difference which model is used.

The stepwise model always gives higher estimates of the TMRCA than the infinite allele model, as the latter can under estimate the number of mutations. According to their website Family Tree DNA's TiP (Time Indicator Projector) tool uses the infinite allele model as opposed to the stepwise model for all STR markers.

How to count simple differences
As an example, using the stepwise model the first 12 markers between two men are presented in the table below. They have one difference so the GD = 1. This could be written as 11/12

	Marker positions 1 – 12											
Test-taker 1	12	25	15	10	12	13	12	12	12	12	13	28
Test-taker 2	12	25	15	10	11	13	12	12	12	12	13	28

When we check markers 13 to 25 we can clearly see three more differences using the stepwise model, since, using this model, the difference at marker 13, between 17 and 19, is counted as two. There were no differences between markers 26–37. So, the count of differences at the 37-marker level is four, thus they have a GD = 4. This can be written as 33/37.

	Marker positions 13 – 25								
Test-taker 1	17	9-9	11	11	25	15	20	30	14-15-16-17
Test-taker 2	19	9-9	11	11	25	15	19	30	14-15-16-17

This match might suggest that the two men are related. But how does a GD of 4 equate to a genealogical timeframe and TMRCA? The simple answer is that you need to consider several other factors: mutation rates; probability; length of a generation and the number of markers tested. In cultures where surnames are passed from father to son, additional evidence (context) ought to be sought to better qualify the DNA match beyond the two men sharing a surname. Interpretation should be based on as wide a range of information as possible. Here is an example using the infinite allele model. Each difference, no matter how large, is counted as one unique event. Using the stepwise model there would be eight differences, but using the infinite allele model there are only five.

est-taker 1	12	25	15	10	12	13	12	12	12	12	13	30	17	9-9	11	11	25	15	20	30	14-16-17-17
est-taker 2	12	23	15	10	11	13	12	12	12	12	13	28	18	9-9	11	11	25	15	20	30	14-15-16-17
ount		1			1							1	1								1

Evaluating matches
The following example from matching at Family Tree DNA has had personal information redacted. The test-taker bears the surname Macdonald, his earliest ancestor was Donald McDonald married circa 1785 in Latheron, Caithness. He has Y-DNA haplogroup of R-L165 and carries the terminal SNP Y15959.

111 MARKERS - 6 - MATCHES					
Genetic Distance ↑	Name	Earliest Known Ancestor	Y-DNA Haplogroup	Terminal SNP	Match Date
3	▓▓▓ MacDonald Y-DNA111	Donald McDonald m.1785 Latheron, Caithness	R-M269		12/13/2013
6	▓▓▓ MacDonald Y-DNA111 FF BigY	John MacDonald of Achscoriclate 1752-1840 Caithnes	R-Y17559	Y17559	8/4/2011
8	▓▓▓ MacDonald Y-DNA111	William MacDonald m.1802 Brawlbin, Reay, Caithness	R-M269		3/7/2013
9	▓▓▓ McDonald Y-DNA111 FF	Alexan MacDonald b.1779 Halkirk, Caithness d.1883	R-M269		10/5/2013
10	▓▓▓ Mackay Y-DNA111 FF	George William Mackay	R-M269		3/10/2017
10	▓▓▓ MacDonald Y-DNA111	Farquhar MacDonald b.1746 Reay, Caithness d.1842	R-L165	L165	8/11/2012

Download: **CSV**

Figure 2: 111-marker STR matching at Family Tree DNA. © FTDNA

The left-hand column is headed 'Genetic Distance' and in the third column information on the test-taker's most distant known ancestor (MDKA) is presented (if added by the test-taker). The terminal SNP is also noted. This will only be stated if the individual has undertaken extra SNP testing. The importance of such testing will become apparent as we explore Y-STR matching further.

In the example above the closest match has a genetic distance of three when 111-markers have been tested. How should this be evaluated?

- Is the surname the same? In this case it is.
  Family Tree DNA state that: 'A 108/111 match indicates a genealogical relationship. Most matches at this level are related as 9th cousins or closer, and over half will be 5th or more recent cousins. This is well within the range of traditional genealogy.'
- Is the match from the same geographical area? Yes.
- Is the MDKA of the match part of the known documented genealogy of the family? In this case they actually share a common ancestor in 1833, five generations ago.
- Is the terminal SNP the same between the two men? No, the match only has the R-M269 designation, as he has not undertaken any SNP testing.

In this case, with a genetic distance of three and other corroborating evidence, it would be interpreted as a close and genealogically relevant match. Depending on the level of confidence required, expressed as a probability of 50%, 90%, 95% or 99%, the two test-takers would be expected to be related in the following number of generations or less.

Genetic distance	Probability	50%	90%	95%	99%
3	Generations	6	10	11	14

https://www.familytreedna.com/learn/y-dna-testing/y-str/two-men-share-surname-genetic-distance-111-y-chromosome-str-markers-interpreted/

The prediction is rather conservative, as it is known through documentary evidence that the men share a common ancestor only five generations in the past, who was born in 1833. The greater than expected genetic distance of three is caused by two random mutations that have occurred in the test-taker's line since 1833. This has been proven by comparison with other test-takers in the list of matches that identified what are known as off-modal mutations.

Off-modal mutations can be identified by comparing the STR results of closely connected men. By identifying the most common value for each marker found in this group of men, what is known as the 'modal haplotype' is established. Any values which differ from the modal haplotype are off-modal mutations. This is helpful when seeking to identify STR markers, which have mutated more rapidly in some individuals. These off-modal markers can assist in better defining the relationship between individuals.

When several test-takers in a group share one or more off-modal markers, this forms an STR signature for the group. The two 'Smiths' in the table share four off-modal markers for their haplogroup. Their YCAII forms a signature in the large R1a subclade L448. Their DYS447 is a very rare off-modal that identifies one particular subclade within L448, namely R-YP984. Then the other two values are particular to the Smith surname subgroup within it. All together these four values create an STR signature that can quickly identify new test-takers who share them all.

	DYS439	DYS464	DYS447	YCAII
Smith 1	10	15-15-16-17	21	19-21
Smith 2	10	15-15-16-17	21	19-21
Modal hg R	11	12-15-16-17	23	19-23

Identifying an 'in-betweener'

What if you do not have documentary evidence to link you to your Y-DNA matches? You may share the same surname, but do not share any genealogical evidence linking you with the match. At other times two individuals may appear rather distantly related according to STRs or not match at all, although circumstantial evidence points to a closer relationship. Both these scenarios can occur if each test-taker carries off-modal mutations. How can the gap be bridged?

Genetic distance between two test-takers will provide a framework in which TMRCA can be estimated, but how can that TMRCA be improved? An 'in-betweener' can bridge the gap in genetic distance and improve the TMRCA prediction. The more individuals that carry the same value at a particular marker, the higher the probability that this value was the 'ancestral value'.

Who is an inbetweener? If you are comparing the haplotypes from two lineages you should seek to test at least one further individual from each lineage. By doing so it may be possible to identify any recent mutations that might be increasing the genetic distance. In the following example, there is a genetic distance of six at thirty-seven markers between the two kits. Family Tree DNA would not show this as a match according to their matching algorithm.

Kit	Most Distant Known Ancestor	Genetic distance
294722	William MacDonald, Breacrie, Strath Halladale, Sutherland	31/37
46281	Donald McDonald m.1785 Latheron, Caithness	

Using documentary evidence, a proven second cousin once removed of kit 46281 was tested. He can be used as an 'in-betweener' to compare with the other two kits. The comparison using the in-betweener revealed that he had a closer match with kit 294722 as the match was 33/37. This is still, on the face of it, a fairly distant match.

It is interesting to see what happens when additional markers are tested. The table below summarises the matching at all levels.

	46281	263343 inbetweener
294722	31/37 – 60/67 – 100/111	33/37 – 62/67 – 101/111

Increasing the number of markers tested narrowed the genetic distance between the two kits with a documented relationship and the comparison kit 294722.

Comparison of the two related kits (46281 and 263343) revealed that over 111-markers three mutations had occurred since the birth, *circa* 1834, of their common ancestor. These consisted of two mutations in kit 46281 and one mutation in kit 263343. Since the three mutations had occurred relatively recently in time, they made the relationships between the three kits appear more distant than they actually were.

This case study illustrates why it is important to test beyond thirty-seven markers, but also test other extant lines to identify random mutations that may affect genetic distance and TMRCA.

STR tools
Dean McGee utility
The Dean McGee 'Y-DNA Comparison Utility, FTDNA 111 Mode BETA' can be used for calculating the genetic distance and TMRCA for a group of haplotypes. It is a quick and easy way to calculate genetic distance and TMRCA without manually counting STR mutations.

The haplotypes can be copied from project pages at Family Tree DNA or formatted manually from individual STR results pages or other sources. Once the haplotypes are pasted into the utility, it will produce various tables: a) a table of haplotypes that includes the modal haplotype for the set of results; b) a table illustrating genetic distance; and finally c) a table illustrating TMRCA in generations or years depending on what was selected, between each kit. The output data from the utility can also be used by phylogenetic analysis software to generate diagrams and charts that infer relationships. Even though STR haplotypes have inherent limitations, use of the tool can help get a handle on the genetic distance between kits that might be just outside the matching threshold set by the testing company.

The McGee utility ought to be used to explore possible relationships between haplotypes, but do not take the output as concrete evidence. It has limitations as it is based on using STRs without SNPs, so the TMRCAs are only predictions.

There are a number of criteria that need to be pre-selected before running the utility, any of which may generate slightly different output. These include the genetic distance mutational model, the mutation rate, probability and generation length. Varying any of these may result in different outcomes. For instance, there is considerable discussion within the genealogical world regarding the average age when men fathered children. Tweaking generation length, if known, can refine the output from the utility. However in most cases this is not known and the average 30–33 years is a good estimate.

In conclusion, the estimated time to a common ancestor can be refined by increasing the number of markers tested, especially true for 25- or 37-marker haplotypes which ought to be upgraded to 67-markers. By adding more participants, mutations which are more recent and 'personal' to an individual can be identified, when compared to the ancestral haplotype.

The ancestral haplotype can be determined by triangulation. This uses the haplotype data of direct-line descendants known by documentary evidence to be connected. At least three haplotypes are required to triangulate and deduce the ancestral allele (value) for each STR marker. Once known, the ancestral haplotype can be used for comparison instead of individual haplotypes and those test-takers with no documentary evidence can learn where their lineage fits within the emerging phylogenetic tree for the lineage.

Other utilities the test-taker can explore include FTDNA's own TiP (Time Indicator Projector) tool, which estimates distance in generations between two test-takers, and NevGen http://www.nevgen.org/, which predicts your subclade by entering your haplotype.

STR limitations
STR testing clearly provides test-takers with the opportunity, under the right circumstances, to identify and confirm the surname of an

individual, confirm a genealogical connection and even identify the ancient origin of the lineage by the identification of a haplogroup or subclade designation. However, filtering and narrowing down matches to tighten up research findings requires test-takers to upgrade the number of STRs tested and work in collaboration with other test-takers to identify the ancestral haplotype, off-modal mutations and confirm a terminal SNP.

STR matching thresholds

Testing thresholds can prevent matching being flagged up and thus important matches may not be identified. That is why belonging to surname and haplogroup projects is so very important. Administrators are able to group your result according to how you and others match each other within a group using its ancestral haplotype or by using SNP testing that has been undertaken.

Minimum STR matching thresholds at Family Tree DNA

The following list indicates the greatest genetic distances regarded as matches by FTDNA at different levels of testing.

12 markers   11 out of 12 (A genetic distance of 1)*

*For 12 marker matches, 11 out of 12 matches are only shown when both test-takers belong to the same surname or group project. However, customers who are adopted and belong to the Adoptee Project are provided with matching to the entire Family Tree DNA database as they cannot know the best surname project to participate in.

25 markers	23 out of 25 (A genetic distance of 2)
37 markers	33 out of 37 (A genetic distance of 4)
67 markers	60 out of 67 (A genetic distance of 7)
111 markers	101 out of 111 (A genetic distance of 10)

STR matching threshold case study

As an example, Archie Shaw-Stewart, a documented descendant of Sir John Stewart of Blackhall and Ardgowan (*d.c.*1412) tested to see if he matched other Stewarts with documented descents from Walter Stewart,

6th High Steward of Scotland (1296–1327), who was one of the commanders of Robert the Bruce's army at the Battle of Bannockburn in 1314. Sir John Stewart of Blackhall and Ardgowan was the son of King Robert III of Scotland, who was a grandson of Walter Stewart.

When his markers were returned it appeared that he did not match the main Stewart line. At 12 markers he matched eighty-three men, six of whom were Stewarts or Stuarts. Matches at 12 markers can indicate a close connection, but may also simply indicate sharing a very distant connection several thousand years in the past. When his matches at the 25 markers level were assessed it revealed he only had six matches, none of whom were Stewart/Stuart.

At the 37-marker level he had one single match, though this was to a Stewart. Typically, men who descend from the High Stewards of Scotland can be expected to have in the range of 60–170 Stewart matches as so many men have tested from this lineage. When his result was compared to that of Earl Castle Stewart, who shares a common ancestor with Archie in King Robert II (1316–1390), it was seen that there was a genetic difference of eight over thirty-seven markers.

If we were to leave testing at the 37-marker level, or fail to undertake further testing with a different type of marker, the SNP test, we would have failed to discover that this man is indeed a descendant of Walter Stewart.

This is an extreme example of an individual experiencing multiple personal mutations that push his matching beyond the threshold employed – in this case – by Family Tree DNA. In fact, without knowledge of similar cases, the false conclusion might have been drawn that there had been a break in the male line due to illegitimacy. This case was cleared up by the test-taker undertaking several SNP tests, first for the SNP called L745, which defines a branch in the subclade R-DF41 to which the High Stewards belong, and then taking a Next Generation Sequencing test called Big Y-500 (FTDNA). This latter test confirmed he carried SNP markers unique to descendants of James Stewart, 5th High Steward of Scotland.

This case demonstrates that if there is no corroborating information, or the test results appear to go against what is expected, it is important not to jump to conclusions, but undertake strategic testing of specific SNP markers. If Archie Shaw-Stewart's SNP testing had been negative for the Stewart SNPs, then testing another descendant of Sir John Stewart of Blackhall and Ardgowan would have been necessary to see if it was possible to identify when the break in the male line occurred. Happily, it was not necessary to pursue this. The usefulness of SNP markers will be explored further in the rest of this chapter.

Using Y-SNPs in genealogical research
STRs and SNPs
Y-STR testing has proven a very powerful means to identify genetic families in the direct male line, winning the interest of surname researchers because of the ability of the Y chromosome to track the patrilineal surname line, or the 'Y-line'. But as more and more people took Y-STR tests it became clear there were certain things they cannot do well. They could not build an accurate 'phylogenetic' tree, that is the branching tree from a common ancestor, whether a historical person or a prehistoric distant ancestor. This is because of two major problems with the way STR mutations are read:

- *Back mutation*: mutations reverting to their previous value. If an STR with value 17 mutates to 18, and then three generations later mutates again to 17, these two mutations will be invisible and will appear as if there were no mutation at that location.
- *Parallel mutation*: two branches separately descending from the same ancestor each mutate the same way on different occasions. This can look to modern eyes like a single sub-branch defined by a single mutation, when they are really two separate and unrelated mutations that just happen to be at the same marker.

These two hard-to-spot processes are the two largest contributors (along with random genetic drift) to what project administrators term 'convergence' – the illusion that two haplotypes are closely related because they resemble each other when in fact they are only distantly related. For an MRCA who lived within the last 400 years or so, there are good chances that testing many lines can tell which mutations were independent, repeated or reversed, but the further back one goes, the more the extinction of lines of descent is likely to hide this information from view.

By the late 2000s Y researchers began to experiment with SNPs. On the Y there is no recombination to erase a SNP's existence, meaning this type of mutation has stability across many generations. Unlike STRs, SNPs could build a true phylogenetic tree down to living test-takers, sorting convergent STR haplotypes by the SNPs the test-takers had, or had not, inherited. Until 2013, however, it was not possible to rely on SNP testing for two reasons. Firstly, very few of them were known, and the ones that were, were predominantly identified with ancient or prehistoric haplogroups. This led to them being seen as relevant to 'deep ancestry' – ancient migrations and peopling of the world, not recent genealogical history. Secondly, the methods for finding and sequencing them were expensive and destructive of the test samples. Enthusiasts would test single SNPs in a hit or miss fashion to find their 'terminal SNP', but costs added up quickly, and most of these SNPs only identified branches from times long before the interest of most genealogists.

What was needed was a means to read all the SNPs on a Y chromosome in a single test, at an affordable price. The technology became available from 2005 in the form of 'next generation sequencing' (NGS) tests, and by 2013 NGS Y tests were being marketed to genealogists.

Types of SNP test
Genealogists in 2019 may encounter SNP tests in four different testing scenarios:

Test type	What they do	Available from?	Pros	Cons
Singleton SNP test	Target region of Y to see whether one SNP only is present or not present	FTDNA YSEQ	Confirming membership of a subclade, especially when STRs show convergence	Hit and miss. A negative can leave you knowing little more than you started with. Cheap as one-off tests, but costs can mount if several are required.
SNP panel or pack	SNP chip with a selection of SNPs that define a subclade and its branches	FTDNA YSEQ	Confirming membership of a subclade and identifying your branch within the subclade in a single test	Can only test SNPs on the chip. No new SNPs, including private SNPs, can be discovered. Can become out of date if new SNPs not added.

Next generation sequencing (NGS)	Targets the full sequence on particular regions of the Y	FTDNA (Big Y-700) FGC (Y Elite)	Gives absolute membership of subclade. Discovers new SNPs and new branches	Cost. There are trade-offs between coverage of the Y, read depth and speed of delivery, so test-taker needs to decide which is most important.
Whole genome sequencing (WGS)	Reads the entire genome, at different levels of coverage	YSEQ (15x, 30x, 50x) FGC (15x, 20x, 30x) Dante Labs (30x)	Analysis of the entire genome becomes possible in a single test	Cost. Speed of delivery. How to analyse the huge amount of data (this is developing). Read depth is still less than Y-NGS testing.

Table 1: Types of SNP test available to the consumer (2019).

The test you would choose depends on your testing goals, and how much you are willing to spend. NGS testing can discover new SNPs in your own descent line, while SNP packs and singletons can only test you against already discovered SNPs. If your STR results suggest you are quite distant from your nearest matches, then an SNP pack may not be able to link you to a recent branch, and NGS testing, though more expensive, will probably be more cost-effective. Another consideration is that the costs of some WGS tests are now approaching the specialist Y NGS tests, giving you all your autosomal and mtDNA data as well as the fullest possible Y read (see next section). The 'x' figures for the WGS tests (e.g. 15x, 20x, etc.) represent the 'read depth of coverage', the average number of times a location is read in the test. At 5x, many locations will not be read at all (as this is an average), but observers suggest that a 15x or 20x WGS test performs comparably to a specialised Y NGS, in terms of SNP discovery on the Y. (See the section 'Next Generation Sequencing testing' for more about coverage).

However, the companies selling WGS tests do not currently have large matching databases. Only the Big Y-700 among commercial NGS tests can offer this to test-takers at the moment, although there are also excellent third-party options for having WGS data analysed for Y-SNPs and matched against other test results. But first we will take a little detour to look at why reading *all* the Y chromosome is a far from straightforward matter.

The geography of the Y chromosome
The Genome Reference Consortium (GRC) publishes a reference

sequence of the entire human genome, regularly releasing new builds as the reads become fuller and more accurate. The current build is GRCh38, often referred to as hg38, and within a few years this will be replaced when build hg39 is released. With a reference sequence you can map an individual's genome to see which *sites* are variants from the reference sequence, being potential SNPs. In one sense, every chromosome is a sequence of the four bases AGCT, and it should be a simple matter to read the order they fall in. But there are obstacles to achieving a fully accurate read: many regions of the genome are highly repetitive, and reading the genome involves splitting it into small chunks, many of which may look very similar and so it can be difficult to fit them together correctly.

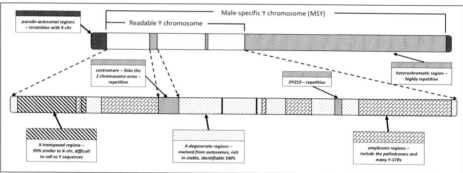

Figure 3: 'Mosaic' diagram of the regions of the Y chromosome. Adapted from Skaletsky et al (2003). © John Cleary

Let's look at the geography of the Y chromosome in more detail. Figure 3 presents a classic diagram to identify the Y chromosome as a sequence of discrete regions, each with a different character. The upper 'sausage' represents the full length of the Y. It is one of the shortest chromosomes, but over half cannot be sequenced at all with current technology. This is the heterochromatin, presumed to take just over half the length of the Y. At each tip are the pseudo-autosomal regions (PAR1 and PAR2), two short regions that behave like the autosomes as they recombine with the X chromosome at conception. They can be sequenced, but it is impossible to know whether a variant read is on the Y or the X, and recombination can remove a variant from the descent line – unlike regular Y-SNPs, which pass on down the patrilineal line.

In between the two PARs is the male-specific Y (MSY), which does not recombine with its pair the X.

The white section left in between these difficult regions is referred to in genetic genealogy as the 'readable Y', and is the target of NGS testing. This is expanded in the lower 'sausage' in Figure 3, but even this roughly 40% of the Y also has a complex structure. The best regions for finding variants callable as reliable SNPs are the ones together referred to as the 'X-degenerate region'. While 'degenerate' may sound alarming, this region traces itself evolutionarily to the emergence of the X and Y chromosomes from autosomes; these regions have diverged from the X so that they can be easily differentiated from X chromosome sequences. This is good for calling mutations as it reduces doubts that a variant is on the X, or a different part of the genome. In contrast the areas collectively known as the 'X-transposed region' are less useful for variant calling. This is a block of DNA that transferred from the X to the Y in early hominid history, but recently enough for these sequences still to show 99% similarity to a similar region on the X. Variants may be called on this region, but there may be greater doubts over whether they are verifiable Y-SNPs.

The 'ampliconic region' can furnish good SNP calls, but also contains special sequences of the Y known as palindromes, in which long sequences are repeated more or less exactly. A variant found on one of these can exist in one of two locations (or more in some cases), and it may be impossible to determine which of these is the true location. This in itself is not fatal and some analysts do call such variants as Y-SNPs, noting that they exist in an unverifiable position on the Y and may be encountered with the formula ZZ22_1 (which the author is positive for). ZZ22_2 is the alternative location, and the SNP is present in only *one* of the two. The palindromes consist of two virtually identical sequences, and periodically one palindromic arm will overwrite its twin, copying itself over any changes that may have appeared on the other arm. Any variants that had appeared on the recipient arm will simply disappear from that point forward for all descendants of the person in whom the overwriting – called gene conversion – happened. ZZ22_1 could simply disappear from the genome of some descendants, introducing an element of uncertainty over its value as a branch marker in a descent tree. There are SNPs that appear to come and go among members of a haplogroup, which may be an effect of gene conversion.

Y chromosome genealogy searches for stable variants that do not disappear so they can be tracked through numerous generations as reliable branch markers. The aim is to identify markers that indicate the carrier must be a descendant of a particular past ancestor, whether close or distant in time. Variants called from the problem regions have a higher risk of disappearance in a later generation, leaving descent lines unmarked, or appearing frequently, if multiple loci are being read mistakenly as the same SNP. This can happen in certain other repetitive regions of the Y, two of which are marked on the diagram above. The region DYZ19 acts like a very large STR, in which micro-regions may be unstable, and as they are repetitive, a variant's location may be impossible to determine exactly. The centromere links the two arms of the Y together, and is another repetitive region. This was sequenced as part of the hg38 reference sequence build, but in an inferential rather than direct way, so doubt is expressed in some circles about variant calls made in it. Nevertheless, testing companies are calling variants found in these two regions as SNPs, and so some caution is needed when evaluating the test results. A quick check on whether new variants fall into one of these positions is offered by the testing company YSEQ (see Figure 4).

Please do __not__ suggest SNPs in the following hg38 regions:
chrY:1..2781479 (pseudo autosomal region 1, PAR1)
chrY:10072350..11686750 (synthetic assembled centromeric region, CEN)
chrY:20054914..20351054 (DYZ19 125 bp repeat region)
chrY:26637971..26673210 (post palindromic region, actually gradual start of Yq12 repetitive region)
chrY:56887903..57217415 (pseudo autosomal region 2, PAR2)
Those sections of the Y chromosome suffer from frequent recombination events and are therefore not useful for phylogenetic studies. Unfortunately we can't provide primers for those regions.

Figure 4: Advice from YSEQ.com on which new variants may be unsuitable for analysis via single SNP testing. https://tinyurl.com/yavr8msl.

Exploring and mapping the Y sequence

So, having taken this extended expedition through the wild geography of the Y chromosome, we can move on to look at how it is sequenced. One last point – there is a mapping reference system for all chromosomes, which starts at the left side of the diagram and numbers each locus on the chromosome in order until we reach the right side. The Y has approximately 58 million loci, varying slightly from build to build. The 'readable Y' falls roughly in the range 2,780,000 to 26,000,000, with the heterochromatin stretching beyond that for 30,000,000 loci (or possibly more, as it is not possible to exactly determine its length, and it may be highly variable in different men). The locus number can be used as a coordinate in much the same way as coordinates on a map.

A very useful resource for Y test-takers is YBrowse, which was created for and supported by ISOGG – try it at http://ybrowse.org/. If you want to look up the location of a Y-SNP, you can enter its name in the search box. You can also enter a locus to see whether there is a known SNP at that site. The Y coordinate needs to be entered in a particular way – try entering this locus, and use the format as shown here:

chrY:20577481..20577481

You have just entered the hg38 coordinate for M269, one of the most widespread SNPs among European-descended people. If you are a man in the widespread haplogroup R1b, you are very likely to be positive for this ancient SNP. Now try entering the following into the search box: L91. This is a defining SNP in the G haplogroup, and was found in the Y chromosome of Ötzi 'the Iceman', an ancient European found mummified in the Tyrolean Alps in 1991. If you have this SNP on your Y, you will be a (very distant) relative of Ötzi. You should see something like Figure 5, and you can notice that L91 has alternative labels (PF3246 or S285): a common problem, as many labs like to name the SNPs they find, and many of them have been found more than once. The additional label rs755612010 is the reference code for this SNP in the academic database of SNPs, dbSNP (not generally used in genetic genealogy).

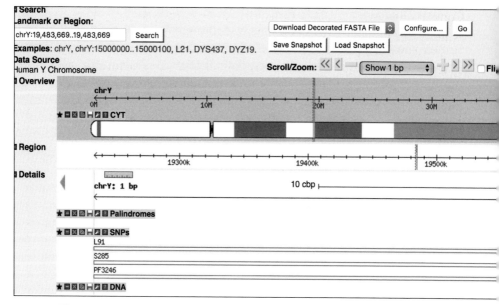

Figure 6: YBrowse window showing result for G-L91. © ISOGG YBrowse and Thomas Krahn

Now go across to the zoom function. You are looking at just one base pair (bp) on the Y at the moment, so select 9bp. You can now see four base pairs either side of your SNP. Now try zooming to 100bp, and 500bp. Are there many other SNPs on either side of L91? With this tool and coordinate system, you are ready to start investigating the SNPs you may find in a SNP sequencing test, for yourself or another testing partner. If you find your results show an apparently unnamed new SNP, you can check it in YBrowse to see whether there are any names for it. You can check the names of your known SNPs to see basic details about them, and whether they are also known by other names.

Next Generation Sequencing testing

Next Generation Sequencing (NGS) is a method of reading DNA employed by genomic science since 2005, which began to impact genetic genealogy in 2013 with the creation of the Full Genomes Corporation's (FGC) Y Elite and Family Tree DNA's Big Y tests. These have evolved over the years since, acquiring new features and increasing read lengths, and as technology continues to develop so will they.

Consult the ISOGG Wiki (https://isogg.org/wiki/Next_generation_sequencing) for the latest trends in this fast-evolving field.

The core principle of NGS is that a long DNA strand cannot be read by current technology, but short ones can. So the first stage is to smash the strand up into fragments, which are sequenced individually, and then placed against a map of the genome – the human reference sequence discussed above. This way, the genome of the individual can be assembled from the reads (that is the individual fragments) and the sites where they vary from the reference sequence can be identified – leading to the lists of variants that test-takers see in their results. The current NGS tests used by genealogists can read 150 base pairs (bp) from each end of the fragments.

By reading multiple overlapping fragments, in principle the entire genomic sequence can be read. It is also possible to target particular regions of the genome, and this is what the major Y-NGS tests do. Of the test types in Table 1, FGC's Y Elite and FTDNA's old Big Y-500 target different lengths of Y chromosome coverage, which was the primary difference between them. Big Y-500 was found by many project administrators to deliver a quicker turnaround and has a large results database of around 20,000 results, but covered a smaller region of the genome. FGC covered a much larger stretch of the readable Y, and consequently discovered more SNPs per test-taker. But it does not offer a matching results database, and its turnaround times are found often to be longer. FGC does, however, offer a results analysis service, also open to customers of the Big Y test. The test data is summarised in Table 2.

The decision whether to take a Big Y or Y Elite has changed with the launch of the new Big Y-700 in February 2019. Now both Big Y-700 and Y Elite 2.1 (the current versions of these tests) target the same coverage of the Y, achieving around 90–95% of the readable Y chromosome. For existing STR test-takers with FTDNA, the Big Y-700 may meet their needs, as only upgrading is required. With both tests now, there are good chances of identifying one SNP mutation every 82–98 years, (though this is subject to random variation) with benefits for recent genealogy research. If more SNP resolution is required, then it would be necessary to move on to specialised long read tests (see p144) or high-resolution WGS at much higher cost, though with even greater SNP discovery potential.

NGS test	Big Y-700 Family Tree DNA	Y Elite 2.1 Full Genomes Corp
Average depth coverage (no. reads per base pair)	20–30x	30x
Read length	150 bp	150 bp
Total sequence length (no. base pairs read @ at least 1x)	23 million bp	22 million bp
Proportion of readable Y chromosome	95%	90%
Callable Y chr. sites (min. 4 reads above set quality threshold)	14–15 million bp	14 million bp
STR coverage	Big Y-700 offers a minimum of 700 STRs – the 111 panel STRs plus at least 589 additional STRs, up to maximum 838	FGC extract approx. 300 STRs in their analysis
STRs from third-party analysis	Up to 800 STRs can be extracted by YFull.com, incl. 96 of FTDNA 111 panel. Not currently known how YFull extra STRs may overlap with Big Y-700 STRs	Up to 800 STRs can be extracted by YFull.com, incl. 107 of FTDNA 111 panel
Results service	Own platform with matching database and minimal analytical tools. Raw results available in BAM and VCF format.	Spreadsheets with analysis supplied to test-taker. Raw results available in BAM format.

Table 2: Comparison of two main NGS tests for the Y chromosome. Information drawn from ISOGG Wiki, URL above, Y-DNA Data Warehouse statistics at https://ydna-warehouse.org/statistics.html, FGC specifications at https://www.fullgenomes.com/qanda/ and analyses by YFull.com.

In 2019, high-resolution WGS tests are beginning to approach both specialist Y-NGS tests in cost, and in performance. Though none of the companies offering WGS tests have matching databases, their raw data can be downloaded to third-party analysts who do. Their depth coverage (average number of times a base pair is read) may look lower at 15x, 20x or 30x than the two Y-NGS tests, but this is more evenly spread across the genome, so producing results on the Y that are comparable to Y Elite (20x and upwards). This is fast becoming an attractive proposition for Y specialist test-takers too, as this also includes all autosomal and mtDNA data, bringing the prospect of all areas of DNA being covered in a single test. The costs are likely to continue moving downwards, the depth coverage increasing, and more user-friendly analysis tools are also likely to be on the horizon.

Working with NGS results: native platforms

Though more expensive than STR panel or SNP pack tests, the available NGS tests have attracted interest from many genealogists because of what they offer for solving genealogical brick walls. STRs have instabilities of back and parallel mutations, but SNPs tend to be one-off (per branch) and permanent (at least in the context of the length of human history). Many researchers are hoping to identify unique SNPs within their family lineages and branches that they can use to identify other members of their family networks, with the SNPs as 'hard' markers of membership.

In this section we will look at how this is being done with NGS test results. Test-takers can start by examining their results in the 'native' tools supplied by the testing company's own website. Then raw data – usually in the forms of BAM or VCF files – can be downloaded and submitted to other third-party sites, which are specialists in analysis of the data.

The tools provided by the testing companies vary greatly and in all cases some additional analysis is likely to be required to derive full value from the data your NGS test generates. YFull and FGC both offer analysis packages. The presentation of the analysis is clear to those familiar with NGS results data, but new test-takers may need some assistance – and haplogroup project administrators are often the best to go to for this.

Most Y-NGS tests at the moment are through the BigY system, now known as the BigY-700, because of the 589-750 new STRs offered along with the SNPs and the existing 111 STRs since 2019 (though it should be noted that the 'new' STRs are still experimental and the matching system is not yet fully developed, as with the established 111). Initial experience suggests that the main significance of the additional STRs may be to help identify signature markers, important in establishing test-takers' membership of specific branches of families. As with other NGS tests, results will come in two main forms:

- *Named variants (known SNPs)*: these have been reported before and may exist on one of the several trees being built from SNP data. These are likely to have a name, e.g. Y9089, (a SNP a couple of thousand years old, and only found in a small number of tests so far); P312 (a major branch marker in the R1b haplogroup common in Western Europe, estimated at around 5,000 years old); or P305 (a very ancient SNP in the haplogroup A1, and at around 130–160,000 years old appeared early in the history of *homo sapiens*, the majority of men consequently carrying it).
- *Unnamed variants (novel variants)*: these may be unique to you; or you may find that other test-takers in your subclade carry them, and they will then become shared, recent SNPs. These may be listed by their Y coordinate plus the mutation, showing the original base and the base it has mutated to – in a form something like 4902003 A>C (the base at this hg38 coordinate has mutated from A to C, adenine to cytosine). This is a private SNP possessed by one of the authors, which another close family member does not share, so it is a genuinely private and recent variant.

The testing companies used to leave novel variants that were not shared, and private to an individual, in the coordinate + mutation form, saving names for shared variants that could be entered on the haplotree of male-line descent. But more recently, and probably partly as a result of competition among testing companies to be seen to be the first to award names to SNPs they 'discover', almost all novel SNPs are now being named by testing companies, or, if not, by third-party analysts. The one in the bullet point above, despite originally appearing in a Big Y test in 2014, and being found only in the author so far, has recently been gifted a name – BY58304. Some readers may find names like this scarcely more memorable than the long coordinate numbers. However, they make it easier to store variants in a database, especially when new reference sequences may cause all the coordinates to change. Test-takers also like having 'names' for their SNPs, as they become more real to them, and there is the possibility they can be added onto the evolving haplotree (though this happens only when they are confirmed by a second matching test).

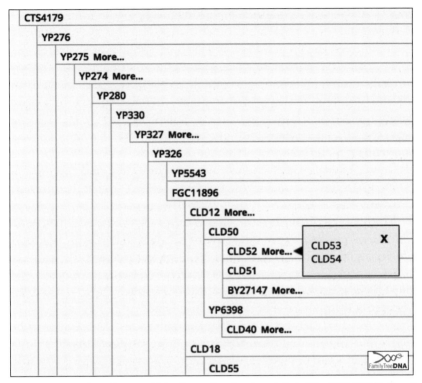

Figure 6: extract from the FTDNA haplotree showing the subclade R1a-CTS4179 (believed to have originated in Norway c.3000 years ago, and is associated with the Macdonalds of the Hebrides in Scotland). © FTDNA

The Big Y results page offers a few tools to help test-takers explore their test results, by far the most important being the FTDNA haplotree (Figure 6). A haplotree, as it sounds, is a tree of haplogroups, and it can stretch right back to the 'Y chromosomal Adam' marked by haplogroup A00 at the apex of the tree over 200,000 years ago, down to living people taking tests today.

Technically, haplogroups are the ancient and large descent groups marked by letters of the alphabet like R, E, J, O and A (to mark some of the most common). This system was created in 2002 by the Y Chromosome Consortium (YCC) to label the major branches in the tree that had been discovered by that time, (and these letters are nothing more than labels for significant branching points – there is no difference between an R or a J haplogroup other than their respective places in the human Y tree). The branches below each haplogroup are usually referred to as subclades, or sub-branches, although the terms are often mixed in daily usage. What a Big Y can do is identify your subclade by discovering new SNPs that become new branch markers from more recent times than the ancient markers labelled by the YCC in 2002. This way, the human Y tree is built out and downwards towards modern times filling in the branches of the tree – or at least the ones where there are living male-line descendants who can be tested and their recent SNPs discovered. So the biggest strength of NGS Y tests is that they are discovery tests.

The extract of the tree in Figure 6 is very well developed with branches identified by just one or two SNPs nested inside the branches above. There has been substantial NGS testing to reach this point of development. Genealogists are particularly keen to identify Y-SNPs that must have appeared inside known historical genealogies, so these can become indicators for membership of a historical family network. In Figure 6, CLD12 and its 'downstream' subclades are thought to be SNPs that appeared in medieval Scotland, in the descendants of John MacDonald, Lord of the Isles, who died in 1386, making these powerful indicators for descent from John MacDonald.

One last thing to note in Figure 6 is the box next to CLD52, at the end of one branch. This shows two more SNPs, CLD53 and CLD54: these are equivalents of CLD52 in branching terms. That is, the three SNPs, which are independent mutations, have always appeared together in the same test-takers. This means they cannot be put in order of age, and they cannot be separated each onto their own branch level. They almost certainly all did occur in different men, in different generations, but the side branches have either all died out, or they have not been found to test yet. This is referred to as a 'SNP block', and represents one branching point in the tree – but it might also represent many generations, anything from 1–12, or possibly more. SNPs appear randomly, may come rapidly or very occasionally, and generations could pass without a new Y-SNP. But one day a test-taker could appear who had, say, CLD52 and CLD54 but not CLD53. These negative results are very important, as they can re-branch the tree. At the moment we have:

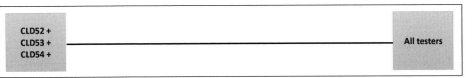

But if there was a new negative result for CLD53, this would now become a branching tree:

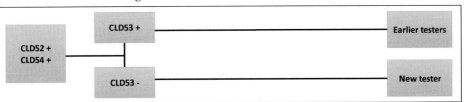

This way, the negative and positive results together build the phylogeny – or the tree-branching. Genetic genealogists refer to this as block-splitting – finding the order recent SNPs appeared by finding the branches that lack one of them, putting the branching point at that place.

At the time of writing, FTDNA has the most comprehensive haplotree from NGS tests, as the BigY has the largest NGS database of Y results, at over 20,000. However, as more WGS testing is offered by other companies there is a risk that no single platform will host a comprehensive tree, creating a challenge for the future of how to maintain all results in one place. WGS test results will most likely add to trees on multi-test-taker third-party analysis sites (see next section), but these can only contain the subset of test results submitted to them. FTDNA's BigY haplotree contains every BigY test result so far, though no others – and there are SNP-rich parts of the Y that BigY-700 has only started to reach. One attempt at building a platform-neutral, comprehensive Y tree is the ISOGG Tree at https://isogg.org/tree/ (though it has its own particularities of presentation, style and criteria for admission).

NGS results – third-party analysis
While there are good analysis tools on the testing company sites, which should be the first call for a new test result, they also have limitations. Many test-takers request their raw data from the testing company,

which comes in the form of a BAM – Binary Alignment Map – file. This large file (often up to 0.5 GB or over) contains all the positions read in the test, the number of reads for each, and records the alignment of the reads against the reference sequence. Downloading this to your own computer is advisable as you are then able to archive it for safe keeping – using an offline external hard drive is the best option. It is then your own decision whether, when and how you share that data with other researchers or platforms. The first third-party analyst you encounter could therefore be yourself, or a project administrator who is working with you.

The testing company will already have identified most of your novel variants, but since there are differences in setting thresholds for SNP calling, getting multiple opinions is a good idea. Among the common third-party analysts are:

YFULL.COM

A specialist Y-NGS analytics company. They check and verify all variant calls, may call additional variants using different thresholds, and assess all calls according to quality. They offer an attractive and easy to use graphical user interface, including a haplotree of all SNPs they call. Their database is not the same size as the Big Y database, as they only receive a subset of BAM files, but they have around 19,000 kits in their database in 2019, including BAMs from other companies and academic research. A small one-time fee is charged for data processing, but the kit is then dynamically matched afterwards with no further charges.

FULL GENOMES CORP

As well as testing, they accept BAM files for further analysis from other companies. The same analysis spreadsheet set as for their own test is provided, and the one-off fee is comparable to YFull.com.

THE BIG TREE

At the moment this is a benefit for haplogroup R1b test-takers, but it is expected to be offered to other haplogroups in time, so keep an eye on it if you are not in R1b. It is a free resource offered by volunteer enthusiast Alex Williamson. The Big Tree was created at the launch of Big Y in 2013, though it accepts files from other testing companies if they are in the correct format. It uses VCF files, which are a spreadsheet-like derived file type that lists the variant calls found in the BAM file. It is not as complete as the BAM file, but experience finds it contains the majority of SNP calls from a test, and the Big Tree has developed the most comprehensive NGS-test-based haplotrees for the R1b subclades R-P312 and R-U106/S21. It is also very attractive to look at and easy to navigate around. Check out the front page of the Big Tree at http://www.ytree.net showing the main branches immediately below it. Now go to this sub-page: http://www.ytree.net/DisplayTree.php? blockID=18. If you search for Y9089 you will see this SNP in its tree position. You can also compare it to the position for the SNP on FTDNA's and YFull's trees to get a feel for how these platforms can differ.

Y-DNA DATA WAREHOUSE
This new initiative is linked to the Big Tree, and is also run by volunteer enthusiasts. This is now the means to upload new results to the Big Tree for those eligible and the team is collecting any haplogroup R data that test-takers may wish to volunteer for analysis (in time it may be extended to other haplogroup test-takers). As well as the Big Tree, this is also supporting a major initiative by co-author of this book Iain McDonald in developing a system for estimating the ages of Y-tree branches found in NGS testing, and the Warehouse team can be expected to develop further applications to understand Y-NGS data in future.

Estimating TMRCA from SNPs
We saw above how to estimate time to most recent common ancestor (TMRCA) from STRs for a group of related test-takers. Having built a tree from SNPs, you may want to estimate approximate ages for the branching points marked by your SNPs. Some methods have been developed to do this – but always remember that SNPs occur *randomly* and are not a 'clock'. Age estimates from SNPs come with very wide date ranges, or confidence intervals.

A few different systems for estimating ages have been developed, but they operate on the same system using similar factors:

1. Count the SNPs that have occurred *since* the branching point you want to age-estimate in *all* test-takers who meet at that branching point. Count in full down each line for each test-taker, so you may count some SNPs several times.
2. Calculate the mean number of SNPs for each line:
   Total number of SNPs ÷ Number of test-takers
3. Multiply by the interval in years that SNPs occur. This is an estimate too. A common figure is that, when following a line down from ancient times, Y-SNPs occur in average intervals of *c.*125 years, covering all Y regions where the Big Y-500 calls SNPs (or 82-98 in the new Big Y-700):
   Years per SNP x Mean number of SNPs = approximate age (years)
4. Round the result to the nearest fifty (if since 1000CE) or nearest 100 (if older than 1000CE). Remember – this is only an estimate!

See Figure 7 for a worked example from the descendants of Stewarts. The private SNPs from the branching point can be counted from the Non-Matching Variants (NMV) list in your Big Y results. Notice that S781 is a shared SNP for two of them, so must be counted twice, for each line: 13+9+7+0 = 29 NMV.

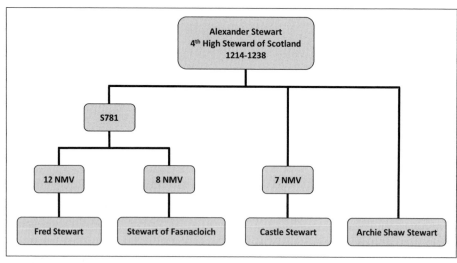

Figure 7: Counting SNPs for age estimation, using a section of the Stewart descent tree as illustration,

Big Y500 - Results			

Named Variants	Unnamed Variants	**Matching**	

Match Name		**Non-Matching Variants**		**Shared Variants**	
Name Search		SNP Name Search			
👤 Fred Stewart (S781+)	✉ 💬	A889, BY12072, S781, 2925930, 6527750, 7436075, 11333624, 17124651, 19451426		323703	
👤 Stewart of Fasnacloich (S781+)	✉ 💬	S781, 2925930, 7030498, 7436075, 8791113, 9309047, 14564299, 14794843, 16661006, 17124651, 17170726, 19451426, 21661609		233822	
👤 Earl of Castle Stewart (S781-)	✉ 💬	2925930, 7436075, 10018527, 12548054, 12721412, 17124651, 19451426		232575	FamilyTreeDNA

From Archie Shaw Stewart's Big Y matches. © FTDNA

The four test-takers have twenty-nine SNPs between them below the branching point at the Stewart ancestor. The calculation then is:

$29 \div 4 = 7.25 \times 125$ (SNP interval) $= 906.25$
Round to the nearest 50 > 900 years TMRCA

Nine hundred years takes us back to 1118, and Alexander Stewart was born in 1214 – about a century out. These are just estimates, and may be quite accurate for ancient haplogroups. But when working with a small number of cases in genealogical time we should allow a margin of error of a couple of centuries either way in all cases – and in this case our result falls into the acceptable range. Some analysts (YFull, Y-DNA Warehouse) are developing more complex systems for SNP-TMRCA, but these also remain estimations. Always check the confidence intervals that the analysts supply, and not just the headline number.

SNPs: from deep ancestry to genealogical markers
We have had a comprehensive overview of reading the Y chromosome, testing SNPs, platforms for analysis and phylogenetic tree building. But

the fundamental question a genealogist test-taker will want to ask is 'How does this help me discover more about my genealogy?' She will be interested in the time since the medieval adoption of surnames (*c.*700 years ago) or since the development of good records for tracing descent (*c.*450 years ago). In the early days of SNP testing, when SNPs were mostly tested individually after being discovered in academic research programmes (and were therefore widespread in populations), the general goal was what some termed 'deep ancestry', ancient or prehistoric, since widespread Y-SNPs are likely to be ancient. As recently as 2013, the year the first Y-NGS tests were launched, many enthusiasts hunted for their 'terminal SNP', e.g. whether it was a 'son of R-L21/DF13' (see the historical tree diagram Figure 8, right-hand branch).

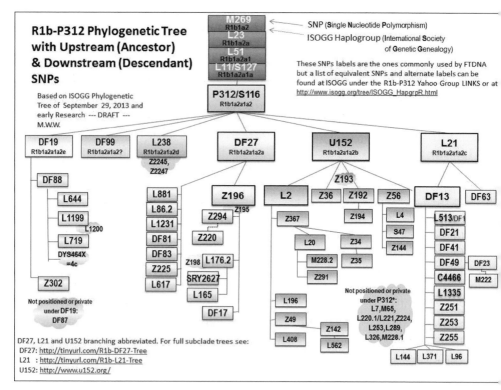

Figure 8: SNP tree for R-P312 in 2013, just before the launch of the Y Elite and Big Y tests, designed by Mike Walsh for the R1b and All Subclades Haplogroup Project. © Mike Walsh

The number of SNPs being found was already proliferating by 2013, but every single one on the tree above is ancient. The Big Tree (previous section) shows the current view of the R-P312 SNP tree, and the YFull tree can be used to find age estimates for these ancient SNPs. What followed in the several years that followed has been referred to as the 'SNP tsunami', transforming this view (which fitted onto a single neat diagram on a single page) to one that demands today's huge trees.

With the discovery threshold moving forward to historical times, the same methods that were used to arrange these ancient SNPs in a phylogenetic tree can be applied to SNPs in the historical era. These modern age phylogenetic trees are also frame trees for lineages that can capture the branching of a family from before the appearance of records, or when documents may have disappeared leaving gaps in the record – the 'brick walls' that family historians are familiar with. Here is an example of a Y testing project that is starting to smash down some of these walls.

The Jacobs family project knows the identity of their emigrant ancestor, one John Jacob who appeared in Anne Arundel County, Maryland, as an indentured servant in the 1660s, but the one big thing the descendants do *not* know about their founder is where he originally migrated from. The project recently moved into Y-SNP testing, having been early adopters of Y-STR testing, in an attempt to crack this mystery. Four Big Y tests discovered a number of SNPs in a subclade of R1a, and these can be built into a SNP tree (Figure 9) by their patterns of sharing. In this case we can see that the first two SNPs are shared by all, so these must be 'upstream' of the founder. The others are all unique to one test-taker ('private'), and so must be in separate 'downstream' branches. One test-taker has no private SNPs at all, while the other three have three or four each.

Descendants of three sons of John Jacob have been tested and there are separate SNP signatures for each. Two descendants of one of the sons, Joseph, have been tested – the two in the middle of Fig. 9 – and their differences tell us that the BY63123 block must have appeared since Joseph, since the * test-taker does not share them (the asterisk represents having no defining SNPs beyond the upstream block). Beyond that, it is impossible to state where in the respective lines these SNPs appeared – they could be anywhere from the test-taker himself up to the last branching ancestor who must have been negative.

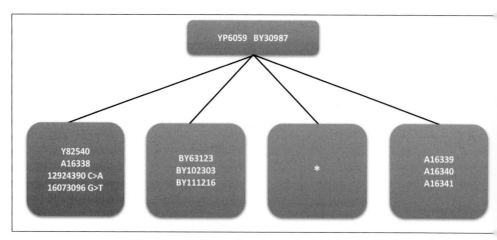

Figure 9: Outline SNP tree from Jacobs Big Y tests.

But all of these branching SNPs are genealogical – because they appear inside a known genealogy. The project should continue by testing another man in each branch, with a more recent common ancestor than the highest person in the line. If some of the private SNPs are shared and some are not shared, then – in the same way as the diagram on p133 – blocks can be split, and SNPs can be ordered within the line. These SNPs then become powerful markers of branching within a descent line, but also potential indicators of whether a person belongs to the line or not.

The SNPs at the top –YP6059 and BY30987 – shared by all the group are also genealogical, but in a different way. So far, they are shared by all Jacobs, but it is possible that another person *not* descended from John Jacob could test positive for one or both. If that happened, then this would be a strong indicator that that person and the Jacobs were genetic cousins, and it might help to establish where the emigrant ancestor came from. These two SNPs would then be shared by the Jacobs descendants and another surname group not descended from John. At the moment it remains a Jacobs indicator, but it could still be shared by other surnames. On the other hand, the other SNPs on the tree are entirely markers of descent from John Jacob – true genealogical SNP markers.

Follow-up
To make the most of Y-NGS results, the SNPs, the signature STRs and the known genealogical information should be blended onto a tree, creating a Mutation History Tree (MHT). For further information on how to build an MHT for your descent line, see Maurice Gleeson's blog post on the topic at http://gleesondna.blogspot.com/2015/08/building-mutation-history-tree-with-str.html. Dave Vance has developed a very useful application called SAPP for generating MHTs at http://www.jdvtools.com/SAPP/. This takes a little bit of training, but once mastered it will draw a tree mainly based on STR information but taking account of SNPs and information on common ancestors shared by test-takers within it. SAPP can only reflect the information you put into it, so it is best used to generate hypotheses for further research – several alternatives are possible and small changes can flip what is presented between them.

The future of Y testing
At the time of writing, we have benefited from an extraordinarily exciting time in Y testing in which the nature of building a genetic Y-line tree has changed fundamentally through the SNP tsunami. The next several years promise to bring equally massive changes, which will enrich all aspects of genetic genealogy, including Y testing. Here are some new testing systems that may impact on sequencing the Y:

- *Whole Genome Sequencing*: this is a 'future' that is fast becoming the present, at the time of writing in 2019. This uses NGS techniques to read a person's complete genome instead of targeting parts of it, as the Y tests do. The technology is not new, but the costs have been prohibitive until recently. The other factor holding things back is the question of what to do with the huge quantities of data the test generates. Today's autosomal SNP chips with 700,000 SNPs read just 0.02% of the entire genome, as opposed to only the readable Y chromosome, and even the Y Elite reading 23,000,000 positions on the Y covers just 0.75% of it.

  However, there are utilities that will extract from a WGS results set a complete Y-BAM file that can be analysed by YFull or FGC, or an autosomal file compatible with the testing companies' chips, which can be uploaded to GEDmatch for direct comparison with existing kits. The main issue is the read depth on offer by the testing companies, but 15x or 20x coverage tests are said to produce results on the 'readable Y' that are comparable to the Y Elite for length coverage and SNP discovery. The price for a 15x has come down close to that of the two Y NGS tests. Competition and evolving technology is expected to bring it down further, so that there may be no difference between the established Y tests and a reasonable coverage WGS. While the analysis of data may remain a challenge, there is something to be said for having all one's DNA read in a one-time test, dispensing with the cycles of upgrades and retesting familiar to genetic genealogists.

• *Mass Y-SNP chip*: Today's SNP packs handle a hundred or so significant SNPs, so they are designed to either identify a test-taker's 'deep clade' or which branch of a particular haplogroup they belong to. One consequence of the SNP tsunami could be the designing of a Y-SNP chip (or microarray) which could contain several hundred thousand Y-SNPs, similar to the autosomal testing chips. While this would not be able to discover new SNPs, and would be 'frozen' at the state of the haplotree at the time of design, it would be able to place any Y test-taker on their branch of the haplotree, right down to historical times – and at very low cost.

• *Synthetic long read technology*: current NGS methods are based on short read length fragments of around 150 base pairs. Newer techniques are being developed that allow these to be compiled into much longer read fragments of up to 10kbp – kilobase pairs, or 10,000bp. The first experimental long-read Y tests have been conducted by FGC in 2017–18, although the costs remain very high. This technology offers the promise of more accurate mapping to the reference sequence, and even the possibility of building *de novo* sequences – that is direct sequencing without needing a reference sequence to map the reads onto. The biggest breakthrough that this technology may create is better ability to read repetitive sequences, because the longer reads can bridge much longer sets of repetitions, whether of STR sequences or other repetitive regions, allowing variants to be called on them. While this is beginning to appear on the market in 2019, it may be some time before the costs fall sufficiently and the process is well enough understood to make an impact on genetic genealogy.

- *Single Molecule Real Time Sequencing*: this is 'Third Generation Sequencing', which is marked by reading a single DNA molecule in real time, instead of amplifying and breaking up the molecule to read multiple overlapping fragments. The 'nanopore' technology offers a possibility of using portable hand-held devices for sequencing and very long read lengths, though currently the rate of error is still high at 13–15%.

Ultimately, these new technologies may revolutionise approaches to genetic genealogy, but they will have far more profound applications in the field of human health and diagnosis. They will lead to new dilemmas over what should – and can – be kept private, and what can – or will – be released into the public domain. To keep up, genetic genealogy will need to develop its own attitudes towards what can be done with WGS data, where it can be uploaded, and whether any editing of the data file is necessary before its results are shared in the sites familiar today or their successors in the years to come.

In 2018 and early 2019, Family Tree DNA introduced a number of new tools to their BigY platform, to help test-takers in analysing their results. As they greatly increase the power of the BigY (renamed BigY-700 in February 2019, with a promise to add an additional 200 STRs to the 500 already guaranteed to test-takers) they will benefit from a brief introduction here.

On p133-35 we introduced the FTDNA haplotree as a resource for test-takers to see how their identified SNPs relate to other SNPs on the tree. The tree is now available on a public platform at https://www.family treedna.com/public/y-dna-haplotree/A. It is searchable by branch name or matches' countries of origin. Branch names consist of haplogroup letter and a SNP that defines a branch on the tree, for example R-L448 or J-FGC1.

The list of Named and Unnamed Variants (see p132) is now accompanied by a graphical Y-chromosome browser on the BigY results pages. This lets you see an image of the 150bp reads in your test stacked up like overlapping stones in a wall. The majority of positions on the Y that show the same value (A, G, C or T) as the reference sequence are coloured blue or green, while any result with a variant call is pink. When a column of pink can be seen running down the whole stack of reads it reveals a SNP at that position, and more information can be found by clicking on the pink variant calls.

An innovation in 2019 is the Block Tree. Modelled on the Big Tree of Alex Williamson (see p136-7), it uses a similar method to display SNPs in a vertical tree layout. It shows all the SNPs that share a branching point on your neighbourhood of the tree – which can range from a single SNP to blocks of ten, twenty or even more. The blocks are drawn to occupy more space, the more SNPs they contain, giving a visual sense of how far back in time a shared branching point split from a sibling branch on the tree. Some of your matches will be visible on the neighbouring branches, though many of them are masked if they have greater than thirty SNPs different to you. Hopefully this limitation will be lifted in future, so that the new Block Tree will be able to develop the full power to map our branches of the haplotree that the Big Tree already offers to its R1b users.

Chapter 6

mtDNA TESTS

Alasdair F. Macdonald

The mitochondrial test (mtDNA) has had a much lower uptake by the public, perhaps because of its more limited application for genealogical research. Similar to the male-specific Y-chromosome test, the mtDNA test analyses just one ancestral line, although both men and women can take the test. Mitochondria are found within all our cells, but outside the cell nucleus where our twenty-three pairs of chromosomes reside. One of its main purposes is to provide energy for cell function.

The number of mitochondria found in a cell depends on its type. Those that need more energy, such as muscle or nerve cells, contain thousands, while others may contain only a few hundred. Each mitochondria contains 2–10 copies of the complete mtDNA genome inherited from the individual's mother and escapes recombination (the random shuffling of parental DNA) because the father's mitochondria in his sperm do not persist after fertilisation. Therefore, only women can pass this type of DNA to the next generation. The mitochondrial genome only contains thirty-seven genes and compared to nuclear DNA is very small, consisting of 16,568 base pairs (the building blocks of DNA), while the smallest nuclear chromosome, chromosome 21, spans about 48 million base pairs.

Your mother inherited her mtDNA from her mother, who in turn inherited it from her mother, who inherited it from her mother and so forth back into the mists of time.

The mitochondrial genome is circular in shape, though if unwound it would look the same as nuclear DNA and take the form of a ladder with rungs made up of base pairs. The genome consists of two regions, the Coding Region where genes are located and the Control Region, which itself is divided into two segments, hypervariable region I (HVR I) and hypervariable region II (HVR II). The mutation rate in the Control Region is higher than that within the Coding Region. Although mtDNA does not recombine at fertilisation and is passed unchanged to the next generation, when it is copied errors can occur. These differences in the DNA sequence can be caused by the replacement of one base with another, for example A replaced by T, or by the deletion or insertion of an extra base pair in the sequence.

Similar to the Y-DNA haplogroups, distinct mtDNA lineages have been identified by mutations that have occurred at certain locations in the sequence and carried forward into subsequent generations by daughters. However, unlike Y-DNA haplogroups, the chronologically oldest mtDNA groups are not prefixed by the letter A, B, then C and so on. Due to the nature of research into mitochondrial DNA, early studies were on Native American matrilineal ancestry and when researchers published their findings they simply used the first letter of the alphabet when giving the group an identifier. Therefore, such lineages are within subclades of haplogroups A, B, C, D and X.

Haplogroups have a geographical focus and association, and therefore are useful for exploration of ancient matrilineal origins. For example, haplogroup K1 was formed approximately 22,000 years ago and has its origins in Eurasia, the Arabian Peninsula and the Levant. Haplogroup U emerged about 50,000 years ago from the Middle East, with one subclade, U2a, found predominately in Central Asia (Turkmenistan) and South Asia (India and Pakistan). As mtDNA only represents genetic inheritance of one ancestral line it cannot be used to infer your admixture (ethnicity).

However, the legacy of an ancestor can live on in our DNA. Billy Connolly, the Scottish comedian, explored his ancestry with the help of the popular television series *Who Do You Think You Are?*. It discovered that his third great-grandfather John O'Brien had married an Indian woman called Matilda when serving with the British military in India.

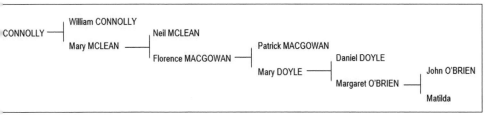

Figure 1: Billy Connolly's matrilineal ancestry

When Billy later took a DNA test it revealed that all his nuclear DNA, his twenty-three pairs of chromosomes (which includes his male Y-chromosome), were entirely European and more specifically from the British Isles and Ireland. His mitochondrial DNA, however, recorded the legacy of the Indian girl Matilda passed unchanged down his matriline. He shares her mitochondrial DNA, which is haplogroup U2a1b, rarely found outside of the Indian sub-continent, with its highest frequencies in the state of Uttar Pradesh in northern India and within the Dravidian family of languages in the south of India.

mtDNA tests

In parallel with Y-chromosome tests, those analysing mtDNA have improved over the years. Originally, mtDNA tests were low resolution, testing the Control Region consisting of HVR I and II which is only 10% of the mtDNA genome. Such tests were limited to discovering the biogeographical origin of your matriline and typically not useful for genealogical questions. Several companies now sequence the entire mtDNA genome, something you only need to do once to obtain results that will be valid for relatives who share the same matrilineal ancestral line. This latter point is important to remember when considering the apparent extra cost.

Taking a full sequence test enables you to get a more specific subclade designation as well as better potential genealogical matching. The full sequence test is necessary for genealogical questions as all mutations in the mtDNA genome can be identified and compared with other test-takers. The mutations are identified by comparing your results to a reference sequence. In fact, there are two reference data sequences to which your mtDNA will be compared. These are the Revised

Cambridge Reference Sequence (rCRS) and the Reconstructed Sapiens Reference Sequence (RSRS). The former is the most commonly used and compares your sequence to the first-ever full mtDNA sequence, which was from a European woman who belonged to haplogroup H2a2a1. The RSRS was created by a group of geneticists to 'root' the sequence in what they believed was the mtDNA sequence of the earliest human, Mitochondrial Eve. When comparing test results, the same reference sequence needs to be used.

Your results

Test results are presented in two ways: a list of your mutations when compared to the reference sequence used, and a list of your matches. The list of differences will include those that define your mtDNA haplogroup, while others are more recent and will be useful for genealogical matching. In the example below from Family Tree DNA, differences when compared to the rCRS are shown for HVR I.

HVR1 DIFFERENCES FROM rCRS		
16069T	16126C	

© FTDNA

There are two differences at locations 16069 and 16126. The letter suffixes indicate the value that you carry at that particular location. At location 16069 the value carried (derived) is 'T'.

HVR1 REFERENCE SEQUENCE		
	Show All Positions	
Position	CRS	Your Result
16069	C	T
16126	T	C

© FTDNA

FTDNA also provide another way to look at the results showing the original or ancestral value in the reference sequence and the derived value carried by the test-taker. At location 16069 the value changed from a 'C' to a 'T'. Results are presented for all three regions, HVR I and HVR II and the Coding Region.

The Coding Region includes your mtDNA genes. If a mutation occurs in one or more of these it can have implications for certain genetic conditions. Having a mutation within a gene does not mean you will develop a genetic disorder, but it might indicate you are a carrier of a condition. Therefore, for privacy reasons many test-takers keep their Coding Region hidden to project administrators. As mitochondrial DNA is not personal – our mtDNA genome is shared with maternal kin such as our mother, grandmother, brothers and sisters and cousins – we ought to not publish or put online results for the Coding Region.

mtDNA matching

Family Tree DNA, the largest test-taker of mtDNA for genealogical as opposed to ancient origins, has over 308,000 mtDNA records in its database, of which 147,000 are full sequence results. As the mtDNA genome is so small there are fewer opportunities for differences between individuals when they are compared. Consequently, even an exact match with another individual does not mean you share the same matrilineal ancestor recently. It could have been many generations in the past.

Test companies have matching thresholds that filter results. With exact matching on HVR I and HVR II FTDNA predict a 50% probability that the most recent common ancestor (MRCA) was within twenty-eight generations. That means that 50% of the time increasing the probability would make the TMRCA stretch further into the past.

FTDNA's analysis of mitochondrial DNA result probabilities	
mtDNA test	**Probability of sharing a maternal ancestor within this timeframe**
HVR1	Exact match: 50% chance within 52 generations (or 1300-1560 years)
HVR1 + HVR2	Exact match: 50% chance within 28 generations (or 700-840 years).
Full sequence	Exact match: 50% chance within 5 generations or a 90% chance within 16 generations.

© FTDNA

If you have taken a full sequence test, FTDNA has set the matching threshold to three differences when comparing two individuals. Once again, the more confidence you desire in the prediction, the greater will be the number of generations to the most recent common ancestor.

# differences between the results	50% probability that the MRCA lived no longer ago than this number of generations	75% probability that the MRCA was no longer than this number of generations	90% probability that the MRCA was no longer than this number of generations
0	5	9	16
1	11	18	25
2	18	26	35
3	24	34	44

Figure 2: Number of predicted generations to the most recent common ancestor

Although a genetic distance of three is used by test companies, and it is very unlikely an individual with more than three differences is related within a genealogical time frame, there is one condition that can cause individuals to fall outwith the matching threshold. The condition is called heteroplasmy.

Heteroplasmy
Each mitochondrion within a cell contains many copies of the mtDNA genome. All mitochondrial DNA mutations go through a state of heteroplasmy. This means that mitochondria with different allele values at the same location exist at the same time within the mitochondria. There are two types of heteroplasmy.

Sequence heteroplasmy involves the coexistence of two strains of DNA that differ at a single nucleotide or SNP. For example:

Strain 1: ...AGTCT**G**GATTC...
Strain 2: ...AGTCT**A**GATTC...

Length heteroplasmy involves the coexistence of two strains of DNA that have different lengths for tracts of repeated nucleotides. For example:

Strain 1: ...TGAATCCCCCCCCCTTGAA...
Strain 2: ...TGAATCCCCCCCCCC**CC**TTGAA..

If more than 20% of mitochondria within a cell have heteroplasmies then the testing companies can pick up the problem. In each generation, children whose mother carries a heteroplasmic genome can inherit three possible mtDNA genomes: a) the heteroplasmic genome b) only the ancestral genome, or c) only the descendant genome. Each child of the mother has the same spin of the dice. FTDNA have summarised the possible outcomes:

a) The child has a heteroplasmy at the same position as their mother. The child inherited some mitochondria with the ancestral genome and some with the descendant genome. Thus, the child has some of each in his or her cells. The proportion of ancestral to descendant genome can vary in each generation and in each child.

b) The child has only the ancestral genome. Only mitochondria without the mutation were passed on to the child. If the child is female, then her children will also inherit only the ancestral genome. The new mutation is then lost in her descendants.

c) The child has only the descendant genome. Only mitochondria with the mutation were passed on to the child. If the child is female, then her children will also inherit only the descendant genome. The new mutation is then fixed in her descendants.

Therefore, heteroplasmy may last for many generations. Between fifteen and seventy generations is normal for humans. However, about 120 generations (3,000 years) are required for there to be a 99% chance that the new mutation has become fixed in the descendants who have it.

How will you know if you carry a heteroplasmy? Like other types of mitochondrial DNA mutations, heteroplasmy is written with the original value, the location of the mutation, and the new (mutated) value. However, the mutated value is denoted by a symbol (see table) that informs which different values were found in the same mitochondria.

Symbol	Meaning
U	U (Uracil – an RNA base
M	A or C
R	A or G
W	A or T
H	A or C or T
D	A or G or T
N	G or A or T or C

Symbol	Meaning
S	C or G
Y	C or T
K	G or T
V	A or C or G
B	C or G or T
X	G or A or T or C

If you have a heteroplasmy you will recognise it by the symbol (a letter) that is not A, C, G or T.

For example, let's look at one location on the mitochondrial genome, position 73. In the rCRS the value is 73A. If a heteroplasmy is identified at position 73, where there are two heteroplasmic values, for example the original value A as well as a G value, the result is written as G73R, 'R', being the symbol used when a mixture of A's and G's are present in the same mitochondria. This means that mitochondria in the same sample have been found that are 73A and 73G.

Why is this important? Imagine that you are seeking to confirm that two or more individuals share the same sixth great-grandmother. If there is heteroplasmy present, individuals will not show as exact matches. If both individuals have one or more heteroplasmies then their genetic distance might fall outwith the matching threshold altogether. The FTDNA full sequence test match list will count each heteroplasmy as a genetic distance of one step.

Heteroplasmies at some locations within the Control region (HVR I and HVR II) are more common. A heteroplasmy occurring in the Coding Region might well be unusual and important to identify close matches who also share that same mutation.

Physiological issues – If you find that you have heteroplasmy or a mutation at a position that is, or may be associated with a physiological issue, then the heteroplasmy may potentially produce the same issue or may produce a lesser form of it because not all of the mtDNA has the mutation.

Testing strategy

Although mitochondrial DNA is a mirror of the Y-chromosome, by following a single direct lineage, it does not have the advantage of having a fixed surname that descends in parallel. Even so utilisation of well-researched genealogy in the form of a descendant tree is necessary in order to identify individuals who carry the mitochondrial lineage under enquiry. We have seen earlier how mtDNA can be used to confirm the biogeographical origin of Billy Connolly in India. If you suspect one of your direct matrilineal ancestors was from a particular ethnic group such as Jewish, Native American, Gypsy or African, then a mtDNA test may provide the evidence.

Genealogical questions that can be answered from mtDNA tend to be more limited and specific. It can be used to identify from which of two possible women a person descends. However, this would only work if these two women were not related on their matrilineal line. More often the test is simply used to identify if two or more individuals share the same matrilineal ancestor. If the ancestor is within the last 150 years and there is no evidence of individuals sharing more than one common ancestor, then an autosomal test might suffice. However, a full sequence mtDNA test can be quite powerful, confirming connection further back, but does need the testing of more than two individuals.

Example 1

One of the best known applications of mtDNA to link individuals is that of Richard III of England (1452–85) whose remains were discovered buried under a car park in Leicester, England. Traditional genealogy identified living descendants of his sister Anne of York (1439–76), as the genealogy of her noble descendants was so well recorded. Samples for comparison were from Wendy Duldig, who is twenty-one generations removed from Richard III, and Michael Ibsen, who is nineteen generations removed from Richard III on the female line. Richard III and Anne of York shared the same mother, Cecily Neville (1415–95), from whom they inherited their rare haplogroup called J1c2c. Michael Ibsen and Wendy Duldig both carry the mutations that define this subclade.

To identify if living individuals are descended from one of two unrelated women (Sally or Jane), you would need to identify at least three individuals using traditional genealogical research – one woman descended matrilineally from Sally and another from Jane. This would establish the mtDNA result for each ancestral woman. The third woman we will call Mary, who is unsure of her maternal descent, would be compared to Sally and Jane to see if her mtDNA matched. If Sally and Jane belonged to a common haplogroup subtype it might not be possible to distinguish from which line Mary descended.

Example 2

Christian Tuach was born *c.*1810 in Inverness, Scotland. She was married in 1847 before civil registration in Scotland and her marriage in the parish records does not mention her parents. On her death certificate in 1877 her parents are listed as Tuach and Isabella MacLennan. No further information is known about Isabella MacLennan, but autosomal matches suggest a connection to Contin or Applecross in Ross-shire in Scotland. Christian Tuach has matrilineal descendants living in the present day who carry the mitochondrial DNA of Isabella MacLennan. Testing one of them would hopefully provide a match to an individual also related in the matrilineal line to Isabella MacLennan and help focus research.

Example 3

An mtDNA test can also be used to prove or disprove a connection. If a woman died in childbirth and there were already a number of children, it was common for the father to remarry, often quite quickly. If the birth was before civil registration it might not be clear which spouse the child was descended from. If the child was a female and had female descendants and her half-sibling sisters also had descendants to the present day, it would be possible to compare their mtDNA to establish the correct parentage.

In summary, mitochondrial DNA is useful for biogeographical ancient origins, to identify recent ethnicity in the female line and in certain circumstances to confirm whether individuals share the same matrilineal ancestor.

Chapter 7

CHOOSING BETWEEN TESTING COMPANIES

Alasdair F. Macdonald

Choosing a test company can be a challenging decision, as many vendors offer similar unique selling points, such as the ability to create an online tree and access to billions of documentary records. Others highlight the ability to discover where you come from or smart matching to help you with your genealogy. Every test-taker has their own experience with vendors, so it is wise to ask friends who have already tested or do some basic research using online forums.

With certain types of test, in particular autosomal cousin-matching tests, it is important to have your data in more than one database. Often this will mean testing with more than one company, however, as it is a competitive market. Certain of the large vendors, such as Family Tree DNA and MyHeritage, accept data transfers from other companies. Ancestry and 23andMe do not accept data transfers.

No matter the size of the company, we ought to be cautious about assuming our test data and results are going to be available permanently. As with all commercial companies competing in the open market, some DNA test vendors will ultimately succumb to market pressures or be absorbed into larger entities. In recent years the field has lost companies such as BritainsDNA, DNA Heritage (database acquired by FTDNA), Genetree and Relative Genetic (acquired by Ancestry).

Although choosing the best test company for your particular aims is very important, you should also consider the longer-term legacy of your results and raw data if a company goes bust. Once you have tested you also ought to ensure you have a beneficiary's contact details added to your kit profile and ensure you download and save your raw data file(s) to your computer as well as a backup location. You should also download and save on a regular basis your list of matches from the various tests you have taken. Adding the login details for your kit(s) and those you administer to your will is also worth considering so that access to the data and results is not lost to future generations.

Before choosing a company you ought to be aware which test is right for the question or area of research you are interested in. Bundled DNA tests that analyse all three types of DNA (Y-DNA, mtDNA and atDNA) rarely meet all your requirements, as they tend to compromise between cost and resolution of test. This may mean that at some point you will need to test with more than one company in order to test for a particular type of DNA, for example the Y-chromosome. Such all-in-one tests are, however, a good introduction to testing if you are just curious, with no specific questions, or to give as a gift to somebody.

DNA testing for genealogy can reveal unknown relationships and family secrets. Familial relationships may not be reported as expected and new close relatives can be discovered. The power of genealogy tests to reveal close familial relationships is the primary reason it has been so successfully utilised by the adoption community, particularly in the United States. Genealogy tests cannot, however, be used for legal purposes as there is no 'chain of custody': in other words, there is no proof the test came from the stated individuals. In such cases specialist relationship or paternity testing is required at an accredited testing laboratory. These can be used to solve a dispute about child maintenance and apply for contact with a child, to apply for a visa so that a child can settle with a relative, or find out who inherits an estate when someone has died.

Because the field of genetic genealogy is constantly developing, it is difficult to give specific advice on which company to test with, so the following guidance focusses on generic issues.

Issues to consider before testing
Here are some general criteria you ought to consider before buying a DNA test:

- *Database size*: What is the size of the database? Not all companies offer a relational database where you can contact matches. Also, does the company sell their kits predominantly in certain regions of the world, such as North America, and thus lack data from European countries? If it is an autosomal DNA test then you should consider having your data in multiple test company databases to maximise your chance of picking up close matches. You also ought to ensure your data is uploaded to the free GEDmatch site, which accepts data files from all the major vendors.
- *Explanation of the actual test*: Is it clear how many marker positions are being tested and the coverage of the test? When was the test launched? The field is advancing very fast and products can be limited in their usefulness two or three years after launch. For example, the Geno 2 Genographic test was informative for ancient origins when originally launched, but very soon became obsolete, although it is still available for sale today.
- *Explanation of results*: None of the companies are particularly good at providing explanation and interpretation of test results, although some do provide useful help pages, forums to ask questions, or a Learning Centre. The company that strives and manages to succeed in this area will be providing real added value for their customers.
- *Contacting matches*: How easy is it to contact your matches? If the test company are primarily offering biomedical testing, experience suggests that matches are less likely to respond compared to companies where the only focus is genealogy.
- *Tools*: Does the company provide tools to help you evaluate and analyse your matches? For autosomal testing a chromosome browser is an essential tool and one that Ancestry refuses to provide.
- *Hidden costs*: Beware of hidden costs. These fall into two types: shipping cost for the test kit and subscription to access all features and services. The latter in particular is due to the way certain vendors are offering parallel online services for access to record sets along with their genetic testing.
- *Privacy*: All the major vendors take this seriously, but smaller companies might be more of an unknown quantity. Check out the terms of service and whether the company is GDPR compliant (General Data Protection Regulation). GDPR has strengthened the

conditions for consent and companies are no longer able to use long, unintelligible terms and conditions full of legalese. This means your private information is safer and you can withdraw consent at any time.

- *Research and third party access*: Does the company ask you to opt-in so they can use your data for 'research' and give access to third parties? Be aware that you do not need to give such permissions to access your results for genealogy. Remember that your test raw data belongs to you and you have the right to access it anytime, limit who sees or uses it and if you so desire have it destroyed (right to be forgotten).

- *Storage of your DNA sample*: How long will the company store the DNA sample? This can be important when testing elderly relatives if the sample is the one and only opportunity to preserve their DNA.

- *Does the company have strategic partnerships?*: Companies are partnering to offer more diversity and breadth of content. For example, LivingDNA partners with FindMyPast and Family Tree DNA partners with MyHeritage, so that test-takers can access large genealogy collections and resources.

- *Projects*: This is an extremely important aspect, particularly for surname, lineage and haplogroup research. Projects need relational databases and the best company for these is Family Tree DNA. They are the primary test company for both Y-chromosome and mitochondrial testing and provide the opportunity for individuals to participate, collaborate, and volunteer to administer research projects. Projects are provided with free online webpages, resources and management tools.

- *How easy is it to upgrade or take a completely different type of test?*: Be aware that although several of the major vendors may have massive databases counting into the millions of test-takers for autosomal DNA, they do not offer either Y-chromosome or mitochondrial testing. Companies that do all-in-one tests are only testing a limited number of Y-DNA SNPs. They might be very useful for understanding your ancient Y-line origins, but will be insufficient for almost all genealogical questions. If you are testing for admixture and biogeographical origins (ethnicity) do not assume that the large companies necessarily have the best data set for the region of the world where your ancestors originated. For example, LivingDNA have the best regional breakdown for individuals whose ancestors came from Great Britain and Ireland.

• *Y-chromosome testing*: Although Family Tree DNA is the primary test company for Y-DNA projects, there are several other companies that offer top-quality products but have no comparative database. These include YSEQ and Full Genomes Corporation.

• *Adoption*: All the major test companies are useful for adoption research. We would recommend having your results in all the main databases: AncestryDNA; Family Tree DNA; LivingDNA; MyHeritage and 23andMe. This will mean testing independently with several of the companies as they do not accept data transfers.

• *Customer support*: Experience by test-takers can be very subjective and the response from companies is very varied. As with many companies it is becoming much harder to talk to a member of staff directly even when a telephone number is provided. At the very least companies ought to provide a visible email and contact form.

• *Turnaround time*: This question is again rather subjective, as companies are constantly reinvesting in technology and are subject to the fluctuating volume of kits affecting processing capacity and the implementation of their own quality-control procedures. As a rule of thumb, results ought to be returned for all types of test in around eight weeks after being entered into processing. Some NGS or WGS tests may take significantly longer. However, the test companies are generally quite good at posting the expected delivery date, even if the reason for any delays might seem problematic.

• *Cost*: Autosomal testing is very competitive and generally low cost for a single test from all the main vendors. However, to make the most of your test result and your matching to other test-takers you really need to test other family members to identify DNA segments from your recent ancestors that you have not inherited. This will result in an overall financial commitment more in line with testing an individual for their Y-DNA or a full sequence mtDNA test. All-in-one tests again test reasonably cheaply for markers that have already been discovered, so limit the amount of information for genealogy purposes. Next generation sequencing (NGS) tests will in the future provide the raw data for multiple products. This is already the case with NGS testing for the Y-chromosome, which can test for both STR and SNP markers. Although a more expensive initial outlay, such tests can discover new markers useful for primary research.

Biomedical testing
Biomedical tests often have genealogy testing bundled with them. Such tests report on: health risks, for example for breast cancer or dementia; carrier status, for example for beta-thalassemia or sickle cell anaemia; wellbeing, for example for lactose intolerance or muscle composition; and finally traits, for example for hair colour or skin pigmentation. The main issue to be aware of with such testing is giving away permission for your data to be used in 'research' and passed onto third parties. Also test-takers at these companies tend to be testing for the biomedical report and not genealogy, so response to matching enquiries can be quite low.

Links to comparisons of test companies
ISOGG provides a number of useful links to the current range of products offered by the main test companies for genealogy. As these comparison sites are maintained by volunteers they may not remain up to date.

General list of all test companies –
https://isogg.org/wiki/List_of_DNA_testing_companies
Autosomal testing –
https://isogg.org/wiki/Autosomal_DNA_testing_comparison_chart
mtDNA testing –
https://isogg.org/wiki/MtDNA_testing_comparison_chart
Y-DNA STR testing –
https://isogg.org/wiki/Y-DNA_STR_testing_comparison_chart
Y-DNA SNP testing –
https://isogg.org/wiki/Y-DNA_SNP_testing_chart

Chapter 8

PROJECTS

John Cleary, Iain McDonald

What DNA projects are

DNA test results can tell us little on their own and many test-takers derive most value from sharing their results within projects. Though mainly associated with Y-DNA, there are types of project associated with all three types of test – Y, mt and autosomal DNA. Projects provide a platform for comparing results, to investigate the evidence for genetic relationships and a forum for discussing research with your DNA matches and genetic relatives. While they can be organised independently of the testing companies, most are usually encountered on the companies' results platforms. This means useful tools for analysing the results can be provided by the companies' IT services and they also provide safeguards that your data will be handled according to ethical guidelines and best practice to protect privacy.

The most common method for establishing a project is to organise it around experienced test-takers known as administrators – or 'admins' – who review the data, welcome and orientate new members and can advise on what your results may show, as well as on further testing possibilities. The projects are supported by the companies, but the admins are never employees: they are volunteers who, like you, have taken DNA tests, and have gone on to develop some degree of expert knowledge about genetic genealogy which they can share with their members. While most admins are enthusiasts, as with any voluntary pastime it can be taxing and admins come and go across time. If you develop an interest in project work then you could consider offering your services, initially as a volunteer co-admin and eventually take charge of administering projects yourself.

Company or platform	Project type
Family Tree DNA	**Projects**: surname (Y), haplogroup (Y and mt), geographical (Y and mt), heritage (Y and mt)
Family Tree DNA	**Autosomal projects**: Family Finder Projects allow test-takers descended from a common ancestor to pool information and use online tools (but not generally about public display of information)
Ancestry.com	**DNA Circles**: created automatically when three or more test-takers share a common ancestor and are DNA matches
YFull.com	**Groups**: for test-takers who have submitted their NGS Y test data (Big Y, Y Elite or WGS) to YFull. Operate mainly as haplogroup projects, test-takers can join any which are relevant
YSEQ.com	**Groups**: for test-takers who have taken a single SNP, SNP panel or WGS test with YSEQ. May be organised on any basis (mainly haplogroup) and allow test-takers to view the results of potential matches
Independent	**Websites/Social Media**: Many active researchers run their own sites which may function as effective projects. These may come and go depending on levels of interest and enthusiasm from the organisers

Table 1: Types of project and the companies and platforms that support them

Family Tree DNA – types of projects
Family Tree DNA was the trailblazer among genetic testing companies in creating projects for its test-takers to share and explore their results. Five main types of project run by FTDNA are:

• *Surname Projects*: for members with a particular surname, or who match people with a particular surname. This reflects the fact that Y-DNA testing is particularly good for investigating surname history.
• *Haplogroup Projects*: for members of particular large Y haplogroups like

R-L21 or E-M35; or mitochondrial haplogroups like the K mtDNA Project.

- *Geographical Projects*: for a particular region like the Finland/Suomi DNA Project.
- *Heritage Projects*: which organise around broader community or historical subjects, such as the Scottish Prisoners of the Civil Wars.
- *Family Finder Projects*: for descendants of a common ancestor or from a defined region like a parish to pool their results in looking for shared atDNA.

Projects are structured around a public results table on a web page in which the marker results are arranged in spreadsheet style, with numbers to identify the test-taker, and (usually) information on the earliest known direct male- or female-line ancestor. Additional information can be added at the choice of the project admins, including the surnames of the test-takers and countries of origin. Active admins develop criteria to group the test-takers within their projects according to how similar their results were, and to the likelihood of descent from a shared direct ancestor. Other features for members include Background and News pages, and in 2015 a new social media-style discussion forum – the Activity Feed – was added in an attractive redesign of the project platform. Admins can turn individual results or the whole results table on or off to public view, and test-takers can also set their results to be visible to members, the general public, or no one at all, as they prefer.

In general, Y-based projects are encouraged to be public as they create visibility and draw in more test-takers if the project can be seen by surname researchers who have not tested. If you are hoping to attract more matches to your Y haplotype or mt sequence, then having them on public view in a project can help to achieve it.

The following are examples of two major types of projects, membership of which can often complement one another.

Example Surname Project: Cummings
To study an example project, see The Cumming/Cummings Surname Project, where some background information is supplied about the surname at: https://www.familytreedna.com/groups/cummings/about

The project has 303 members at the time of writing, making it a medium-sized DNA project. From the Project Statistics tab we can see that 124 of these members have tested up to the Y-67 level, and 208 have tested some Y-DNA. 134 have taken the Family Finder test – which is a clue to why ninety-five members have not done a Y test: this project has an open policy to encourage all Cumming/Cummings descendants to join if they are interested in the surname, whichever test they may have taken. However, only Y-DNA results are displayed, since they are the ones most relevant to the surname history. 205 members have entered their furthest known paternal ancestor and 181 their maternal. Project admins should encourage all test-takers to enter this information. Finally, fifty-nine members have taken the advanced Big Y test, or around 28% of the members who have taken any Y-DNA test, a reasonable percentage, and one that is increasing as interest in this test grows.

Publicly visible results can be seen at:

https://www.familytreedna.com/public/cummings?iframe=yresults

(Note that some test-takers have elected to keep their results visible only to other project members.) The surname is a multi-origin surname, with many Y haplogroups visible in the results page, and the admins have grouped the members according to their terminal SNP, where this is known. The largest single lineage has eighteen members, and has been labelled:

R1a - Lineage 1 [R-Z284>L448 ('Young Scandinavian')>YP355> YP609>YP618>YP984>YP983]

'Young Scandinavian' is a nickname given some years ago to the R1a subclade marked by the SNP L448, thought to have originated in Norway some 3,000 years ago, though it is not so much used today. More significant is the SNP data presented as a descent chain, which all of the members of this group have (or are predicted to have, if they were to test for SNPs). The last SNP in the sequence is YP983, which is the terminal SNP for the entire group. It is noticeable that thirteen of the members of this lineage have a terminal SNP label in green, implying that they have taken the Big Y test or single SNP tests to identify their terminal SNP.

Some of these show different terminal SNP labels, for example YP3932 or YP992 – and these can be deduced to be SNPs further downstream, shared by some but not all of the group, forming subclades within the larger group. Some admins split these into separate groups, but this project's admins have kept the larger group together.

To see why, follow the link to the colorised results display at https://www.familytreedna.com/public/cummings?iframe=ycolorized (Figure 1 shows a monochrome snapshot of part of this page, but see the Project page for the full colour view.). Notice the shaded cells – the purple cells indicate an STR value that is lower than the modal (most common) value for the group, and the red cells indicate one that is higher. This coloured information gives an at-a-glance overview of where mutations have appeared in the group, and whether any of them could be shared branch markers.

Finally, this subgroup has been very successful in posting most distant known ancestor (MDKA) information, which helps to place its lines in place and time. Some of the members have gone further than others in giving birth and death dates, and places where the MDKA either lived or was born. Adding places as well as dates is especially useful when trying to build lines back towards a common origin and is strongly recommended. Conversely, members in other parts of the project page offer little or no ancestral information. This means the admins have nothing to go on other than the DNA results and so the task of relating them to other matching members is harder.

mes Cummings, b. 1806 and d. 1892	R-Z283	13	24	15	11	11-14	12	12	10	13	11	31	15	9-10
mes Cummings, b. 1806 and d. 1892	R-YP992	13	24	15	11	11-14	12	12	10	13	11	31	15	9-10
mes Cummings, b. 1806 and d. 1892	R-M198	13	24	15	11	11-14	12	12	10	13	11	31	15	9-10
mes Taylor (~1800 Loudoun, VA - ? Loudoun, VA)	R-YP3932	13	25	15	11	11-14	12	12	10	13	11	30	15	9-10
hn Cummins	R-YP992	13	25	15	11	11-14	12	12	10	13	11	30	15	9-10
lliam Cummins b. 1785 VA d. 15 Sep 1851 OH	R-YP3932	13	25	15	11	11-14	12	12	10	13	11	31	15	9-10
muel Ballard Cummins, b. 1784 and d. 1852	R-YP3932	13	25	15	11	11-14	12	12	10	13	11	31	15	9-10
hn Thomas Cummings, b.1859 d.1916	R-YP983	13	25	15	11	11-14	12	12	10	13	11	31	15	9-10
ert Drake Bennett b. ~1818-19 Wilson Co. TN	R-Z283	13	25	15	11	11-14	12	12	10	13	11	31	15	9-10
ert Drake Bennett, b. ~1818-19 Wilson Co. TN	R-YP983	13	25	15	11	11-14	12	12	10	13	11	31	15	9-10
muel Ballard Cummins, b. 1784 VA d. 1852 IN	R-YP3932	13	25	15	11	11-14	12	12	10	13	11	31	15	9-10
mes Cumings b. VA circa 1755 d. OH 1821	R-YP983	13	25	15	11	11-14	12	12	10	13	11	31	15	9-10
omas Cummings, b. 1732 and d. 1798	R-YP992	13	25	15	11	11-14	12	12	10	13	11	31	15	9-10
mes Cummings, b. abt 1804 and m. 1828	R-YP3934	13	25	15	11	11-14	12	12	10	13	11	31	15	9-10
hn Cummins b 1720 d aft 1787 Southampton, FC, PA	R-M198	13	25	15	11	11-14	12	12	10	13	11	31	15	9-10
gh Noble Cummins, b. 1760 VA and d. 1860 WV	R-M173	13	26	15	11	11-14	12	12	10	13	11	31	15	9-9
arles Cummins, b. abt 1750 and d. btwn 1810-1820	R-YP983	13	26	15	11	11-15	12	12	10	13	11	31	15	9-9

Figure 1: Extract of the colorized results table from the Cummings Surname Project at FTDNA. © FTDNA

Example Haplogroup Project: R-U106

See project page at https://www.familytreedna.com/groups/u106/about

R-U106 is a very large subclade within the R1b haplogroup. It has been associated with the northern European region, and loosely with Germanic languages. At the time of writing there are 5,481 members, and 2,667 have taken the Big Y, almost 50%. This is higher than the above surname project, which is not surprising, as members of haplogroup projects are more likely to have an interest in advanced SNP testing to build their downstream subclade trees.

The colorised results page is at https://www.familytreedna.com/public/U106?iframe=ycolorized. Note that project results pages only display 500 lines per page as a default, which includes the subgroup labels and the modal lines. But it can be very slow to search through page after page in a large project, so you can increase the page size to show all results by entering any number in the Page Size box. On the regular results page, as there are 5,481 members, 6,000 should be enough to include all of them along with the group headings. On the colorised page we need to include the lines for the modal, maximum and minimum values too, but 7,000 seems to bring the full page up. At busy times this can be a slow load, and you may need to reload once or twice.

Once the full page is loaded, you can search for any name in the MDKA information or test-taker's number you like, or any other information on the page, using the CTRL+F or CMD+F search function of your computer. Let's search for some Cummings and see if there are any in this haplogroup.

[05] Z30>Z27>Z345>Z2>Z7>FGC7559>FGC904>CTS10893>CTS4099>FGC909, FGC918>																					
MIN		13	23	14	11	11-12	12	12	12	13	13	29	16	9-9	11	11	25	15	19	29	15-15-16
MAX		13	23	14	12	11-14	12	12	12	14	13	30	17	9-10	11	11	26	15	19	30	15-15-17
MODE		13	23	14	12	11-14	12	12	12	13	13	29	17	9-10	11	11	25	15	19	29	15-15-17
John C. Clark, b.c. 1756, St. Mary's County, MD	R-FGC909	13	23	14	11	11-12	12	12	12	13	13	29	16	9-9	11	11	25	15	19	29	15-15-16
John Rock Smith b. 1615 d. 1706	R-U106	13	23	14	11	11-14	12	12	12	14	13	30	17	9-10	11	11	25	15	19	29	15-15-17
Ephraim Smith, b. 1816, Merrick, Nassau, NY	R-FGC909	13	23	14	12	11-14	12	12	12	13	13	29	17	9-10	11	11	25	15	19	29	15-15-17
Gideon Cummings, b. 1795 d. 1832	R-FGC909	13	23	14	12	11-14	12	12	12	13	13	29	17	9-9	11	11	26	15	19	30	15-15-17

Figure 2: Extract from colorized results table for the R-U106 Project. © FTDNA

There are six test-takers with the name Cummings in their MDKA information – a further reason why it should be entered, so people with the same name can find you. Two of them are in groups on their own (at least in the public view), while three others form a group together, repeating what we can see in the surname project. But the one in Figure 2, descended from Gideon Cummings, 1795–1832, has gained something by joining this haplogroup project that he cannot gain from the surname project: he is grouped with three more people who share his subclade – here marked by the SNP labelled FGC909. The John Rock Smith descendant may share this SNP too if he tested it, seeing the similarity of his STR results. This adds to what this test-taker can see over being a member only of a surname project, extending his matches to people with other surnames who may have deeper ancestral connections – or signs that there may have been a surname switch sometime in the past. Either way, this is an alternative view of his matches that gives further clues on where else to search.

Haplogroup project admins tend to be experts on the deep genealogy of clusters of surnames, whose ancestry reaches back into the distant past before today's surnames were in use as hereditary names. They often have interests in historical and prehistoric migrations that predate the 'genealogical era'. For anyone who is considering upgrading a Y test, taking a SNP test or the advanced Big Y, the advice of the relevant haplogroup project admin is very much recommended, as they can advise on the most likely testing course to help achieve your goals.

Family Finder Projects (or sections within surname projects)

Although they are less visible than the Y and mt Projects, Family Finder Projects are playing an increasingly important role as autosomal testing gains in popularity. These exist at Family Tree DNA in two ways. Firstly, administrators of surname projects are often open to accepting new members, both female and male, who have taken only the Family Finder test, but descend from a recent common ancestor who carries the surname of interest. This is often used as a cross-check against relationships within the lineages the surname project is exploring, building the trees out to check connections within and across them.

Many active test-takers are also now creating specialist Family Finder Projects, using the surname project platforms. These are typically created to investigate the descendants of a named common ancestor that the group believes they have in common. Unlike surname projects, there is no public display of results (Y, mtDNA or SNP results pages may be visible, but these are unlikely to be informative unless the admins are collecting results in the two direct male/female lines).

However, the project can make use of the resources Family Tree DNA provides to analyse their common results, and the public web pages can be used to post news, trees and reports on project findings. The Activity Feed can also be used for the circle to discuss their discoveries and theories about their shared ancestry.

Project goals

The many varied types of projects available across Family Tree DNA and other platforms can enhance the enjoyment of the tests that members take and open up new discoveries from sharing results. Do bear in mind though that the projects are run and administered by volunteers – other test-takers like yourself who may have enthusiasm for their topic but differing amounts of time to give to tending their project. If you feel you are waiting a long time to receive help, do not complain. Better is to offer to help. Projects always need fresh hands to help with the work and carry the methods on to new places and people.

If you gain little from the projects you join, you can also leave them. Do give a constructive reason in the departure email if you do, as that helps improvements to be made. Remember that projects are not really places to 'find matches' – you can see all your matches already by looking in your account. What projects do is provide access to advice, create visibility for your shared research, and create a place where information can be exchanged about both the genetic and the genealogical research.

Family Tree DNA – administrator ethics

If you find you are developing a strong interest in aspects of genetic genealogy, or in a particular surname or haplogroup, then consider offering your services as a co-administrator in the first instance. Being an admin comes along with responsibilities and new ones must accept the rules and principles of ethical use of the data they have access to – and implement this in their administration of the projects. There is a full description of responsibilities and rules of conduct for FTDNA administrators on the GAP (Group Administrator Pages) pages at https://www.familytreedna.com/learn/project-administration/gap-guide lines-ftdna-projects/. ISOGG has also drawn up its own guidelines on best practice for DNA project administrators.

YFull.com and YSEQ – Groups

Although Family Tree DNA has done the most among testing companies to promote public and semi-public projects for their members, it is worth taking a quick note of other project-type activity among genetic genealogy companies. YFull.com is an analysis platform rather than a testing company, but it provides a user-friendly graphical interface for reports on the Y NGS results, like Big Y results uploaded to it, and it has created a platform for 'Groups'. These function rather like projects, and can be based around haplogroups, surnames, geographical areas or heritage themes. YFull members may choose to join one or more groups, which give named administrators the possibility of seeing their reports, as with FTDNA projects. As the Big Y is predominantly a SNP test, there are group pages for test-takers to see which SNPs they share with other group members. YFull extracts up to 780 STRs from Y NGS data, so there are also STR results pages for each group which function similarly to haplogroup projects at FTDNA.

YSEQ.com is a small, recent start-up based in Berlin, which specialises in single Y-SNP tests or in creating bespoke panels of SNPs for a haplogroup or surname project. YSEQ also provides a group system on its platform that allows its test-takers to share their results with others.

Autosomal DNA projects

As autosomal testing becomes the dominant approach to genetic genealogy, at least for most newcomers to the field since 2015, autosomal projects are developing new forms of collaboration for genetic genealogy research. We have looked at FTDNA's approach to Family Finder Projects above, and here we will look at two more project-like activities – one company-based, and the other harnessing the power of social media.

Ancestry DNA circles

Ancestry is currently the testing company with the largest database of atDNA customer results and it has developed a number of innovative tools to assist customers to understand their DNA results. DNA Circles are not projects in the way discussed above, nor are they created by the actions of test-takers. Instead they emerge automatically, when three or more Ancestry test-takers who have trees linked to their DNA results are discovered by Ancestry's matching system to have a likely shared ancestor. The platform then creates a DNA Circle containing these test-takers, and the Circle can grow as more are added, in the same way. This provides a means for test-takers who share DNA and possible ancestors to explore their shared links further.

Independent projects – harnessing the power of social media

Circles can also be created by test-takers themselves – aided by sharing sites where test-takers from one company can upload their DNA to another where they can compare their results to tests from another company. Currently MyHeritage and FTDNA welcome uploads from the other companies, but the biggest sharing site of all is GEDmatch. com at https://www.gedmatch.com. GEDmatch is an open-source sharing site, where test-takers can upload their autosomal data and GEDmatch calculates matches and the amounts of shared DNA the test-taker has with those matches. You can share your GEDmatch number with your matches to explore further the properties of your shared DNA. It is important to read the GEDmatch Privacy Policy if considering using this site, as it is completely open to all kinds of uses, and test-takers should only upload their DNA results if they are personally happy with the levels of privacy and openness it offers. It is also important to note that GEDmatch does not reveal test-takers' own DNA – it works through showing the shared match lists and the quantities of shared DNA with individual test-takers.

Starting up a project

Decide on its scope

A dedicated, motivated individual will quickly learn more about genetic genealogy than their peers – by the time you finish this book you will already know more than most! At some point, many people will want to set up a project around their special interest.

First, you must define the project's scope. It is important to set clear boundaries in time and space, both for yourself and for the people you are declaring an interest in. A project may range from the relations of one person (e.g. tracing one's own ancestry, or descendants of a historical individual), to the ancestry of entire countries and beyond.

Many projects focus on a family surname, a geographical region, a period of time, or a type of person. Remember that your interests tend to broaden with time, and that the amount of data may increase substantially with new and deeper tests, so start small.

Identifying existing projects

Equally, it is important not to duplicate research. Find out what is being done already: many areas of interest are already being covered by one or more projects.

Existing projects can be protective of their membership and interests, because they have worked hard to pull a community together and also because they are human. Administrators have usually invested heavily in learning their subject, researching their project and educating their membership. Rightly or wrongly, they are used to being the experts.

A new project *within* the remit of an existing project is tantamount to a breakaway republic: only advisable if there is no meaningful government. You may be better off helping the existing project from within, e.g. by helping with administration, or forming a sub-project (website, special interest group) within the main project's body.

Consequently, the interaction between some projects can be more about 'international relations' than about genetics. Expect a cautious welcome to your new project from more-established ones: it is important to create a rapport with them and set clear, mutually agreed boundaries from the outset.

To be or not to be (a new project)

Working within existing projects has advantages. A large community base means you can share ideas with experts and draw on the expertise, knowledge and contacts those projects can provide. This way, you learn the ropes of project administration and build up a group of like-minded people with similar goals. Getting your face (and goals) known in an existing project is ideal for finding people who can help you with your own line of enquiry. Many administrators of larger projects began in this way.

However, this generally means living with the structures, precedents and ideas set by that project, which may not match your expectations. Going it alone allows you to set up a project to cover exactly what you want, and research it in exactly the way you choose. There are several ways to go about this.

Forming a project

Projects vary in size and form. At their simplest, they are a bunch of people who email each other. Many small projects use Facebook groups or other social media channels. Large projects have thousands of members, their own discussion forums, software packages, and very direct relationships with the testing companies.

Size is not everything. Some projects have hundreds of members sharing only a Facebook group. Some surname projects only have a handful of members. Your best choice of medium depends on: 1) your ability to effectively use and control that medium; 2) the time and effort you can commit; 3) what help you can get from existing projects; and 4) the relative importance genetics has in your research.

Each medium comes with its own advantages and disadvantages. The most thorough is a fully-fledged project with one of the testing companies (e.g. Family Tree DNA). However, you should be aware that the more formal you make this arrangement, the more responsibilities you accrue (see below).

Administering a project

What is an administrator?

A good administrator manages a project, but takes on many roles:

- *Researcher*: Good administrators are experts in their project's topic, conduct and manage meaningful research into it, and disseminate that research to the wider community.
- *Advisor*: Most people have very little idea how to interpret their test results. They often look to administrators for help and advice about existing tests and further testing. Good administrators know the people and tools to go to for help. Great administrators are those that help develop and write those tools!
- *Intermediary*: Administrators have the ear of the testing companies, and can often help fix users' problems, e.g. understanding why tests have been delayed, identifying problems with existing tests, or shaping new tests.

- *Confidant*: Admins are given personal genetic and genealogical data. Moral and legal obligations require respecting the privacy of that data and obtaining permission to use or publicise it.
- *Politician*: Administrators are often also tasked with dealing with interactions between users, either privately, or via a public forum. They must balance conflicting evidence and resolve conflicts where possible, and calmly and fairly deal with different and minority views.

Admin responsibilities

Administrators have substantial responsibilities regarding users' data. This may include their names and contact details, plus detailed genetic and genealogical information. Some people will volunteer the passwords used to access their kits, and sometimes this data belongs to someone who is not the kit administrator. Your project's success, your personal reputation, and that of the whole of genetic genealogy, all rely on this information being used responsibly. Confidential information must remain confidential, and informed consent obtained before you make any data public.

Availability and appointing co-admins

A crucial part of administration is your time commitment. People will expect an active, controlling voice, who will analyse data and place people within the project quickly and effectively, and answer their (often complex) queries within a few days at most. If you anticipate long periods where you are busy or absent, you may want to appoint a co-administrator.

A co-administrator is a partner. Sound them out before agreeing to anything. Do they have the time to commit to the project? Can you rely on them to step in when you are unable to? Can you work closely with them? Will they back you up? When you disagree, can you resolve any conflicts amicably? You want help, not a liability.

Recruiting members

DNA is a comparative science. More project members means better comparisons and more information. Not all members are equal: some bring money to test deeply, some occupy key positions in your tree or have historically important results. It is important to appeal to all the people in your project but target your recruitment in these important areas.

An initial announcement on discussion forums, mailing lists and social media groups will find interested people who have already tested. If you can view genetic matches to your members (e.g. as a Y-DNA project), contact them and invite them into your project as appropriate. Particularly for autosomal projects, recruitment can come through genealogy sites, boards and discussion lists.

Throughout, be mindful of your goals: you are a researcher, not a DNA salesperson. You have a responsibility to ensure members spend their money wisely, rather than simply testing because you want more data, and you should be able to justify to your (potential) members the value of taking the tests you recommend.

Managing relationships and groups

Once you have your members, you will need to analyse their data. One of the simplest ways is to split people into groups. Your choice of groups depends on the primary aims of your project. Most projects choose to split data by haplogroup, but a split by surname or geography may be more useful for some.

The fineness of this splitting should be appropriate to your group, and will likely be related to the smallest unit you want to work with. For well-tested individuals, grouping by SNPs involves simply locating them on a phylogenetic tree. For less-well-tested members, this may require identifying any Y-STR matches they have at close genetic distances, or comparison with a haplogroup project.

You may also wish to keep a personal database with genealogical or personal notes, where items like haplogroup, surname and geography can be sorted at will. However, you then have the burden of keeping it up to date, and the responsibility to ensure the data is stored and managed appropriately. This (legal) responsibility for data security becomes even more important if you wish to put this database online.

A day in the life of an admin

An admin's job is never done. It mostly involves 1) welcoming new members and establishing a rapport with them; 2) placing those members into groups; 3) moderating discussion between your members, if you have a discussion group; 4) advising on new tests; and 5) discussing test results. If you are lucky, you might also have a group fund to administer. Of these, advising on new tests and discussing results normally takes the bulk of the time.

A reasonable expectation might be at least 20 minutes' work per day for every 100 people in your project, spread among your co-admins. Membership lists tend to increase, rather than decrease, and there will be increased demands on your time when there is a glut of test results, or when a new product or discounted sale is announced at one of the major companies.

Sources of information

Administrators should be able to find information when they need it. By engaging with the administrative and 'super-user' community, you will find many resources to help you. Most importantly, maintain good contacts with projects near you: e.g., surname project administrators should work closely with geographical, haplogroup and special interest projects that serve their members. Local history organisations may also have specialist knowledge. Wider community resources include the International Society of Genetic Genealogy (ISOGG), for statistics, comparison tables and articles. Discussion forums (e.g. Anthrogenica) can answer more advanced and specialised questions.

Problematic situations

Project members are drawn from the general public. Inevitably, this includes the fringes of many social spectra: people with atypical beliefs, people in unusual situations and, worst of all, combinations of the above. Simpler situations include testing deceased relatives using previously submitted DNA samples. Special care has to be taken not to waste the sample, and your advice should reflect that.

Many members do not want to be disturbed; others want the world on a stick, and an update every five minutes. You will find angry customers who have been sold DNA testing on false pretences and people who think they are experts in every field who give out bad advice to your members. And you will have to find ways to deal with each of them. Below are a few common examples and suggestions, but there are as many problems are there are test-takers. Good luck!

Examples: 'My haplogroup doesn't match that of my cousin! What does this mean?'

'I'm descended from Sir Joe of Bloggs, why doesn't my haplogroup match the current Earl of Bloggs?'

Background: A common situation is having to inform people of non-paternal events (NPEs) in their family: situations where the recorded ancestor does not match the genetic ancestor. This may be due to poor research by a genealogist, or fabricated primary sources by long-dead bards. It may be due to societal changes, such as adoptions, or of a bastard child taking his mother's surname. However, sometimes it may uncover marital infidelity. Cuckoldry rates are 1–2%, meaning any medieval ancestry has about a 40% chance of being wrong, even with robust documentation. Delicate situations can occur if this happened in living generations, so this issue should be approached with care.

Suggestions: First, obtain a copy of the paper trail back to the common ancestor. This can highlight misunderstandings in the Y-DNA inheritance process, and allow you to corroborate the family tree with other sources, looking for weak links. Next, ensure the test-taker is aware of the possibilities and risks raised above, and ask if they and their family want to investigate further. If they do, testing another cousin closer than the previously supposed common ancestor can narrow down the point where the NPE occurs: try to target a cousin near any weak spots or, failing that, about halfway back to the supposed common ancestor, repeating the process as necessary to find the NPE generation.

Example: 'My surname is McBart, so I must be descended from Bart the Mighty.'

Background: People 'know' the origin of their surname, despite the fact that many surnames have dozens or even hundreds of different genetic origins. Especially in the Gaelic tradition, surname inheritance could be more to do with allegiance than strict paternal transfer of genes.

Suggestions: Keeping a few choice examples up your sleeve is good: e.g. only a quarter of MacDonalds descend from the Lords of the Isles.

Examples: 'I've got my DNA results back, but I can't work out how these tell me who my great-great grandfather was.'

'I paid all this money and I don't even match anyone else with my surname!'

Background: Some people are angry because they expect too much from DNA testing. They expect it to break down their 'brick walls' and extend their family tree, when often this is impossible with the available data.

Suggestions: Try to give test-takers realistic expectations, and stress that DNA testing (particularly Y-DNA or mtDNA) is not about going link-by-link back into the past. Instead, emphasise that it gives a broader view of ancestry over many generations, and identify any combinations of further testing that would help in breaking down specific brick walls (see also Chapter 9).

Developing your research
Having looked at the daily life of an admin, we will look in this section at some of the ways projects can help members with their research and the tools admins have for carrying out their functions.

Working with GAP
The Group Administrator Pages (GAP) provided by Family Tree DNA deliver a collection of tools to admins to investigate the collective results of members. Among these tools are:

- *Genetic Distance (GD)* report: admins can see GDs up to 30 for all levels of testing, in contrast to the 1/2/4/7/10 GD levels that test-takers can see in their own results page. This is especially useful in those cases when test-takers cannot see some potential matches because of a greater than usual divergence of their STRs.
- *TiP Utility*: the probability that two members are related within a certain number of generations (up to 24) can be viewed, and this can be a useful tool for creating genetic families.

In a successful project the admins will build and maintain a relationship with members. Across time, previously active members may become less active, inactive, or die – in which case their accounts may be taken over by beneficiaries or become dormant. New members join, and new discoveries may lead to inactive members getting interested again. What good admins can do is put members in touch with each other – admins are in a position to identify connections, alerting the members concerned.

Grouping Genetic Families

One of the primary roles of a project administrator is to create 'genetic families' among the members. This is taken to mean groups of matching test-takers who are also likely to be descended from a common ancestor within the 'genealogical era' – that is historical periods when surnames were used and descent is open to research with genealogical methods. Individual test-takers can see their close matches, but admins can use their overview to see networks of test-takers who match each other beyond the 4/37 or 7/67 limits of matches. For example, you may have three members with the following connections:

• Alan matches Brian at 4/67
• Brian matches Chris at 5/67
• Alan matches Chris at 8/67 – so neither will see the other in their matches

Brian is the 'link' in the matches here. Alan and Chris can both see Brian, but they cannot see each other. It is the administrator's overview that allows a genetic family to be built from this data, and all members can then compare their results in the project results pages. However, the admins should examine the matching haplotypes from a number of different perspectives before confirming a genetic family from a group: there are many subclades in which there are many closely overlapping haplotypes. This is due to the phenomenon of convergence, discussed in Chapter 5. Two test-takers who do *not* have a common ancestor within the historical era may find themselves matching within the 7/67 level, because changes in their haplotypes begin to bring them closer together again. Test-takers in populous subclades such as R-M222 may have a very large number of matches within this level, but who will not be within a genetic surname family.

When the haplogroup is rare and an STR signature appears to identify a branch absolutely, the admin can be more confident that a match indicates membership of a genetic family. Genealogist Maurice Gleeson has developed a system which he refers to as 'markers of potential relatedness' (MPRs – see Table 4) to use as criteria to decide whether a group of matching test-takers can be declared a genuine genetic family. (And of course, every conclusion from genetic data should be considered as tentative until further research can strengthen the suggested genealogical connections). These MPRs are based upon both genealogical research of the paper trail and indicators from DNA testing, and can help to establish whether someone belongs in the genetic family or not.

Markers of Potential Relatedness

1. The members have the **same surname**
2. The **Genetic Distance (GD)** between two members indicates a close or very close relationship
3. The **TiP24 score is >80%** compared to the group modal haplotype
4. There is a clear **Genetic Distance Demarcation** between project members within a genetic cluster & project members outside it
5. Presence of **"rare" marker values** or a relatively **Unique STR Signature** among genetic group members
6. **SNP testing** is consistent among the members of the particular group
7. **SNP predictions** are consistent (**Matches' Terminal SNP Analysis**)
8. The **same surname variant** is predominant in a genetic group
9. The **same MDKA location** is present in the particular genetic group
10. The **same MDKA** is present in the particular genetic group

---

Table 2: Maurice Gleeson's Markers of Potential Relatedness. Checklist of criteria to help determine whether a group of test-takers who match each other form a genuine genetic family. Reproduced with kind permission of Maurice Gleeson. Further details at: http://dnaandfamily treeresearch.blogspot.it/2017/06/criteria-for-grouping-people-into-y-dna.html

Inevitably, grouping people into genetic groupings will bring into consideration test-takers who have different surnames to the main group, which may be coalescing around a single surname. A common abbreviation used by many project admins is NPE. Drawn from genetics, this stands for 'Non-Paternity Event', and represents a case in which a child being raised by a parent is not a genetic offspring of that parent. Some project admins are uncomfortable with this term and soften it to 'Not the Parent Expected', and in autosomal DNA circles there is common use of MAP for 'Misattributed Parentage' or MPE for 'Misattributed Parentage Event'.

Whichever term is preferred, admins will need to make decisions about NPEs and whether or not to add them into genetic families. Working with NPE cases can be a rewarding task for admins in working with their project members (who do not all need to have the surname of interest).

Working with the members

Surname projects will often contain members who are very experienced genealogical researchers, members who may not have much experience or knowledge of genealogy and many shades between. Project admins do not have to undertake genealogical research for their members and are under no obligation to offer this. However, assisting members with their research can be rewarding, and collaboratively building a database of pedigrees is a major contribution that a project can make to understanding the history of the surname or family in question. It is also worth bearing in mind that project members may be the persons who took tests on their own DNA, but can also be family members who ordered tests for their relatives to further their own research. Many family history researchers order Y-DNA tests for male relatives in lines they want to research, and it is common for active autosomal DNA researchers to order tests for several relatives. The member an admin interacts with may be the kit handler or manager rather than the test-taker.

Many test-takers do not understand fully how necessary it is to build a database of genealogical information to go along with their test result. This is classically in the form of a tree of direct ancestors in the lines of interest reaching back to the MDKA, or 'Most Distant Known Ancestor'. Early Surname Projects were often very active in collecting male-line pedigrees for their members, though as the number of projects and test-takers has proliferated in recent years, this activity has ebbed somewhat.

In a Surname Project using mainly Y-DNA, the main aim is to collect pedigrees of direct male-line ancestors. Ideally the lines should collect male-line ancestral names with dates of birth and a place of birth or residence during the ancestor's life. If dates of death or alternative places can be added, this is valuable information. A member may wish to expand a full genealogical tree for their own interest, but the direct line data is of most value to the project – and this should be verified with documentation of source records. The member should be encouraged to enter the MDKA name, dates and place name in their earliest known ancestor field, as this makes their result immediately more useful to other matches they will have. In an mtDNA project, if an admin is working on historical era matches, the same process can be applied to building a pedigree of a direct female line, which can be linked to a female line MDKA in the same way.

Working with NPEs can be fulfilling for project administrators. A line can be built and verified in the same way, and earliest ancestor names or place names of residence can begin to offer clues to where the surname switch may have occurred. Identifying the place and time of the NPE allows the descent lines of the genetic family to be extended and the NPE-test-taker's link to the matching genetic family to be established to the satisfaction of all concerned.

Communicating with members, hearing their stories and working out what their research goals are (not always clear when a test is ordered) is an important task that project admins can undertake. Without it the test-takers may find there is little to support them in making sense of their results. An active and knowledgeable project admin can bring together a disparate collection of individual researchers and build them into a group. Some admins write and circulate a regular newsletter to members to announce and discuss new findings, and this is a recommended course of action for those with the time to do it.

Working with members in autosomal projects
A lot of the activities described above for Y or mtDNA projects also apply to autosomal projects, though these tend to have a less public profile, as discussed above. They tend to exist for a family circle of descendants from a particular shared ancestor, and, as with surname projects, a detailed tree is essential. As autosomal DNA covers all lines of descent from that ancestor, test-takers should build trees up to *all* of their most distant known ancestors, in all lines. These assist connections to be made with other test-takers' ancestral lines. If two people are genuine matches with each other, as discussed in Chapter 4, then they will share an ancestor. By maximising the reach of your ancestral tree, you may find a connection on another person's, or find surnames that lead you to a common ancestor above the MDKA. An administrator of an

autosomal project is much more likely to be a member of the family cluster, so in helping other members to *build* and *verify* their trees they are also undertaking advanced genealogical research within their own extended family network.

Collaborating with other projects

Genetic genealogy needs to be a collaborative activity if it is to progress. In conventional genealogy an individual working alone might make substantial progress in discovering documents to uncover further and further ancestors, but with DNA testing, the infrastructure of projects, advice from testing experts and sharing of results and family information with close matches are all essential.

It is just as useful for projects to collaborate with each other, as information useful to solve one question may be in the hands of another project. Here are some cases in which projects can usefully collaborate:

• Two surname projects may collaborate over an NPE case.
• A surname project collaborates with an autosomal project over a shared interest. A good example of this is the Clan Irwin Surname DNA Study (which has a Y-DNA surname project page at https://www.familytreedna.com/public/irwin/default.aspx?section=yresults and a project web site for informing members at http://www.clanirwin-dna.org). This collaborates with the Irwin Autosomal DNA Project, for any descendant of an Irwin (Irvine, Erwin, etc.) ancestor who wishes to research descent from that ancestor down any of their descent lines. As this is a major surname associated with the Scottish Border Reivers, there is a heritage interest for genealogists trying to make a connection with them.
• A surname project has one or more genetic families who belong to one or several subclades with haplogroup projects. The members of the genetic family may wish to undertake SNP testing and see how their genetic family may attach to a cluster of genetic families. The members should be encouraged to join the haplogroup project, but there is also scope for the surname project and haplogroup project admins to collaborate on interpreting that genetic family – as it will be one cluster among the various clusters of the larger project. Haplogroup project admins tend to be experts on SNP testing and

building phylogenetic trees, while surname project admins are the experts on the history of their surnames, and each can leverage the expertise of the other.

Group funds and collective sponsoring

A final, but very important, issue to discuss in relation to project management is the money. DNA tests cost money, and a large number of test-takers will have funded their own tests. But if a project wants to develop a testing programme that may involve upgrading test results to higher levels, or recruiting new test-takers to explore further lines, there will be a cost involved. The FTDNA project platforms have a function known as the General Fund (GF), and admins may choose to show this on the public pages or hide it from view. Anyone – members or interested members of the wider public – may donate funds for the benefit of the project, these donations being allocated to a particular project and listed in its GF. When payments are made for tests, these are also listed in the GF.

Two types of donation can be found in the GF. There are open donations for the use of the project, and admins can apply these to any test purchase they wish, as long as the funds exist to cover it (part-payments can also be made). In this situation, the serving admins are *de facto* trustees for the fund and can apply it as they see fit, as long as the project benefits.

The GF is also a means by which several people can share in the costs of a test. Each person uploads their share to the GF with a note of the purpose of the sum sent. The kit handler then places the order and does not make a payment; the admin applies the agreed funds to the order. If the order is fully covered it goes ahead to the lab, but if an amount is still left to be paid, the kit handler needs to top off the full cost, and the order is completed.

Sharing the cost of tests is strongly recommended for progressing a project, and the GF offers a means to do this easily and with clear understanding of the amounts due from each person contributing. If an expensive test such as a BigY is needed in a lineage which had – say – ten members, it is quite likely that one or two carefully selected BigY tests will be sufficient to answer most of the questions the whole group has. All members of the group would benefit and an equal contribution from each member will allow the tests to go ahead with a relatively small contribution from each. Using the GF in this way allows research into the whole genetic family to advance.

Surname projects: mapping and researching the name of interest
A common approach to DNA testing in a project is to allow the course of the project to grow organically. New test-takers in the countries with large-scale buying of autosomal tests have an excellent chance of finding themselves part of a family network on receiving their results. The rate of Y-DNA tests has not reduced either, and a common experience is for a new test-taker to take a 'fishing trip' test to see what they find, and if they match people with the same surname to join the relevant project and find themselves grouped inside a genetic family. The genetic families within projects grow by accretion, some slowly, some quicker, but largely depend on the regular appearance of new test results for growth, and the occasional action of a member to test a suspected Y match.

A more systematic approach was proposed by Chris Pomery in a pair of classic articles in 2009–10, based on the systematic collecting of data on the distribution and descent lines for the surname of interest, then sampling surname bearers by descent line to cover the whole surname distribution in its country of origin:

> The goal of a documentary-led surname project is to reconstruct all its constituent family trees back from the present day to their point of historical origin in time and space. Documentary projects tend by their very nature to seek to answer the question – where does this surname come from? (2010, p4)

Basing surname project work mainly on results from an emigrant society such as the USA will lead to the full genetic variety connected with the surname of interest being missed. This is a result of the 'founder effect': for example, if you are researching the surname Roth, only a subset of Roths will have left their German or other European homelands to settle in the USA. Even though the name is fairly common in the USA, these name-bearers can only ever be in possession of that subset of Roth DNA that was brought with the emigrants. The

German, Austrian, Swedish and other Roth name-bearers will have a much larger pool of DNA variation – and using the Pomery methodology, the aim would be to map and sample it all. This allows strong conclusions to be developed about the origins of the name.

Descendants of American, Australian or other historical era emigrants may feel that the question of where in the 'old countries' their ancestors migrated from is more interesting to them. This is a fair question, but again to answer it a broad sample of surname-bearers in the origin country is needed. They will be less interested in the process of placing emigrant ancestors in their homelands, so a different motivation would still be needed to encourage name-bearers in the origin countries to undergo DNA testing. Estimates suggest around 80% of DNA test-takers with the major companies are from the USA, with progressively smaller numbers in other English-speaking countries and fewer again in other countries around Europe and other regions.

Pomery first estimated the number of Pomerys (and variants) in the UK and Ireland in the year 2000 to be around 2,500, from which he identified 326 initial trees. By testing his way systematically through these trees, and conducting exhaustive genealogical work, he coalesced these into just fifty-five trees by 2010, obtaining DNA tests from forty-four of them. Just over half fell into five genetic families, while twenty of the lines were represented by singleton genetic signatures, showing a large amount of variation even within a small surname. There were also eight trees found only in the US and Canada that had no living UK descendants. Pomery's method is worth reading in full; the text below notes new utilities that were not available to Pomery a decade ago when he was working on his project.

Systematic searching for surname branches
Mapping the distribution of a surname to locate living representatives of its trees and potential test-takers was done in the 2000s by analysing name lists like electoral registers and telephone directories (for modern times) and the free online 1881 census for earlier historical times. Today, these modern listings are less reliable as – in the UK at least – people tend to opt out of publicly accessible lists of phone numbers or voters. But there are a number of excellent resources for surname mapping which can fill the gap.

Steve Archer's Surname Atlas http://www.archersoftware.co.uk/satlas01.htm is a nifty CD-ROM mapping application (Windows PCs only) which maps surname distributions from the 1881 census. It goes down to registration district level for England and Wales, and historical county level for Scotland, giving some fine-grained views of where names and variants can be located. It does not cover Ireland, but the gap is more than filled by John Grenham's excellent Irish Ancestors site that does something similar using data from the Griffiths Survey of 1848–64, at https://www.johngrenham.com/surnames/. This is a pay-per-view site, but a handful of gratis searches are offered each day.

An excellent free surname distribution site is the Public Profiler developed at University College London in 2008–10, again using the 1881 census. The breakdown is by postcode regions, so not as fine-viewed as the Surname Atlas, but does have the advantage of also providing a modern surname distribution from the UK 1998 electoral registers. GBnames maps surnames within Great Britain at http://gbnames.publicprofiler.org and its companion site WorldNames http://worldnames.publicprofiler.org maps surnames from a range of countries across the world, drawing on telephone directories and national electoral registers from the period 2000–05.

Identification of potential test-takers
Once the locations of surname bearers are identified, genealogical research – aided by local historians – can identify the descent trees within each district. Then the search can begin for testing candidates that represent each tree.

There are two broad approaches to doing this. You may want to use directories and electoral registers to find people with the surname in your target area, make contact with them as a genealogical searcher and build trees backwards from the present in the conventional way. You can discover relationships between present-day people in that way, and later sample among them for test-takers. The main point is that just inviting people to test without undertaking the tree-building back to their MDKA will not help as much as being able to attach DNA results to particular MDKAs, to discover the numbers of genetic families represented by the surname.

The second approach would be to take all the surname bearers in a district from a nineteenth-century source – like the 1881 census – and then research in two directions: up, to find the MDKA for each person in the census; and down, to find present-day descendants. This will in addition lead to descendants who have left the area, or emigrated, widening the pool of potential test-takers.

A big change since Chris Pomery's papers on dual documentary/ DNA projects has been the massive proliferation of online records for genealogical searching, along with that of online family trees, at subscription sites like Ancestry.com, membership sites like Geni.com or Wikitree.com, and many others. There is a strong chance today that you will identify many of the key ancestors that you are tracing on sites like these, but you should be very careful with the information you find. While some of these online trees are well researched, many give no sources, or refer only to other trees, and errors and false information can be repeated many times across the internet. To counter this, you can develop the skill of verification: looking for documentary evidence for each link in the line up or down from the key ancestors you are investigating. A newly researched or thoroughly verified tree provides a strong foundation for the DNA testing to come.

Approaching potential test-takers

Having established the geographical extent of the surname you are interested in and built a set of reliable or verified trees, you are ready to sample the modern-day surname-bearers for DNA donors. The trees you have constructed will show how to select the test-takers so that each line will be sampled at least once. Later in the research a second test-taker may be desirable for some or all of the lines, depending on what the initial results show. An ideal second test-taker is a distant relative of the first, as close relatives (first cousins, brothers) are unlikely to show much difference from each other.

Ideas about how to go about contacting matches were provided in Chapter 4, some of which might also be appropriate in contacting potential test-takers. In each case, have an information statement ready that is clear, concise and interesting to capture the attention of your potential DNA donors. Try to involve them in your study and create a newsletter with results and findings to keep them informed about what their DNA has helped to discover. Some people may not be interested, may be suspicious and not willing to take part in DNA testing. This must be respected – but leave an information statement and contact details with them in case they reconsider later.

If you are finding it difficult to convince important descendants to test, maybe because there are only a few qualified descendants remaining to invite, you could consider appointing a third-party support service to help. The University of Strathclyde Genealogical Studies Programme has recently created its DNA Partnership service, having acquired experience in approaching new test-takers in sensitive projects and managing the testing process in a sympathetic manner that reassures anxious test-takers the process is secure and safe for them. If you are seeking to invite a specific descendant to test as part of a Y-DNA project and would welcome this type of support, the University can offer a service to DNA project administrators. Certain criteria should be met, usually that the individual has a documented descent stretching back to before 1600, but other approaches may be considered. Contact scosh@strath.ac.uk for more information on this service.

Funding and costs will always be a major headache. If you are approaching people to contribute to your research project, you cannot expect those new test-takers to foot the bill. You need to have a source of funding ready, even if it is the Bank of You. Here it is worth considering a final benefit of projects – membership in a project at companies that support them, like FTDNA, brings a small project discount. Have the project already set up and enrol new test-takers in it as they order to get the discount. Remember too that the companies offer regular sales, which have become part of the rhythm of the DNA testing yearly cycle: a winter season sale now happens every year, and other sales for at least some of the tests you may want to order have occurred in late summer, around DNA Day in April, and to coincide with Mothers' or Fathers' Day.

Try to make the project or study something which all test-takers feel they own – in doing this, you may find some of the test-takers you recruit become involved and can begin to shoulder their own share of duties like project administration, fundraising, interpreting results, researching trees and recruiting new test-takers. An active project is a healthy one, and while it may feel as if the work will never be finished, many can enjoy the process of moving it along.

Chapter 9

AN INTEGRATED APPROACH TO DNA TESTING FOR GENEALOGY

John Cleary, Iain McDonald, Graham S. Holton

Combining DNA tests

To recap, individuals may test autosomal, mitochondrial or Y-chromosomal DNA. atDNA efficiently finds close relations, up to about fourth cousins. Beyond this, variations in the fraction of DNA inherited from any one ancestor and pedigree collapse (distant inbreeding) mean the accuracy of matching declines.

Unfortunately, mtDNA and Y-DNA mutations are rare, which limits how accurately they can identify relationships. A full mtDNA sequence may only be able to identify whether or not someone is related to you within the last 500–600 years. The market-leading Y-DNA test (Family Tree DNA's BigY-700) averages one Y-SNP mutation every 82-98 years, and one Y-STR mutation about every sixty years; but since these are just averages, the actual mutations may have occurred over a shorter or longer timespan.

Consequently, identifying relationships within the last 200 years or so is more accurately done with atDNA. Here, Y-DNA or mtDNA cannot reliably pinpoint the timing of an ancestral connection, but they can be used in conjunction with atDNA to identify on which lineage the connection lies. Most commonly, it is used to trace the origins of adoptees, foundlings, illegitimacies and similar events. Such situations come under the overall term 'non-paternity events' (NPEs). Broadly speaking, these are any situations where the paper genealogical records do not match the biological inheritance of DNA, regardless of whether children were legitimate or illegitimate, hence sometimes receiving the more accurate moniker 'not the parent expected'. Nevertheless, a family's virtues may be at stake, so care must be taken when dealing with NPEs (see Chapter 8). The remainder of this chapter includes descriptions of how to research these types of events using a combination of DNA tests.

Matching a person to two or three types of test

At the time of writing, there is only one effective place where Y-DNA, mtDNA and atDNA tests can be systematically compared: within a Family Tree DNA account. The Advanced Matches tool, available from an individual test-taker's home page on FTDNA, makes it possible to identify individuals who match the test-taker on more than one of these tests, depending on which tests have been taken. For example, this will list any individuals who match the test-taker on both a Y-DNA37 test and a Family Finder test. As more and more people take multiple DNA tests, this facility is likely to become increasingly useful in narrowing down the possible ancestral lines which should be investigated in the quest for common ancestors shared with matches.

Generalised matching criteria and strategies

As Y-DNA/mtDNA matches are respectively related by the test-taker's purely paternal/maternal lines, the chance of an autosomal match being from one of these lines decreases twofold for every generation into the past. Differing family sizes will mean that you may either have disproportionally many of these matches, or perhaps none at all.

To effectively follow up a genealogical link utilising a combination of atDNA with either Y-DNA or mtDNA, you would need to refine the two individuals' haplogroups to a small enough group that you would not expect to share that ancestry by random chance (e.g. representing less than 1% of the population).

For mtDNA, this often requires a full sequencing test. For Y-STRs, a rough criterion for also finding an autosomal match might be a genetic distance (number of mismatching Y-STRs) no greater than two in 37 markers, four in 67 markers, or six in 111 markers. Matches at 12 or 25 markers generally need further confirmation, except exact matches in rare haplogroups. If you have a next-generation sequencing test, or other test that precisely defines your subclade, a straightforward way to refine the matching is to get your match to test for your terminal SNP using a single SNP test. For example, if you were R-A1234, they should also be A1234+.

Varying levels of proof can come from using these methods, and sometimes testing is simply a case of amassing evidence until you can convince yourself and others.

Case studies

Below are four specific cases drawn from real life. They exemplify some common search scenarios: for a biological parent, for a more distant ancestral surname change, for living relatives descended from various ancestral lines, and for connections to ancient family trees. Some names have been changed to protect individuals' privacy.

The circumstances of each individual's search can mean different approaches may be more fruitful. Furthermore, the price and availability of tests, and the ability to integrate them with others, can change on a day-to-day basis.

These studies provide guiding principles only. Some cases may require hundreds of pounds, dollars or euros of investment to research properly, and hundreds of hours of painstaking research. Hence, you may wish to pool resources and expertise, and consult with an expert before embarking on any expensive venture.

Adoption: Ben Wake's search for his father

The following case uses clues from a Y-DNA test in combination with results from a number of atDNA tests, some of which identified close autosomal cousins, in order to find a biological father.

Ben Wake was adopted at birth, but his father was not named on his birth certificate. He was determined to trace his birth father, so turned to DNA testing. He took a Y-37 test, which found he had a distinctive STR value rare within his haplogroup, R1a, and matches with two or three surnames. The distinctive STR signature strongly hinted at a Scottish and Ulster surname, Little.

Ben's Ancestry autosomal DNA test identified two possible third cousins, Windy and Josh. An Ancestry test on Ben's half-sister Maggie did not match these two, confirming they were related on Ben's paternal side. Windy and Josh were third cousins (3C), meaning all three shared a common ancestral couple – Windy and Josh's great-great-grandparents, Wilhelm Barking and Felicity Cameron (Figure 1) – and the search team began working on the assumption that all three had the *same* relationship to each other. However, this was a potentially misleading assumption: the Shared cM Project's calculator suggests that the 119 cM across eight segments shared between Ben and Windy pointed more to a 2C-type relationship, if not full 2C.

It was decided that a third child of Wilhelm and Felicity, Faith, and her husband Johan Underberg were Ben's most likely ancestors, making him 3C or 2C1R to the other two. The team searched for a descendant on the Underberg side of Johan's brother or cousin to see whether their shared DNA was in the range for the expected relationship. A negative result would rule out the Underberg line as Ben's parental line – and this is exactly what happened when the search team found that Keith W., Johan's brother's grandson, had tested with Ancestry. Keith should be 2C or 2C1R to Ben if the Underberg hypothesis was correct – but he and Ben had *no* shared DNA at all. This effectively eliminated the Underberg hypothesis. Second cousins always share some DNA, and 2C1R do in all but a tiny number of cases. If Ben was not related to Keith, then he was not related to Johan, so could not be a descendant of the Faith/Johan couple.

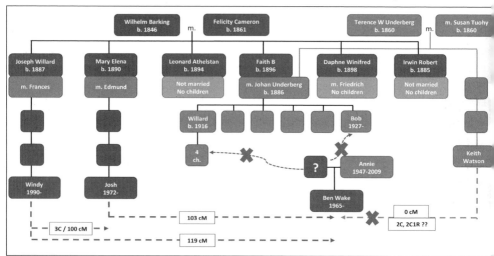

Figure 1: Descendants of Wilhelm Barking and Felicity Cameron, shared ancestral couple of the three test-takers. Shared DNA in cM from the tests is indicated, showing that Ben could not be related to the Underbergs. © John Cleary

The focus of research now moved back to lines descended from Windy and Josh's great-grandparents. Further documentary research revealed that Windy's great-aunt Daphne had an earlier marriage that Windy had not known about, in 1939 (aged 16) to an 18-year-old named Ernest Noel Little. A son was born before they separated. Ben's Y-37 test then became crucial evidence. The research team worried for a time that the small fraction of DNA (119 cM) shared between Ben and Windy, seemingly now second cousins, was too low. Over 200 is typical, but values as low as 46 cM have been recorded for 2C, so this was well within the acceptable range. The final tree is as shown in Figure 2.

It is important to note that Ben's discovery was not categorically *proven* by DNA. The DNA results were *leads* that let the team build a case fitting the evidence better than any other. On Fathers' Day 2016, Ben travelled cross-country and met his father, Stephen Little, in a televised union. He could have asked for another paternity DNA test, but said that when he saw his father it was obvious it was the right man and he knew his search was over.

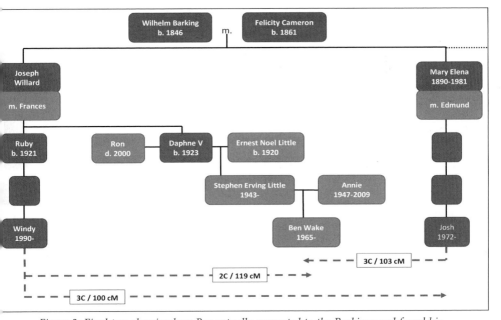

Figure 2: Final tree showing how Ben actually connected to the Barkings and found his birth father, named Little, predicted by the Y-37 test. © John Cleary

While an mtDNA test could be used in a search for a biological mother, surnames would not be predicted and most people's mtDNA matches are not related in a genealogical timeframe. To identify biological grandparents the methodology used above can be followed if the parents' autosomal DNA is available. Otherwise, one needs to rule out DNA matches from other family sources. For example, if tracing a paternal grandfather, a test from a maternal relation can identify shared matches which will be on the test-taker's maternal side and can therefore be eliminated (as done with Ben's half-sister, Maggie).

The next case looks at a parentage search when the break in the line was several generations earlier, a consequence of a discovered, previously unknown, illegitimacy.

Surname changes and illegitimacy: Who fathered George Leonard?

Leona Leonard has spent several years researching her Leonard ancestors from Massachusetts, Wisconsin and Michigan, descended from the English or Welsh settler John Leonard, born 1615, who emigrated to New England by 1638. But when Leona ordered autosomal tests for several family members, and Y tests for her brothers P. and G. to identify their Y haplotype and connect to other Leonards, the Y-STR test brought a surprise. They had no Leonard matches, but instead over forty matches named Cummings. This name was so dominant because they had matched with another early colonial American lineage, which was being researched by a lineage association: the descendants of Isaac Cummings of Mistley, Essex (b. 1601), who arrived in another part of Massachusetts in 1634. In fact, her brothers' distinctive Y haplotype showed beyond doubt that their *genetic* ancestor was a descendant of Isaac Cummings, or of a very closely related parallel lineage.

Leona's research suggested where the NPE ('Not the Parent Expected') event had occurred. Her great-grandfather George Herman Leonard was born in Racine, Wisconsin, in October 1858. His parents Chester Phoenix Leonard and Sarah Atwood had married ten years earlier, probably in New York, and had had a number of children around Wisconsin. Chester seems to have disappeared around 1857–8, marrying again in Michigan and having another son there in 1859, also named George Leonard, before enlisting in the Civil War and dying shortly after. Sarah can be seen living with another man in Racine in the 1860 census, marrying him the same year. There is no evidence of a divorce. This is the focus period for the NPE that led to George Herman Leonard's birth.

Y-DNA is excellent for indicating a likely relationship, but not good at pinpointing an exact family branch. P. was evenly 0–2 steps away from most members of the Isaac Cummings project. Harnessing the power of autosomal DNA when linked to the Y result offers a means for resolving this question.

A search of the 1850 US Census correlated with a number of Cummings Y-STR results generated a shortlist of four Wisconsin Cummings families most likely to include George's father. Fitting the movements of George's parents around Wisconsin to the residences of these individuals highlighted the proximity of two Cummings brothers, sons of Jeremiah Cummings of Dunn, WI, around the time of George's birth. When Sarah later remarried she had another son named Orrin. Interestingly, the name of one of the Cummings brothers was Orin Cummings, who begins to look the favourite to be the father of her genetically Cummings son.

The next stage was to develop an autosomal testing strategy. Leona, brother P., sister D. and their second cousin J. had already taken autosomal tests. We need to set some *hypotheses* – the possible fathers of George from Jeremiah Cummings' family tree. Four possible hypotheses emerge. Hypothesis 1 (H1) is modelled in the tree in Figure 3, and H2 and H3 can be modelled similarly by moving the Leonard line to other positions. This creates a set of family relationships between the three Leonards and other test-takers, which are different for each hypothesis. H4 is to test whether H1–H3 are all wrong, with someone else being George's father.

- Hypothesis 1: *George is the son of Orin C. Cummings.*
- Hypothesis 2: *George is the son of Orin's brother, John Woods Cummings.*
- Hypothesis 3: *George is the son of another son of Jeremiah Cummings (Sanford or Washington, half-brothers to Orin).*
- Hypothesis 4: *George is the son of a more distantly related Cummings.*

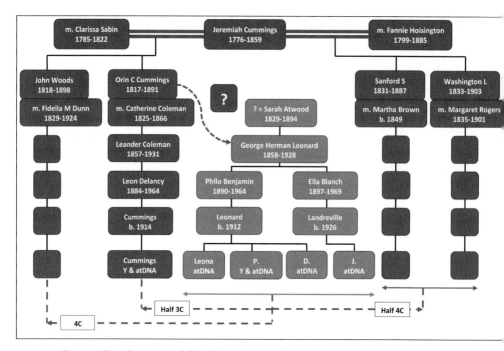

Figure 3: Tree diagram modelling H1, proposing that Orin Cummings is George Leonard's father. Some DNA tests have already been taken as shown, while others need to be ordered.
© *John Cleary*

Forward genealogical research to fill the empty cells on the tree allows tests to be targeted at one descendant each of John and Orin. Descendants of the other brothers can be added later if needed to clarify the picture. The shared DNA expressed in cM will then be compared pairwise between each of the four descendants of George and two new test-takers to see whether the predicted relationships can be discerned. The test-takers should be selected from the oldest generation available, being some type of third or fourth cousin (half or full) to the Leonards. Each hypothesis predicts a set of distinctive family relationships, which pattern as shown in the following table.

Test-taker Pair	cM	H1	H2	H3	H4
Leona – John W descendant	?	4C	Half 3C	Half 4C	5C+
D – John W descendant	?	4C	Half 3C	Half 4C	5C+
P – John W descendant	?	4C	Half 3C	Half 4C	5C+
J – John W descendant	?	4C	Half 3C	Half 4C	5C+
Leona – Orin descendant	?	Half 3C	4C	Half 4C	5C+
D – Orin descendant	?	Half 3C	4C	Half 4C	5C+
P – Orin descendant	?	Half 3C	4C	Half 4C	5C+
J – Orin descendant	?	Half 3C	4C	Half 4C	5C+

The *expected* shared DNA values for each relationship are shown in the next table, drawing upon the work of the Shared cM Project. The nifty calculator created by DNA Painter crunches the numbers for the *actual* pairwise values, throwing up the relative odds that each hypothesis best fits the data.

Relationship	Expected cM (central value)	Range
Half 3C	61 cM	0-178 cM
4C	35 cM	0-127 cM
Half 4C	c. 30 cM	0-98 cM
5C	25 cM	0-94 cM

The hope is that one of the hypotheses will present much greater odds than all the others, giving Leona a firm lead about the identity of George's father. Odds 20 times or more in favour of one hypothesis over all the others, representing more than 95% likelihood, are sought. The success of the testing strategy depends upon a clear Half 3C range appearing, since the more distant relationships are harder to differentiate. The cM numbers can be low at these relationship levels, but as four descendants of George have tested, there may be enough data for a resolution *if* one of these two Cummings men was George's father. If the results are inconclusive, then it may be necessary to find and request further test data.

Relationships further back in time tend to be more difficult to identify, and normally focus on surname changes in the male (Y-DNA) genetic line. Surname changes are historically relatively common. Reasons range from cuckoldry (1–2% of all births), bastardy (up to 10% in the early 1800s), orphanage (highly variable, typically a few percent per generation) to reasons of inheritance, and a variety of other social reasons. These include people wishing either to make a new start or evade the law. A significant number of people will find their surname has changed in the last 200 years, but the social complexities around these NPEs make identifying the original name difficult. Y-DNA testing your autosomal matches is important to rule out particular lineages, but so is appreciating the geography of test-takers' origins and their known genealogical histories.

This and the next example follow cases where surname changes have occurred. In the next case we see how Y-DNA held the key to identifying where the surname changes took place. It also demonstrates the large scale that these problems can grow to and how to effectively pool resources from interested parties.

Ancestral research: Pitman, Wall or Treece?

Captain Thomas Pittman/Pitman is genetically descended from an English Pittman family and is well-documented in Virginia by about 1649. He married a relict of Mr Wall and had a step-son, Joseph Wall. He had other sons and produced a long line of Thomas Pittmans. Early Y-DNA tests uncovered a genealogically close connection between the Pittman and Wall families, but also other isolated American families, including a Mr Treece. Common given names and sparse genealogical records make it difficult to tease out individual families with traditional genealogy, meaning DNA testing is the best method of determining how the Pittman and Wall male lines are related.

Both Pittman and Wall occur frequently in present-day America, along with the various derivations of both: Wall is sometimes Walls, Wallis or Wallace; Pittman can be Pitman, Pitmon, etc. Capt Thomas Pittman's line is among the most successful: over ninety Y-DNA test-takers have his signature haplotype. However, the rapid spread of this family makes it difficult to find distinguishing Y-STR markers to separate family lines, due to the small number of mutations in each generation.

The Pittman and Wall families were first genetically connected by the National Geographic Geno project's 12-marker Y-STR tests. In 2005,

Mr Treece became one of these early test-takers. Normally, 12 Y-STR tests cannot reliably distinguish closely related individuals from those related several millennia ago. Consequently, Mr Treece initially dismissed his Pittman and Wall matches as irrelevant: he 'knew' his ancestry back to 1733 – an immigrant from Germany named Andreas Driess – so he was not expecting to match an English family.

Several years later, Treece upgraded his Y-STR data to 37 markers, and those Pittman and Wall matches remained. It transpired their common haplotype has three mutations in the first twelve STRs, meaning any exact 12-marker matches almost certainly belong to this family. A further, very rare mutation in the 37-marker set makes it certain that any matches are related in the last few centuries.

Mr Treece's German ancestry no longer made sense. By now, Andreas Driess's other descendants had tested and did not match Mr Treece. He was therefore not descended from Andreas Driess, so he began the hunt to find the break in his recorded lineage.

Mr Treece identified distant cousins on his male line and asked them to test. Another descendant of his great-great-grandfather, John Treece (b. c. 1812, Surry County, NC), matched. However, descendants of John Treece's supposed father matched the Driess line.

Mr Treece then upgraded to 111 Y-STRs and the Big Y sequencing test from FTDNA. He also recruited Pittman and Wall test-takers to do the same. The results were analysed by the R-U106 haplogroup project, which determined the ancestral Y-STR motif of the families, and counted the Y-STR and Y-SNP mutations since their common ancestor. The number of mutations was consistent with all the families sharing a common ancestor born around 300–500 years ago, indicating that the Pittman and Wall families were related at around the time of Capt Thomas Pittman. The known Pittman test-takers remaining in England strongly suggest that the Wall family descends genetically from the Pittman family: this was the first surname change.

Unfortunately, the Big Y tests produced mutations that were either recent or old: few formed in the critical range (1649–1812) that would have allowed the early branching structure of the Pittman/Wall families to be determined more accurately.

Treece then returned to his atDNA results. The efficacy of atDNA for relationships this old is low: roughly half of fourth cousins and only a small fraction of fifth cousins are detectable. However, Mr. Treece only needed one member of that family, meaning that small fraction still offered hope.

Database size here matters, as it increases the odds of having a close match in the database. AncestryDNA has the biggest database, and when Treece and his father took an AncestryDNA autosomal test, their many matches included a few male test-takers whose surname was Wall. One particular match, at 37 cM, was from North Carolina.

Mr Treece's BigY results provided some distinguishing SNPs: testing any one of them would place a person inside or outside the Pittman/Wall family. Mr Wall agreed to test one of these SNPs, and was positive, so Mr Treece and Mr Wall's male lines must merge at some point in recent history. Mr. Wall's ancestry does not reliably extend beyond about 1812 either, but suggests his ancestors were also from Surry County, NC.

Both AncestryDNA results were uploaded to GEDmatch for a more detailed comparison. GEDmatch uses a different algorithm, which identified a 55 cM match between the pair, over three segments of DNA, the largest being 33 cM in length. The three matching segments all map to chromosomal regions shared between the two descendants of John Treece (b. c. 1812), indicating that the relationship is on their Treece line. The amount of shared DNA is a typical relationship for 3C1R, but could indicate a relationship anywhere from 2C to 7C. Their paper trails, confirmed by Y-DNA, indicate they cannot be closer than 3C.

While their common ancestor has not yet been identified, these results strongly suggest that the Treece surname was previously Wall, and originally Pittman – i.e. two recorded surname changes within the last 400 years. There is now a clear direction for further research linking the Treece and Wall families, by finding additional autosomal DNA test-takers to match and prove relationships more accurately.

Research into early ancestries

A combination of atDNA and Y-DNA testing can also lead you to a confirmed match with someone whose surname is associated with an illustrious history. Their Y-DNA test could potentially reveal a specific descent from much earlier times than they have been able to establish through documentary evidence. This short final case study is in many ways simpler than the preceding studies, but nevertheless produces very significant results, indicative of how the potential for research into ancestral lines will be widened considerably in the future, as atDNA research links to individuals with far reaching Y-DNA results.

Allyson McAdam took an atDNA test and was identified as a high-confidence match to Ann Stewart Burns. Both of these test-takers live in America and Ann thought she could spot the genealogical connection between them. An online tree showed that Allyson's grandmother was a daughter of a David Stewart. She was able to provide further information from American and Irish sources which clearly showed that her great-grandfather David Stewart was born at Corradooey in Donegal, Ireland, and was a brother of Ann's great-grandfather Samuel Stewart (b. 1855). Having established this important link, initially through atDNA matching, backed up by documentary evidence, it became possible for an ancestral link back through Allyson's Stewart great-grandfather to be made. Since he shared the same male-line ancestry as Ann's brother, Thomas Philip Stewart, the latter's Y-DNA test result would also reveal information about the Stewart ancestry of Allyson.

The Stewart DNA Project is one of the larger DNA surname projects hosted by FTDNA, with over 1,500 members, and with a large body of Stewart test-takers to match against, Thomas's Y-STR results clearly showed that he was descended from the ancient line of the Stewarts, High Stewards and Kings of Scots. SNP testing done over a number of years had established the main distinguishing SNPs for the ancient Stewarts as L744, L745 and L746, while in 2014 a new SNP named S781 was discovered, which occurred in Sir John Stewart of Bonkyl (d.1298) and would therefore be carried by all his descendants. When Thomas undertook further testing to identify SNPs, this revealed firstly that he did not carry the S781 SNP and was therefore descended from Sir John Stewart's elder brother James, 5th High Steward of Scotland. As a result of DNA testing carried out as part of the Battle of Bannockburn Family History Project, another new SNP, Y14197, was shown to be carried by a documented descendant of Sir John Stewart, Sheriff of Bute, an illegitimate son of King Robert II of Scots (1316–90), and a great-grandson of the 5th High Steward. This SNP was not carried by individuals descended from other sons of King Robert. This meant that Y14197 would only be found in descendants of the Bute line of Stewarts, although not necessarily all of them, since it is not yet known whether the mutation occurred in Sir John Stewart himself or one of his later descendants. Thomas also tested positive for Y14197. This verified the fact that he was descended from the Bute Stewarts and ultimately King Robert II, and therefore so was Allyson McAdam.

DNA testing had bridged a gap of around 500 years of documentary evidence between Sir John Stewart, Sheriff of Bute and David Stewart, through the use of Y-DNA, and also, using atDNA, established a link to his great-granddaughter without there being a male line descent.

Chapter 10

ANCIENT DNA

John Cleary

In 2015, DNA from three men and a woman from Ireland was sequenced and some extraordinary conclusions about the prehistoric origins of Irish people were drawn. Three men from Rathlin Island, off the north coast of Antrim, and a woman from Ballynahatty, near Belfast, had their whole genomes read at a lab in Dublin, allowing new ideas to be developed about ancient migrations into Ireland. The woman's DNA looked like that of populations from southern Europe, while the three men had DNA that resembled peoples from northern Europe and the eastern European steppes. This was proposed as powerful evidence that Ireland had undergone massive population replacement during the Bronze Age, which may even have been linked with the arrival of the forerunner of the Irish language.

That it was possible to draw such a conclusion about ancient migrations was because the DNA – and those four people – was ancient itself. These were archaeological remains: the three Rathlin men dating from between 2000–1500 BCE during the Irish Bronze Age, while the Ballynahatty woman had been buried earlier in the Irish Neolithic, around 3350–3000 BCE, shortly after the arrival of agriculture in Ireland. Both periods saw tremendous changes in human culture in Ireland – agriculture during the 3000s BCE and metallurgy in the Bronze Age. Now there was DNA evidence from people who were alive in those times for the replacement of populations during those cultural upheavals, going to the heart of deep debates within archaeology. The DNA was extracted from the four skeletons at the Molecular Population

Lab of the Smurfit Institute of Genetics at Trinity College Dublin, headed by Professor Dan Bradley, one of the labs driving forward the science and technology of ancient DNA (aDNA).

The fact that DNA can be sequenced at all from the long dead is an amazing story of scientific and technical innovation, and aDNA has become a crucial tool for disciplines such as archaeology, palaeoanthropology, population genomics and evolutionary biology. It is now also beginning to make a significant impact in the field of genetic genealogy. Many readers will have heard the story of how a skeleton unearthed in a humdrum carpark in Leicester was identified as that of the English king Richard III, and how aDNA played a significant part in that identification. A wide number of other historical individuals have been identified by similar methods and recently genetic genealogy methods were used in the identification of unknown soldiers who died at the World War I battle of Fromelles. The technology is continuing to advance more rapidly than most can keep up with. At the time of writing in 2019, the powerful combination of whole genome sequencing (WGS) and open databases of mass genetic genealogical data is beginning to create new functions that few had thought possible until recently, raising new ethical questions in their turn (see Chapter 2). And at the more microscopic level, we may also be about to see genealogical uses being created by isolating forensic DNA from personal items of more recently deceased family members, such as hairbrushes or envelopes.

This chapter will survey the history of aDNA, how sequencing it is possible and what the challenges are, and will then look at the impact genealogy and aDNA may have upon each other. For any reader who may wish to set up an aDNA project, some steps and conditions for success are laid out, and towards the end of the chapter we will take a peek at that new future we are beginning to enter. This is a wide and complex field, and a much fuller account of how to set up an aDNA project is available at the ISOGG Wiki https://isogg.org/wiki.

Defining aDNA and a quick run through its history

DNA is the vital molecule at the heart of all living cells, and while a cell lives the DNA within it is repaired and kept whole. But things are very different after death, as the fragile DNA strand begins to decay and break up rapidly. There are no longer repair mechanisms to keep the long chromosomes together and degraded DNA breaks down into progressively shorter strands. The science of forensics has developed methods to isolate, capture and read the DNA of victims of crimes and mass disasters, or DNA found at crime scenes, which may have degraded. Special techniques are required to read the fragmenting strands, which open up the possibility that DNA can be read of formerly living beings whose lives have ended.

Ancient DNA, abbreviated to aDNA, is degraded DNA that is associated with investigating the archaeological past. There is really no clear distinction between ancient and forensic DNA – at least not in terms of the age of the sample. One useful definition of aDNA by archaeologist Connie Mulligan suggests '"Ancient" samples are generally those that were not collected for the purpose of immediate DNA analysis and include archaeological, clinical, and natural history specimens.' As with forensic DNA, aDNA may exist only in traces or low copy numbers (very low numbers of copies of any particular DNA strand, making isolating and sequencing them a challenge).

Forensic approaches to degraded DNA

An aDNA sequence was first read in 1984, when a short sequence from a kind of extinct zebra called a quagga, from a 150-year old museum specimen, was cloned and sequenced. Around the same time, Alec Jeffreys at Leicester University discovered a method he termed 'DNA fingerprinting' using microsatellites, which are the same as the STR markers explained earlier in this book, and which would become the foundation genetic genealogy would be built upon. Jeffreys developed this into a forensic system for crime scene use and identification of persons unknown, and working with aDNA specialist Erika Hagelberg, who had pioneered extraction of aDNA from human bone, used the methodology first to identify a murder victim, and then the remains of the fugitive Nazi Josef Mengele.

Timeline of scientific breakthroughs in the reading of human aDNA, 1985-2017	
1984	DNA cloned from a quagga, an extinct zebra
1985	Svante Pääbo claims DNA extraction from an Egyptian mummy (later challenged as contamination)
	Alec Jeffreys develops DNA finger printing in forensics
1989	Erika Hagelberg extracts DNA from human bone
1991	Hagelberg and Jeffreys identify a murder victim by DNA from her skeleton
1992	Jeffreys and Hagelberg identify the remains of fugitive Nazi Josef Mengele using early forensic aDNA methods
1994	The Romanovs' remains identified by Gill, Hagelberg and others using mtDNA, Y DNA and autosomal STRs. Though mired in controversy for years, the findings are eventually upheld as a landmark application of historical forensics.
1997	First sequencing of Neanderthal DNA by Pääbo and others
2000	Cooper and Poinar establish the "nine gold standard criteria" for doing aDNA research
2005	NGS breakthrough for aDNA with 40kya cave bear skeletal remains
	Poinar reads large sequences of mammoth DNA
2008	First complete mitochondrial sequence of a prehistoric European – Ötzi the Iceman
2010	Draft of full Neanderthal sequence
	Denisovan genome sequenced from a single finger bone
2014	Mixed Siberian-East Asian ancestry of native Americans revealed through aDNA of Palaeolithic Mal'ta Boy
	Richard III skeleton identified partly by mtDNA at Leicester University
2016	Rathlin Island and Ballynahatty Woman sequences using WGS techniques at Trinity College Dublin give hard evidence of ancient population replacement in Ireland
2017	Massive study of 170 ancient European genomes, processed on 'industrial scale' using 1.2 million genome-wide SNP chip
2018	Genome-wide sampling impacts both forensic science and genetic genealogy when the "Buckskin Girl" and "Golden State Killer" are identified using genealogical databases

Table 1: Timeline of scientific breakthroughs in the reading of human aDNA, 1984–2019

In the years since, forensic science has developed an advanced methodological system for its work, organised around criminal investigations and humanitarian relief of mass disasters. The main tools are:

- sets of 15 STR markers on the autosomes (recently expanded to 20) which can identify individuals and very close family members;
- supplemented by testing the HVR part of mtDNA, and Y DNA haplotypes of 17 STRs (recently expanded to 23 or 27 markers, depending on the company);
- forensic databases of haplotypes that can be used to judge whether a particular haplotype produced by a test was a common one, or a very rare one in a region, allowing judgements to be made on how unique a sample might be.

Genetic genealogists accustomed to testing haplotypes of 67 or 111 Y-STRs, full mitochondrial sequences, and autosomal chips with 600,000+ SNPs may feel that the short datasets produced here may not be informative or even entirely safe for making identifications with the certainty demanded by law. However, genetic genealogists carry out a different kind of research – searching a wide field of data for *similarities* to create leads for further research. Forensics aims at establishing an exact match between two samples, and needs to make decisions on what degree of non-exact matching can be tolerated in order to make a legally sound identification. Nevertheless, some forensics specialists have questioned the number, and the types, of DNA markers that are necessary for sound identifications today.

Methods in forensic DNA searching
Forensic labs that read degraded DNA use the polymerase chain reaction (PCR) method, which multiplies copies of the aDNA strands ('amplification') for easier reading. The common genetic genealogical Y-STR tests use the same method. While advantageous for aDNA with its weak and fragmented strands, there is a contamination risk with PCR should the wrong DNA strands be picked up by the PCR and amplified, like DNA left over in the lab from previous procedures, or contaminant DNA from people who handled the samples.

Forensic science has developed standardised forensic test kits, the results of which are searched against the databases and a likelihood ratio is calculated to estimate the probability that the sample can uniquely identify a particular person. This may be expressed as odds (e.g. 2000 to 1 odds for or against a hypothesis) or as a percentage probability figure – and we will see how this was applied to the Richard III case later in this chapter.

Historical aDNA
Most specialist aDNA labs exist in academic institutions and serve the needs of archaeology, population genetics or other scientific research disciplines. Now that aDNA has opened up a means of accessing the actual DNA of past populations (like the Rathlin Island skeletons) rather than attempting to infer it from the DNA of present-day populations, more reliable answers can be found to questions asked by these disciplines. Over the past thirty or so years there have been a number of collaborations between archaeologists, population geneticists, historians and others when identification of an individual has been either an aim, or the primary goal. A special, high-profile case was the identification of Richard III, the last Plantagenet king of England.

This focus on identification of an individual creates an intersection between some of these research areas which has been dubbed 'biohistory', incorporating investigative approaches like radiocarbon dating, autopsies, investigating diet and body chemicals, osteological analysis – and historical aDNA. Because historical aDNA shares with forensic science a strong focus on identification, it has drawn heavily on the latter's methodologies and concepts, although this is beginning to change (in 2019) with recent advances in technology and techniques.

Genealogists may find themselves involved in such projects – possibly as biohistorians developing a project or supporting the identification work with genealogical research. Later in the chapter we will look at how a project can be set up, drawing upon the experience of a number of case studies. But first, returning to scientific aDNA research, let's look at how a revolution in methods brought increasing confidence that very old samples could be successfully sequenced.

Challenges in aDNA: fragmentation and damage
PCR works best when there are large quantities of the target DNA (as

with living samples) and it has not degraded. The repeating STR sequences require long enough strands for the full set of repeats to be counted; thus, fragmentation was a considerable challenge to forensic DNA methods, while, as scientific aDNA moved on, damage became the greater challenge because chemical changes in the DNA strand can undermine the reliability of results.

The main degradation risks include:

- *Fragmentation*: the strands become shorter and shorter so STRs cannot be read, and they become too short for classic PCR primers
- *Damage*: base pairs change, e.g. T may substitute for C
- *Damage*: bases disappear from the strand
- *Fragmentation*: cross-linking, when the double strands of the DNA helix part and reattach at different points on its own strand, or with other molecules

Oxygen and water are devastating for the survival of intact DNA, which survives far longer when neither is present near the sample. Waterlogged graves are bad news for the survival of aDNA, while cool, dry conditions are the best for preservation.

However, this is not all bad news. Modern sequencing methods have developed which work with short strands of DNA, while processes that cause damage are now statistically predictable – so they help to identify a sample as aDNA, distinguishing it from modern DNA, partially solving the next problem, contamination.

Challenges in aDNA: contamination

In early tests of aDNA, contamination was found to be a problem, so methods for eliminating contamination were refined, drawing on forensic science to develop clean room technology and mandate the use of Tyvek white suits when working with samples. Extraction processes had to be carried out independently at two separate labs to ensure false positives were not picked up from contamination in the lab processes.

aDNA scientists talk of *endogenous* and *exogenous* aDNA. The former belongs to the sample, the person or organism being investigated, and is the aDNA that is wanted. The latter is anything that does not belong to the sample, and can originate in a number of sources:

• Mixed burials creating cross-contamination
• Contamination from laboratory processes (e.g. PCR), equipment or previous extractions
• Contamination by handling (current investigators or previous handlers)
• General environment (soil, air, storage facilities)
• Microbial contamination – as much as 60% of a sample may be microbes, and this can be both ancient and modern microbial DNA

By 2000, Alan Cooper and Henrik Poinar's famous protocol ('Do it right or not at all') had established guidelines on how a reliable aDNA project should be conducted, although not all researchers welcomed it, with some finding it unnecessarily rigid. But the arrival of next-generation sequencing after 2005 made contamination issues a little less pressing, as it became easier to tell endogenous aDNA from modern contaminants. But steps still need to be taken to limit contamination risks.

Shotgun sequencing and the return of confidence

The third major challenge that scientists face in sequencing aDNA comes from the low copy number of the target DNA that may exist in a sample. From the time of Cooper and Poinar's protocol (2000), quantifying the amount of endogenous aDNA was deemed essential before starting. Forensics approached the problem by sequencing parts of the mtDNA – because it existed in much greater copy numbers than nuclear DNA – or by increasing the number of cycles of PCR to amplify small quantities up to readable levels (but with a significantly enhanced contamination risk).

The quantity problem can also be approached by careful selection of the type of tissue used to extract the aDNA. Soft tissues like muscle were used in the early days, until Hagelberg and others found ways to extract it from bones. Then long bones such as femurs were favoured until recently, when the petrous part of the temporal bone was discovered to be the best source of endogenous aDNA. This bone, part of the skull which houses the inner ear, is the densest in the human body and is as hard as rock. Once the outside has been shaved away, the dense interior portions are rich in the DNA of the former living person. This bone has now become the source of choice for acquiring aDNA, when it is available, and can provide enough material for more than one sequencing process, should it be needed. Endogenous aDNA can be between 37–85% from the petrous, while other bones may contain less than 1%. Teeth also provide good sources, especially when the roots are intact, or still in their sockets.

In 2005, next-generation sequencing methods (familiar to genetic genealogy through the Big Y, Y Elite or Whole Genome tests) made a breakthrough when DNA from 40,000-year-old cave bears and woolly mammoths was sequenced. NGS (also called 'shotgun sequencing') is especially suited to aDNA, as the first stage in the process is to smash the DNA up into fragments which are read individually and then mapped to a reference sequence. aDNA is already broken and fragmented, so lends itself to NGS, the challenge being to read the smallest fragments. It also needs much less material than sample-heavy PCR, and is much cheaper per megabase (1000 bp) to sequence.

The technical breakthroughs came thick and fast after this, pushing back in time the age at which aDNA could be reliably extracted. In 2008, the full mtDNA sequence of 'Ötzi the Iceman' was read by NGS (5,000 years old). In 2010 the first full draft sequence of Neanderthals (c. 40,000 years old) was produced, and the DNA of the ancient Denisovan people (of similar antiquity) was sequenced from a little finger bone. 2012 saw the sequencing of the 24,000-year-old Mal'ta Boy from Siberia, and then in 2016 came the Smurfit Institute's high resolution coverage of the Rathlin and Ballynahatty people. In 2017, David Reich's lab at Harvard University published its study of 170 prehistoric Europeans, using new 'industrial scale' genome-wide sampling methods to drive costs down to potentially $200 per sample.

Creating a biohistorical project with aDNA

While ancient population research has thrived on the possibilities of NGS, it has made less of an impact on historical aDNA. When identification or kin reconstruction are the goals, forensic methods seem to work well enough. The cost per megabase of NGS data may be relatively cheap, but the total costs of sequencing whole genomes may seem excessive given the typical goals of a historical project. However, some voices warn that if the effort is being made to extract aDNA, then the loss of information through not attempting whole-genome sequencing (WGS) is worse than the costs involved in trying. aDNA is destructive sampling and once sample material has been destroyed in analysis, it can never be analysed again. An innovative WGS method was used to identify the remains of Irish rebel leader Thomas Kent, exhumed in 2015, with aDNA sequenced from his petrous bone. The relatively lower costs of the Reich method, and its particular suitability to aDNA, could make it an attractive method for historical and identification studies in future. As we saw in Chapter 2, WGS or genome-wide methods are beginning to attract the interest of forensic science as of 2019.

In this section, we will look at the steps involved in putting together an aDNA project, and at what may be involved in playing the role of the biohistorian in projects like Leicester University's Richard III case. A genealogist or historian may know of an item in a museum or a private collection that presents a question of identity, and would be of wide public interest. There may be remains of interest in a grave or crypt that could be exhumed (at least in theory); or there could be incidental discoveries of mass graves of war dead, epidemics or other disasters. The following section also draws upon the experience of a number of case studies of other historical identification projects that have been carried out across the last 30 years of aDNA discovery.

Ethics and the law of ancient remains
Ethical practice in DNA sequencing is a major theme of this book and it may surprise some to hear that it is an issue for aDNA as well. While some writers have mused over whether it is ethical to discover more about the health of Abraham Lincoln or Tutankhamen than they could ever have known about themselves, a more significant issue is that archaeological remains are special, and scarce, and aDNA – along with radiocarbon dating and isotope analysis – is a destructive form of analysis. Destroying a sample to sequence it by today's methods means it cannot be sequenced again by tomorrow's superior and more informative methods, because it will no longer exist. Museums are

committed to the preservation of their collections, and will consider destructive sampling only if it is carried out by properly trained experts and only if the goal of the research is significant, the only way to answer a question, and offering clear prospects of a successful outcome.

Case 1: Clare Priory (2016)
Following the surprise result of Richard III's Y-DNA read, historian John Ashdown-Hill proposed exhuming and testing the remains of Lionel, Duke of Clarence, believed to be buried at Clare Priory in Suffolk, England. Clarence, son of Edward III, was in the same patrilineal line as Richard, and they should match each other if there had been no intervening illegitimacies. Historic England rejected the proposal in October 2016, citing a number of concerns. There was uncertainty that Clarence was actually buried at the site and if so where. As there was also no certainty that any excavated remains from the site would or would not match Richard's haplotype, they decided the project goals were insufficiently likely to generate a clear answer to the research question to justify the damage to a Scheduled Monument.

The Clare Priory case shows that exhuming and testing even archaeological human remains is controlled by complex legislation and licencing regimes, which differ across various jurisdictions. The UK has a stricter regulatory environment over scientific tests conducted on human tissue: consent of the individual or personal representatives is required (and this would certainly make illegal in the UK the testing of 'discarded DNA' that was a key element in the unmasking of the Golden State Killer – see Chapter 2). On the other hand, Ireland has a stricter licensing regime in the hands of the National Museum of Ireland, which has full decision-making rights over whether a human item should be deemed archaeological, exported, reburied or permitted to undergo destructive sampling. A fuller discussion of these issues in the English context can be found in the English Heritage publication *Science and the Dead* (2013).

Case 2: Richard III (2011–2015)

The discovery of a skeleton in a Leicester car park and the successful identification of the bones as Richard III is one of the most celebrated archaeological discoveries of the decade. But before the superb work of archaeologists and geneticists began, amateur and professional historians had been lobbying and raising finance for the work to start. The project also received a major contribution from the genealogical research led by Kevin Schürer, and earlier of historian John Ashdown-Hill, which identified the living mtDNA-carrier descendants of Richard's mother. The initial impetus, including fundraising for the excavations, had come from the Richard III Society. This was a project which benefited from the preparatory work of enthusiasts before the discovery of the remains, and the expertise of archaeologists, historians, geneticists and data analysts following the discovery in a splendid example of biohistorical project teamwork.

The project was also ground-breaking in the way it used statistical reasoning to identify Richard, using Bayesian statistics to estimate likelihoods that certain factors increased or decreased the chances the skeleton was his. All the estimates of probability from radiocarbon dating, the skeleton's age at death, the signs of battle trauma and deformation in the bones, as well as the results from the aDNA extraction, were added into the calculation. Because the Y DNA results had found a mismatch with Richard's expected patrilineal relatives, they made a small negative contribution to the odds. The mtDNA match to the two living female-line descendants of Richard's mother made a contribution on the positive side, but was not sufficient on its own to make the identification certain. Here is how the DNA contributed to the outcome.

Taking all factors together produced likelihood ratio (LR) odds of 6.7 million to 1 that the skeleton was Richard's, which translated into a probability of 99.9994% even taking a sceptical starting point for the analysis. The mtDNA as a factor on its own made a 478:1 likelihood ratio that the skeleton was Richard's, or a 92% probability with the sceptical starting point. This reflects a small probability that the mtDNA sequences could have matched by chance, and not necessarily been unique to Richard's matrilineal line. The Y DNA, because of the NPE it revealed, contributed an LR of 0.16:1 that the skeleton was Richard's, which is actually 6.25:1 odds *against* the hypothesis that the skeleton was his – effectively a negative contribution, but a small one since breaks in the male genetic line are not unexpected over hundreds of years.

DNA testing can play an important part in cold case identification, but the Richard project demonstrated how *all evidence* needs to be evaluated together in a robust statistical analysis. The mtDNA gave a strong lead and the verified matrilineal descent tree is powerful visual evidence in favour, but still constituted just one component of the analysis and not definitive on its own.

Setting up a biohistorical project

Maybe you have an idea for a biohistorical project – you may know of curious remains in a museum collection, or have a question about remains in a tomb. The Barry Surname Project was interested in its connection to James Barry, the 4th Earl of Barrymore in County Cork (1667–1748), a well-known Jacobite, and was able to access his (possible) remains from his crypt on the Barrymore estate. You may also be called upon to assist with genealogical research work that supports a major aDNA project (see Case 3). This can include verifying trees to establish the relationships with reference sample donors, or building new trees down to living people who can be approached as possible reference samples. There is also a role for genetic genealogists to act as consultants to a project, advising on what types of testing strategy may be beneficial, what the limits of DNA evidence may be, and on how results may be interpreted.

A biohistorical project will pass through a number of stages, including:

- Defining the project goal(s) and evaluating the possibilities of success given the specific factors at play: if destructive sampling is to be proposed this needs to be assessed.
- Considering legal requirements, ethical practice and obtaining permissions and approval for project actions from relevant authorities.

- Advising on testing methods, including types of analysis that should be run *before* attempting to extract aDNA, as well as on different methods of aDNA sequencing.
- Identifying reference sample donors, often through genealogical research.
- Reviewing the supporting documentary evidence.
- Building the specialist team and arranging access to necessary technical facilities.
- Raising funding for project actions.
- Analysis and publication of results.

While a genealogist acting as biohistorian may not have the technical expertise to lead on every aspect of the project plan, they may be in a good position to act as project manager, coordinating activities, acting as lynchpin for the team and bringing the technical specialist group together. Both the Richard (Case 2) and Fromelles (Case 3) projects originally came about in part because of the activities of enthusiasts preparing, lobbying and building interest over many years.

Case 3: The Fromelles First World War Dead (2008–14)
John Cleary and Michelle Leonard
Historical aDNA is not only about identifying kings and notable historical figures. A major project which led to the identification of ordinary twentieth-century men was the Fromelles Unknown Soldiers. The battle of Fromelles, 19–20 July 1916, in northern France, led to heavy casualties for the 5th Australian and 61st British Divisions, with over 2,000 dead. A mass grave of Australian and British soldiers was discovered at the site, partly due to the work of retired enthusiast Lambis Englezos. The Commonwealth War Graves Commission and Australian and British governments commissioned Oxford Archaeology to excavate, and forensic DNA specialists LGC to attempt identifications of the dead soldiers, before reburial in a new, specially designed war grave cemetery. 159 of the 250 remains found in the mass grave have been identified, all of them Australian army soldiers. The DNA testing used a strict forensic chain of evidence protocol, extracting the DNA in LGC's degraded DNA labs, using the YFiler 17 and mtDNA HVR test kits and forensic databases as the basis for the identifications.

Volunteer British and Australian genealogists played a major role in the project, in making connections to living relatives of the soldiers who could provide reference samples for the identifications. The UK genealogists researched trees for all 332 missing British soldiers, creating a database with over 18,000 names; the task was even larger for the 1,335 Australian missing. The process involved contacting each of the DNA-suitable relatives identified by the researchers, explaining the project, and asking if they would be willing to donate a DNA sample to a database of reference DNA. A donor database needs to be created securely to protect fully the privacy of the volunteer sample donors. They need to give informed consent to their DNA being held for a defined period and purpose, and no other uses of the database can be permitted. Across the decade of the project, over a quarter of a million DNA comparisons have been made.

The Fromelles Project used a triangulation approach, aiming for 2 Y-STR and 2 mtDNA samples from living relatives to compare against each soldier, although in practice this was often not obtainable. It proved possible to extract both mtDNA and Y-DNA from the recovered remains of the soldiers, with the best results from tooth pulp, and some bones also being useful. The probability was then calculated of how likely the results could have occurred by chance (i.e. in the general population) through comparison with global forensic databases. If the probability was high that a similar haplotype occurred in the general population, then a DNA sample would be less likely to be distinctive to a particular family. In other words, common Y or mt haplotypes made identification difficult – unless the team could find both a Y and an mt match for each soldier. As with Richard III, additional evidence of height and age of death, and artefacts found in the graves, were also considered, and a likelihood ratio calculated that a soldier's sample was more likely to be related to a living reference person than not. If the LR was over a certain pre-set threshold then the identity was declared to be 'acceptably probable' (since absolute certainty is never possible). In this case a positive identification could be made to the families who had donated the reference samples. Though additional evidence was taken account of, unlike in the Richard case none of it was decisive without the DNA evidence, which has proven necessary for all the identified soldiers so far.

Degraded DNA and the future: personal preserved samples

Thus far, this chapter has been considering the role of aDNA extracted and sequenced from remains of deceased persons, either historical people or more recent forensic cases. Typical sample types have been bones (especially the petrous part of the temporal bone), teeth, hairs or surviving soft tissues. Most of these projects imply some form of excavation, exhumation or working with public or private collections in museums and archives and are the preserve of large technical teams in which a genetic genealogist may be playing one role among many.

In recent years the science of extracting degraded DNA has been developing to the extent that it may become possible to extract the DNA of the recently deceased from items they have touched or used in their lives – directly reading the DNA of those who are no longer living, and who have no claims to fame. Though in its infancy and still too expensive (in 2019) to be a common method for most genealogists, mass market procedures are being developed by some companies. For some people, like Anthea Ring (Case 4), it may be possible to find definitive answers to their question only by reading the degraded DNA of a deceased person. This will throw up new ethical and legal questions over what is permissible when attempting to read the DNA of the recently deceased, who should be required to consent to any extractions and what might be published after the investigation is done.

Personal items that could be exploited in this way (some only being practical from the very recently deceased) could include:

- Hairbrushes and combs holding hairs (with follicles) of the deceased
- Letters in envelopes which the deceased may have licked
- Stamps on the same envelopes (that needed to be licked, prior to the age of adhesive stamps)
- Items of clothing that could have hairs, blood marks or other bodily fluids on them
- Razors that may contain hair or blood samples
- Teeth that may have been kept as keepsakes
- Buccal DNA samples taken by an undertaker prior to a funeral

Hairbrushes, envelopes and stamps seem to offer the greatest potential for family historians. In all cases there is a major risk of the aDNA being contaminated. While it can be easy to identify modern contamination in a degraded sample, because aDNA shows distinctive patterns of degradation, it is not as easy to detect ancient DNA contamination by another person in the past. For example, if a post office handler's DNA from the same era as a stamp was licked was picked up in the test, that could be read as the result, and missed as contamination.

Preserving your personal DNA sources

You might have a question that a personal item could help answer, but you may be unable to afford the testing at present. Or you may not have a particular question to answer, but still have some items from deceased (or elderly) family members that you could conceivably want to test one day, when procedures are cheaper and maybe less destructive. It is essential to protect these items from contamination from the environment and other humans, and to try to minimise the ongoing degradation of the DNA they may contain. Some methods for this include:

- Keeping the items in cool and dry conditions away from sources of heat or sunlight (just as you would with vital documents or photographs)
- Storing them in acid-free paper-based archival storage containers or envelopes
- Avoid storage in plastic containers or wrapping, as moisture will build up which can accelerate DNA degradation
- Avoid handling, and do so only with clean archival or rubber gloves, and a facemask is also recommended

The more samples that can be made available to the lab, the greater the chances of a successful read.

Case 4: Anthea Ring (2017–18)
Anthea Ring was abandoned as a baby in 1937 and found in a blackberry bush on the South Downs in Sussex, England. Raised by adoptive parents, she later used genealogy and DNA to identify her birth mother. The same method allowed her to trace her birth father to one of several brothers, who were by that time deceased. The

brothers' family were in possession of 30-year old letters written by one brother and DNA was extracted from the stamps and envelopes by the company Living DNA, finally allowing Anthea to identify her birth father as that brother. The DNA from the first three samples taken was 'too degraded to use' but the fourth sample yielded enough DNA for a definitive identification.

Degraded DNA and the future: forensic science

We saw with the case of the Golden State Killer in Chapter 2 how forensic science, law enforcement, genetic genealogy and cold cases are beginning to interface. The autosomal genetic genealogical databases built by the direct to consumer (DTC) testing companies and the open database GEDmatch.com have become powerful means to identify relatives of searchers, as adoptees searching for birth parents have become well aware. They offer the exact same power to search for relatives of amnesiacs or unidentified persons (known as John or Jane Doe in the USA), that they do for unapprehended violent criminals like the GSK.

The forensic methods based on PCR and STRs reviewed above are little use for identifying persons unknown, because you need to have a close relative for a reference sample – impossible when a body is completely unidentified. Y-DNA can lead to possible candidate surnames for a John Doe, but these are never certain because not all men take their fathers' surnames. Familial searching is usually banned by legal forensic databases, though the UK and some US states permit it. This is because the haplotypes in the databases do not have the resolution for reliable searching once you are no longer looking at exact matches, but allowing small differences to be considered.

The range of the data from autosomal test chips and the growing size of the autosomal databases makes them far more powerful than forensic STR databases for familial searching. Genetic genealogists know they can recognise probable first or second cousins when they see cM matches in the right ranges. Until recently there has been little evidence of interest in forensic application of this power, but the 2018 identification of the 'Buckskin Girl' (see Case 5) may have initiated a much greater interest from forensic science and, potentially, from law enforcement investigating suspects, as well as 'Does'. There are no international standards or regulatory bodies with oversight of this process and hobbyist genealogists who upload their test results, or those of other family members, to these databases may need to consider their attitudes towards such potential uses of databases where their own data, or that of family members, may be held.

Case 5: The 'Buckskin Girl' (2017–18)
A young woman murdered in Ohio in 1981, found wearing a buckskin poncho, was still unidentified in early 2017. A tube of blood had been taken at autopsy and kept in an evidence store, unrefrigerated, for thirty-six years. Despite that, it proved possible to extract 50–75% of the variable DNA used in autosomal DNA tests familiar in genealogy. This was then entered into GEDmatch in the same way as an autosomal raw data file and used to search for familial matches. Different versions of the file with different confidence levels of calling were searched in GEDmatch, but all led to a genealogical lead that allowed a legal, forensic identification of the murdered woman to be made. This was the first publicly recorded use of the GEDmatch database for a purpose connected with forensics and law enforcement and therefore has implications for the users of the database and the uses that they consented to when they uploaded their own data.

Chapter 11

WHAT DOES THE FUTURE HOLD?

Iain McDonald, Michelle Leonard

The future of genetic genealogy offers a mixture of points of hope and potential problems, arising from both the testing companies and the populace. To put together this chapter, we have drawn on information supplied by experts in the field, leading people in the major testing companies and experiences with existing test-takers.

Protecting the future on a personal level
People keep dying. Unfortunately, this nasty habit can have important ramifications for others. Unless you dig them up, or a sample already exists in a lab, it is hard to test DNA from someone who is already dead. Thus it is important to get a sample of DNA from any aged relatives you may want to test in future and send it to a lab for a simple DNA test, after which they will store it securely.

It is also hard to get access to the DNA results of the dead. By default, most companies only allow access to people with the right combination of username and password. Assigning a benefactor who can control your account after your death is a good precaution to take now, even if you feel quite well. This can be done through major companies (e.g. Family Tree DNA, who provide an option to add the name, phone number and email address of a beneficiary under the Beneficiary Information tab within Account Settings). However, precautions should be taken on an individual level, e.g. ensuring your email will be checked by someone after your death, and providing a sealed document with relevant login details for your descendants to manage any accounts, data, subscriptions, etc.

Changes in DNA testing on a societal level

Like it or not, society is becoming more litigious and genetic testing is becoming more widespread and more precise. There is concern among some that positive genetic predisposition to certain conditions could become a factor in medical or life insurance quotations. As further conditions are identified, the number of medically relevant genes will increase. Genealogical DNA databases are also being used increasingly by law enforcement agencies to identify criminals.

Medical aspects are less concerning for Y-DNA. Y-DNA disorders are usually linked to male fertility issues, as the remaining genes have largely lost their functionality. Mitochondrial disorders are numerous, but future issues are likely to centre around autosomal DNA. For future generations, archived autosomal DNA may be an important source of information on both genealogical inheritance and inherited diseases. However, while a person is alive, sharing autosomal or mitochondrial DNA data risks publicly sharing you and your family's susceptibility to inherited diseases. Aside from making private information public, in future this may affect insurance costs, unless data is properly pseudonymised so that it cannot be associated with you. Data should be shared only where you and your immediate family are happy with the level of privacy you retain, and you should make yourself aware of how organisations you share your data with will use it.

More generally, it is becoming increasingly important that persons handling DNA results for others (including genealogists and project administrators) adhere to the same ethical principles of confidentiality and data security that are expected among many other professions. Our ability to continue research relies on people sharing their DNA test results with each other, or at least with trusted intermediaries. Restrictions on this sharing may come either at a personal level, or be imposed by testing companies, by case law, or by broader privacy laws.

Legislation often arises as a result of individual cases of misunderstanding or malpractice. The onus is increasingly on individual researchers, project administrators and testing companies to prevent these situations. We have to balance the desire for privacy of individuals with the fact that most genetic test-takers want to be contacted. The key here is to provide clear, informed, written consent for any action taken. Personal information should remain private, unless the individual has consented to sharing it – this includes individual researchers taking genetic data from relatives, and information in family trees. There should also be a strict separation maintained between personal and genetic data where possible, so that genetic information cannot be traced back to a living individual, except where that individual has expressly consented to that.

Improvements to the status quo
Database size
Identifying relationships relies on a large database and deep testing by those in that database. Predictable improvements come from the recruitment of new test-takers, and from upgrading of existing tests by older test-takers.

Little over a decade ago the prevailing wisdom was that autosomal DNA could not be used for genetic genealogy. Fast forward to the present and autosomal DNA tests are by far the most popular on the market today with over 26 million test-takers across the databases by early 2019.

Family Tree DNA's Y-DNA database has increased by an estimated 200,000 test-takers in the last year, with the number of sequencing tests approximately doubling. And each of these test-takers is typically testing deeper than their predecessors.

It is very difficult to predict how many people may test over the next few years, but it is clear that databases will continue to grow swiftly and database size will play an ever-increasing role in how successfully DNA testing can be used for genealogical purposes. Fuelling this is an increasing acceptance of DNA testing in genealogy, as the answers it can bring become more accurate. This results from test-takers seeking out new matches, wider marketing by testing companies and the wholesale decrease in price of genetic testing.

There will be many benefits to larger databases, including improved admixture percentages as reference panels increase and algorithms become more sophisticated. Additionally, the number of adoption and unknown ancestor mysteries that can be solved will increase dramatically as databases expand. The flipside of that is that many more people will discover hitherto unknown family secrets, making it more important than ever that people understand these possibilities before testing. The number of brick walls broken down will increase exponentially and confirmation of your ancestry via DNA will become easier to achieve. It is likely we will reach the point that most people with ancestry from areas where testing is most prevalent (North America, UK, Ireland, Australia, New Zealand, Scandinavia etc) will find close or reasonably close relatives have already tested when they enter the databases.

Another major benefit could be ancestor identification via DNA testing alone. Testing companies may develop the ability to automate personal family trees for test-takers based solely on their DNA matches. It is likely that the early days of such a system would require substantial trial and error and further traditional research. It would, however, be an amazing development for adoptees, those with recent unknown ancestor mysteries and test-takers who have yet to construct detailed family trees. Ancestry's 'New Ancestor Discoveries' (NADs) beta feature is an early forerunner of such a potential tool. Large-scale sharing of both DNA and family tree data would be required to fully realise this future application; it would be essential to have millions of segments collaboratively mapped back to millions of ancestors so that when new test takers share any of the collectively mapped segments they can be immediately informed which ancestors their DNA segments have been assigned to.

Universal family tree

As DNA and genealogy continue to integrate over the coming years there is great potential for a universal family tree that incorporates traditional family trees with DNA test results. There are several websites already attempting to create universal family trees (i.e. FamilySearch, FindMyPast, WikiTree, Geni) but none have integrated with DNA databases yet and the fact that there are several, as opposed to just one, is a limiting factor. WikiTree and Geni, however, allow you to attach information about tests taken. LivingDNA recently announced the 'One Family One World Project' which aims, over a five-year period, to create a single worldwide family tree based on DNA. It is an ambitious but exciting project and it will be interesting to see how it develops.

Reconstructing the DNA of our ancestors

Reconstructing the DNA of our ancestors will become the goal of many a genetic genealogist over the coming years and is actually already partially achievable. When we undertake chromosome mapping we assign segments of our DNA back to our ancestors and, in essence, reconstruct parts of their genome. The objective is to reconstruct as much as we possibly can, but that largely depends on both how many descendants our ancestors have, and how many of those descendants have DNA tested. No matter how far the technology advances, if your second great-grandparents only had one child there is no way you can ever fully reconstruct their genomes. For ancestors with a large number of descendants, however, it may be possible to reconstruct all or, more realistically, a significant proportion. Rising database numbers will, once again, be essential to this endeavour. The more descendants of the ancestors we wish to reconstruct that test, the more of their DNA we will have to work with and the easier it will become to rebuild their genomes.

Back in 2014 Ancestry experimented with reconstructing the genome of a particular man and his two wives who lived over 200 years ago. David Speegle was a perfect subject for such a study as he fathered twenty-five children with wives Winifred Crawford and Nancy Garren. Using their DNA Circles feature Ancestry identified that a large number of their descendants (stemming from their 150 grandchildren) had already tested. Approximately 50% of the genomes of David, Winifred and Nancy were reconstructed during this study and it is easy to see how useful this could be if replicated across many other ancestors or ancestral couples. It was also determined that one of the three passed down the gene for blue eyes and male-pattern baldness to their descendants. The potential to find out which genes specific ancestors passed down to us could be a fascinating development.

Another interesting and successful attempt to reconstruct a genome was publicised recently when a large portion of the DNA of Iceland's first known black man, Hans Jonatan, was recreated via his living descendants. 38% of his maternal African side was stitched together using segments from 182 of his descendants.

It is likely that more sophisticated tools will be developed in the coming years to assist in the reconstruction of ancestral genomes and convert them into a format compatible with the major testing companies or third-party tools. GEDmatch already provides a Tier 1 tool, named Lazarus, which fulfils this function to a certain extent, but it has a number of limitations. If the eventual outcome could be the existence of virtual kits for long-deceased ancestors in the commercial databases, that would be a game-changer for using DNA for genealogy and breaking down brick walls further back in time, as it would circumvent the current 5–7 generation limitation of autosomal DNA.

We can start reconstructing our ancestors right now by testing as many of their descendants, particularly older generation relatives, as possible, but the ways of going about this will become more sophisticated and perhaps even automated over time.

DNA-only ancestors

There are many places in the world where a dearth of records renders tracing family trees past a particular date almost impossible, yet DNA from our mystery distant ancestors can be traced. We can call these ancestors 'DNA-only ancestors' and over time we might find a place for them on our trees. It is perfectly plausible that we could know basic information about DNA-only ancestors and create simple identifiers for them e.g. 'fifth great-grandfather Leonard lived in Ireland during the early to mid-1700s and had several children including fourth great-grandfather Jeremiah'. Despite the fact there is no documentation in existence that can provide an actual name for fifth great-grandfather Leonard, I could add him to my tree and map DNA segments back to him, especially if DNA helps me identify his other children and their descendants.

DNA phenotyping

DNA phenotyping is the prediction of physical appearance and biogeographical ancestry using DNA alone. This would have seemed like science fiction a few years ago, but it is actually coming to pass right now and in the future could be used to reconstruct the facial features and traits of our ancestors. Perhaps in time we will even be using these techniques in conjunction with reconstructed ancestral genomes we have built ourselves. It is already possible to predict eye colour, skin colour, hair colour, facial structure, freckles and ancestry composition, although the jury is out on the overall accuracy of this technology.

A forensics company named Parabon Nanolabs is currently at the forefront of this field and offers the Parabon Snapshot advanced DNA

Analysis service, which has been used to create 3D facial reconstructions of both perpetrators and victims using crime scene DNA. Just recently a 3D photo-fit Parabon created of a suspect in a murder case helped identify the offender.

This kind of DNA technology has also been used in high-profile ancient DNA cases like Cheddar Man, Richard III and a soldier from the Battle of Dunbar. Not only were the latter's facial features reconstructed, but it was also possible to work out that he had lived in south-west Scotland in the 1630s and had gone through periods of poor nutrition in his childhood.

These DNA techniques are almost certainly going to become a new aspect of genetic genealogy and, in time, regular consumers may be able to obtain digital 3D facial reconstructions for their ancestors. This would be especially interesting for those who lived prior to photography or for whom there are no surviving photographs.

It may not just be the appearance of our ancestors we will be able to predict in the future though – we may be able to learn about other traits and which ancestors we inherited these traits from. This would enable us to build up a more complete picture of our ancestors from their DNA and learn more about ourselves in the process.

This cutting-edge technology is bound to improve and evolve over time with more accurate facial reconstructions and better trait predictions for both ourselves and our ancestors. It will be very interesting to see how it affects DNA testing and the future of genetic genealogy.

Deeper testing

Mitochondrial DNA can now be fully sequenced. Test-takers who have fully sequenced their mtDNA have no new mutations to find and progress can only be made by obtaining closer matches, to get a better understanding of the geographical distribution of one's 'close' relatives.

Y-DNA tests are still getting deeper (see p231-2), but the increasing uptake of sequencing tests is providing the most significant improvements. These create branches (sub-clades) in the Y-DNA family tree progressively closer to the present, allowing more recent ancestry to be explored. We call this 'closing the genetic-genealogical gap'.

On average, the database size has to double before a person finds a match closer than their present closest relation. For Y-DNA or mtDNA, this step typically represents a relationship only a few centuries closer to the present. The genetic-genealogical gap is typically 1,000–3,000 years for most people, so closing it completely may take a long time.

Unlike mtDNA, there are still unread sections of Y-DNA. Current high-definition tests (e.g. Family Tree DNA's Big Y-700) cannot estimate the age at which two people are related to much better than a factor of about two (e.g. between 1,000 and 2,000 years ago). Combining many tests gives slightly better results. A growing fraction of Y-DNA test-takers need advances in technology to find answers more precisely than this.

The potential for new and cheaper tests

With mt-DNA fully sequenced, new technologies are limited to autosomal and Y-DNA. In all tests, we can hope for a reduction in price. Once the sizeable outlay of machinery costs is recovered, the fundamental cost of tests is limited by the staff expense of running and analysing tests, plus the effective 'rent' for the machine's bench space. Many people will pay US$100, but only a small fraction will pay US$500 or more for autosomal or Y-DNA sequencing tests. So the current focus is on making the existing sequencing tests cheaper.

The market for whole genome sequencing (WGS) is driven largely by the medical information in these tests. Genealogy is a secondary priority. Very little has so far been made of the inheritance of autosomal SNPs, and we could see this as a major emerging facet of autosomal DNA research once enough WGS tests are collected.

Improving tests requires either increasing read depth, by effectively repeating the same test more times, or by increasing read length through new technologies. WGS tests can now be bought with between 4x and 60x read depth, and reads of 150 to 250 base pairs. However, for genealogical relationships closer to the present, people may ultimately have to look towards deeper Y-DNA testing.

The Y chromosome has a highly repetitive structure and strong similarities between itself and other chromosomes: it is the length of the reads which currently limits how much of the chromosome can be read. Full Genomes Corp's YElite 2.1 test, WGS tests and Family Tree DNA's Big Y-700 test currently test around 14 million base pairs (Mbp), reaching one mutation per ninety years. Full Genomes Corp is trialling long-read technologies giving 20 Mbp (one mutation every sixty years), but at a price of around $3,000. The full Y-DNA sequence is about 57 million base pairs long. Depending on the mutation rate in these regions, we may ultimately be able to attain one mutation every twenty years.

Simultaneously, complex mutations are now being routinely extracted from sequencing tests. Read length also dictates the ability to extract complex mutations, with at least 700 Y-STRs being extractable from most NGS tests, including Big Y and Y Elite but even Family Tree DNA's Big Y-700 test holds around 750 Y-STRs. Initial results indicate at least 6,000 Y-STRs can be read from longer read tests. Insertions, deletions and multi-nucleotide polymorphisms can increasingly be extracted, meaning that these rarer but still useful mutations can be more generally used in determining the closeness and accuracy of relationships.

If a combination of Y-STR plus Y-SNP data from sequencing tests becomes *de rigeur*, we will approach a situation where one mutation occurs roughly every generation. If long-read technology becomes more standard, we may see typically more than one mutation per generation. If it becomes affordable, we can start to probe individual generations of families, putting together a real family tree in the absence of complete paper records. However, this still appears financially prohibitive for at least several years into the future. Identifying a specific generation will also still rely on finding genetic distances between test-takers on two surviving lines (e.g. descendants of two brothers for Y-DNA tests), which becomes increasingly unlikely as generations pass and lines die out.

Input from the academic community
Major advances can be expected from studies like the 100,000 Genomes project. Meanwhile, existing datasets such as the People of the British Isles project and the Irish DNA Atlas project have yet to be fully exploited. Commercial companies like Living DNA are enlarging their comparison database by testing populations outside Europe.

Many academic datasets come with additional privacy restrictions, because the participants have not given their consent for individual results to be published. Nevertheless, they will provide results including very detailed population distributions and Y-DNA and mtDNA haplogroup trees.

In ancient DNA, the 1000 Ancient Genomes project (Uppsala University, funded to 2021), should greatly expand the number of ancient genomes we have for comparison, while prominent researchers such as David Reich are known to have further data. This will more accurately tie individual Y-DNA and mtDNA haplogroups to specific historical periods and cultures, and better map the migrations that have led to different autosomal admixtures.

Summary

Genetic genealogy will likely never solve some problems and will never replace traditional genealogy. Getting names onto a family tree will always rely on the written record that provides that name. With few exceptions, confidently putting people onto a family tree cannot be done with genetic genealogy alone.

The small but significant risk of dictats from litigation-averse testing companies, or poorly considered, or poorly implemented privacy laws, could restrict or effectively halt the sharing of information, but can be avoided by responsible action within the community.

However, the gap between what traditional and genetic genealogy can provide is closing, meaning the two fields are becoming increasingly inseparable. Testing databases are growing and, at least for autosomal and Y-DNA, tests are becoming cheaper and more detailed in their results. More people are starting to see genealogical mysteries unravelled that would never have previously been possible. The future of genetic genealogy remains bright: never in our history have our ancestors been able to speak to us so clearly.

Glossary

Admixture estimates – estimates of the percentages of individuals' early ancestors who came from specific geographical areas.

Allele – a genetic value that can exist at a specific location in a DNA sequence and is displayed in an ancestral (i.e. on a reference sequence) or variant state. The variant state may also be referred to as *derived* or *mutated* (cf. marker).

Ancestral haplotype – the haplotype of an ancestor, normally deduced from the haplotypes of a number of descendants who have taken a DNA test.

Ancient DNA (aDNA) – degraded DNA from human or animal remains dating from ancient times to the recent past.

Autosomal DNA (atDNA) – DNA contained in the 22 non-sex chromosomes.

Back mutation – a mutation in which a SNP or STR value reverts to a previous value.

BAM file (Binary Alignment Map file) – a large file containing the fullest amount of data available from a Next Generation Sequencing (NGS) test: all the positions read in the test, the number of reads for each and the alignment of the reads against the reference sequence

Base – SEE nucleotide base

Base pair (bp) – a pair of nucleotide bases forming a rung on the double helix found in DNA, consisting of either adenine and thymine (A and T), or cytosine and guanine (C and G).

Callable reads – positions on the genome which can be reliably read in a genetic test.

CentiMorgan (cM) – a value assigned to a segment of DNA indicating the probability that it will recombine. It is not a linear measurement of the segment.

Centromere – a constricted area of a chromosome where the arms of the chromosome are linked.

Chromosome – a structure consisting of nucleotide bases and proteins.

Humans have 46 of these arranged as 23 pairs, contained in the nucleus of each cell.

Chromosome browser – a tool showing a graphic illustration of segments of DNA shared between two or more test takers.

Chromosome mapping – the process of identifying a specific ancestor or ancestral couple from whom a test taker has inherited specific segments of DNA.

Coding region – a region of mtDNA containing genes. It has a slower mutation rate than the control region.

Control region – a region of mtDNA including hypervariable control regions 1 and 2 (HVR1 and 2) which are tested in genealogy DNA testing. This region has a faster mutation rate than the coding region.

Convergence – the illusion that two haplotypes are closely related because they resemble each other while in fact they are only distantly related, due to back mutation or parallel mutation of STRs.

Coverage (for Y-SNP testing) – this can refer to length coverage, or depth coverage. Length coverage refers to how much of the Y sequence is read, expressed as a number of base pairs, e.g. 13.9 million. Depth coverage refers to the number of times a base pair is read, e.g. 20x.

Daughtering out – the extinction of unbroken male lines due to males producing daughters but no sons.

Divergence – the illusion that two haplotypes are distantly related because they do not resemble each other while in fact they are more closely related, due to multiple mutations.

DNA – deoxyribonucleic acid – a molecule carrying all the genetic instructions which govern all living organisms.

DNA fingerprinting – the use of microsatellites (STR markers) to assist in identifying individuals from their DNA. This technique is used in crime scene investigations and forms the foundation on which genetic genealogy is based.

DNA phenotyping – the prediction of physical appearance and biogeographical ancestry using DNA alone.

Endogamy – the practice of groups of people marrying within the same ethnic, cultural, social or religious circles.

Ethnicity estimates – SEE Admixture estimates

False negatives – genealogically significant segments of DNA that do not show up as a match due to an error in the testing process e.g. miscalls or no calls.

False positives – segments of DNA giving the appearance of being genealogically significant, but which have not in fact been inherited from a specific ancestor. They may be common to a particular community stretching back before a genealogical timeframe or caused by a mixture of segments from both parents being read as a single segment.

Fully identical region (FIR) – a segment of DNA that is shared on both copies of a chromosome.

Genetic distance (GD) – the count of the number of mutational steps between different haplotypes.

Genetic genealogy – the application of DNA testing to genealogical research.

Half identical region (HIR) – a segment of DNA shared on just one of the two copies of a chromosome.

Haplogroup – a major genetic grouping defined by at least one SNP mutation occurring at a known location on the Y-chromosome or in mtDNA.

Haplotree (also known as a phylogenetic tree) – a tree of haplogroups and their subdivisions.

Haplotype – a list of the number of Y-STR repeats at a number of locations on the Y chromosome.

Heteroplasmy – the coexistence of two strains of mtDNA in one individual that differ from one another.

Human genome – the whole set of human nucleic acid sequences encoded as DNA, including both genes which code for proteins and non-coding DNA.

Hypervariable region (HVR1 and HVR2) – specific named regions within the control region of mtDNA which are used in genealogy DNA testing. They have a faster mutation rate than the coding region.

Identical by chance (IBC) – a segment of DNA which is IBC is not inherited from a single ancestor, but is identical as a result of a mixture of segments from both parents being read as a single segment.

Identical by descent (IBD) – a segment of DNA is IBD if it has been inherited from a single ancestor.

Identical by population (IBP) – segments of DNA which are IBP are common to a group of people from the same area. They are usually older segments that stretch beyond a genealogical timeframe.

Identical by state (IBS) – segments of DNA which are IBS can be either population segments (identical by population) or false segments (identical by chance).

In common with (ICW) – test-takers who share the same segment(s) of DNA with both an initial test-taker and another match, but not necessarily with one another.

Inbetweener – a test-taker whose result is compared to another test-taker from a specific lineage in an attempt to discover whether the lineage has experienced any recent Y-STR mutations which might increase the genetic distance between individuals.

Infinite allele mutation model – a method of counting the differences between haplotypes in order to establish the genetic distance (GD). It regards each difference between an STR value as the result of one mutational event, no matter what the numerical difference is between the two numerical values. The total of these gives the genetic distance.

MAP (mis-attributed paternity) – the individual recognised as the parent is not the true biological parent. (cf. MPE, NPE)

Marker – often used to refer to the locations on a chromosome read in a test, which may display variant values (cf. allele). In population genomics, the term is usually applied to known variants that are associated with a population, trait or condition.

MDKA (Most Distant Known Ancestor) – the earliest ancestor of an individual who can be identified.

Mitochondrial DNA (mtDNA) – a type of DNA found in the mitochondria of a cell, outwith the cell nucleus. It is inherited by all children from their mothers, but can only be passed on by daughters.

Modal haplotype – the haplotype with the most common value for each marker based on a group of closely connected men.

MPE (misattributed parentage event) – the individual recognised as the parent is not the true biological parent. (cf. MAP, NPE)

MRCA (Most Recent Common Ancestor) – the most recent common ancestor shared by two test-takers in a particular line of descent, from whom shared DNA is inherited. May be more recent than the MDKA (cf.).

Mutation – a change in DNA. The most commonly used mutations in genetic genealogy are STR mutations and SNP mutations.

Named variants (known SNPs) – nucleotide bases having different values to those of the reference sequence used for comparison, which have been recognised as stable SNPs and named.

Next generation sequencing (NGS) – a powerful and fast process of reading sequences of DNA which facilitates the discovery of variants.

No calls – locations at which a definite result could not be established by a DNA test.

Non identical region (NIR) – an area of atDNA which does not match another test-taker on either copy of the chromosome.

Non-matching variants – variants that are found in only one of two test results undergoing comparison, some of which may be novel (cf.) or private variants.

Novel variants (cf to unnamed variants) – nucleotide bases having different values to those of the reference sequence used for comparison, which at present are only known to have been found in one test-taker. Also known as private SNPs.

NPE (non-paternity event / not the parent expected) – the individual recognised as the parent is not the true biological parent. (cf. MAP, MPE)

Nuclear DNA – the DNA present in the nucleus of the cell, contained in the 23 chromosome pairs (cf. mitochondrial DNA)

Nucleotide base – DNA has four nucleotide bases, adenine, cystosine, guanine and thymine, which always pair up in the same way, A with T and C with G. Each of these base pairs forms a rung of the ladder found in DNA's double helix structures.

Off-modal markers – STR markers which differ from the most commonly found values.

Palindromes – special sequences of the Y-chromosome, in which long sequences are repeated more or less exactly. The position of variants occurring in these regions is unverifiable and one sequence may be overwritten by another, thereby deleting a variant that had occurred.

Parallel mutation – when two branches separately descending from the same ancestor each mutate the same way on different occasions, giving the impression of a single branch defined by a single mutation.

Pedigree collapse – this occurs when marriages take place between cousins, so reducing the number of an individual's ancestors.

Phasing – the process of identifying which segments of atDNA are inherited from the mother and which from the father.

Phylogenetic tree (also known as a haplotree) – a tree of haplogroups and their subdivisions.

Pile-up regions (also known as excess IBD sharing) – regions in chromosomes where a large number of test-takers all match each other on the same segment of DNA but no common ancestors can be identified between them. Pile-ups are generally relatively small in cM size and are likely to be population-based segments.

Read depth (also known as depth coverage) – refers to the number of times a base pair is read, e.g. 20x.

Read length (also known as length coverage) – refers to how much of the Y sequence is read, expressed as a number of base pairs, e.g. 13.9 million.

Recombination – the process by which atDNA is divided up and exchanged between pairs of chromosomes at each successive generation.

Reconstructed Sapiens Reference Sequence (RSRS) – one of the standard reference sequences with which mtDNA is compared, to identify mutations. It is an attempt to reconstruct the earliest full genome mtDNA sequence.

Reference sequence – a standardised sequence of the human genome to which test results are compared in discovery of variants. The sequence in use since 2013 is GRCh38 (Genome Reference Consortium human no. 38), also referred to as hg38.

Revised Cambridge Reference Sequence (rCRS) – one of the standard reference sequences with which mtDNA is compared, to identify mutations. It is a revised and corrected version of the original sequence based on the mtDNA of a recent European woman.

Sanger sequencing – a process for reading DNA developed by Frederick Sanger in the 1970s, which allows short fragments of DNA to be copied and sequenced. It is an efficient method for identifying a single variant in a sequence, but is too slow and expensive to apply to whole chromosomes, for which next generation sequencing (cf.) is better suited.

Signature STRs – off-modal STRs shared by a group of test-takers which can provide a distinctive identification for a specific lineage.

SNP (single nucleotide polymorphism) – a mutation of one of the four nucleotide bases.

Stepwise mutation model – a method of counting the differences between haplotypes in order to establish the genetic distance (GD). It counts the numerical difference between each STR value, regarding these as the number of mutational events. The total of these gives the genetic distance.

Sticky segments – DNA segments of significant size which have been inherited down a considerable number of generations without the expected amount of recombination.

STR (short tandem repeat) – the number of times a motif, consisting of a series of nucleotide bases, has been repeated at a specific location on a chromosome.

Subclade (also known as a subhaplogroup) – a subdivision of a haplogroup.

Subhaplogroup (also known as a subclade) – a subdivision of a haplogroup.

TMRCA (Time to Most Recent Common Ancestor) – the length of time to the birth of the most recent ancestor whom two or more individuals are descended from.

Triangulation – in Y testing, this occurs when three or more closely matching haplotypes allow an allele's ancestral value to be ascertained (on the assumption that the non-matching allele is more likely to be the variant form). In autosomal testing, it is a process to confirm whether three people with a half-identical match in the same chromosome pair all share exactly the same segment on the same chromosome within the pair.

Unnamed variants (cf to novel variants) – nucleotide bases having different values to those of the reference sequence used for comparison, which have not been recognised as stable SNPs and named. They are listed by the number of their location.

VCF (Variant Call File) – file type that lists the variants found in the BAM file for a Next Generation Sequencing test.

Visual phasing – an advanced technique using atDNA test results from ideally three full siblings, to identify which segments of DNA were inherited from which of their four grandparents.

Whole genome sequence (WGS) tests – tests which use Next Generation Sequencing techniques to read a complete genome.

X-chromosome DNA – DNA found in the X-chromosome, one of the sex chromosomes (chromosome 23).

Y-chromosome DNA – DNA found in the Y-chromosome, one of the sex chromosomes (chromosome 23). It is only carried by males.

Further Reading

Chapter 1
Druze DNA Project
https://www.familytreedna.com/groups/druze/about/background

Chapter 2
Bettinger, Blaine. (2014) Announcing the creation of genetic genealogy standards. *The Genetic Genealogist.*
https://thegeneticgenealogist.com/2014/05/12/announcing-creation-genetic-genealogy-standards/
Bettinger, Blaine. (2015) Announcing the Genetic Genealogy Standards. *The Genetic Genealogist.*
https://thegeneticgenealogist.com/2015/01/10/announcing-genetic-genealogy-standards/
Boddy, Janet, Neumann, Tim, Jennings, Sean, et al. Key ethics principles. In: *The Research Ethics Guidebook – a resource for social scientists.* Swindon: Economic and Social Research Council.
http://www.ethicsguidebook.ac.uk/Key-ethics-principles-15
Eidelman, Vera. (2018) Opinion: The creepy, dark side of DNA databases. *Washington Post.* 8 May. Opinions
https://www.washingtonpost.com/opinions/the-creepy-dark-side-of-dna-databases/2018/05/08/279e9c2c-5230-11e8-abd8-265bd07a9859_story.html
GEDmatch.com. (2018) *Terms of Service and Privacy Policy.* Revised May 20, 2018. https://www.gedmatch.com/tos.htm
Genetic Genealogy Standards Committee. *Genetic Genealogy Standards.* http://www.geneticgenealogystandards.com/
ISOGG. ISOGG project administrator guidelines. In: *ISOGG wiki.*
https://isogg.org/wiki/ISOGG_Project_Administrator_Guidelines
ISOGG. Project consent forms. In: *ISOGG wiki.*
https://isogg.org/wiki/Project_consent_forms
Jouvenal, Justin. (2018) To find alleged Golden State Killer, investigators first found his great-great-great-grandparents. *Washington Post.* 30 April. Public Safety

https://www.washingtonpost.com/local/public-safety/to-find-alleged-golden-state-killer-investigators-first-found-his-great-great-great-grandparents/2018/04/30/3c865fe7-dfcc-4a0e-b6b2-0be c548d501f_story.html
Judicial Committee of the Privy Council (UK). (2016) *Judgment In the matter of the Baronetcy of Pringle of Stichill*. Trinity Term, Privy Council Reference No 0079 of 2015 Trinity Term. London: Judicial Committee of the Privy Council.
https://www.jcpc.uk/cases/docs/jcpc-2015-0079-judgment.pdf
Pringle, James. *The Pringle Surname DNA Project.*
http://www.jamespringle.co.uk/html/dna_project.html
Rainie, Lee & Duggan, Maeve. (2016) *Privacy and Information Sharing*. Washington, DC: Pew Research Center.
http://www.pewinternet.org/2016/01/14/2016/Privacy-and-Information-Sharing/
Schmidt, Samantha. (2018) Did man serve 39 years for slayings actually committed by 'Golden State Killer' suspect? *Washington Post*. 30 April. Morning Mix
https://www.washingtonpost.com/news/morning-mix/wp/2018/04/30/did-man-serve-39-years-for-slayings-actually-committed-by-golden-state-killer-suspect/
Temkin, Jennifer, Prainsack, Barbara, & Moore, Carol. (2018) Biometrics & Forensics Ethics Group: ethical principles. London: GOV.UK. https://www.gov.uk/government/publications/ethical-principles-biometrics-and-forensics-ethics-group

Chapter 4

ISOGG. Autosomal DNA tools. In: *ISOGG wiki*.
https://isogg.org/wiki/Autosomal_DNA_tools
ISOGG. Visual phasing. In: *ISOGG wiki*.
https://isogg.org/wiki/Visual_phasing
Visual Phasing Working Group.
https://www.facebook.com/groups/visualphasing

Chapter 5

Ardui, Simon, Ameur, Adam, Vermeesch, Joris R., et al. (2018) Single molecule real-time (SMRT) sequencing comes of age: applications and utilities for medical diagnostics. *Nucleic acids research*. 46 (5). pp. 2159–2168. https://academic.oup.com/nar/article/46/5/2159/4833218

Family Tree DNA. *Y-DNA – Standard Y-STR Values Page*. https://www.familytreedna.com/learn/user-guide/y-dna-myftdna/y-str-results-page/

Heather, James M. & Chain, Benjamin. (2016) The sequence of sequencers: the history of sequencing DNA. *Genomics*. 107 (1). pp. 1–8. https://www.sciencedirect.com/science/article/pii/S0888754315300410

Jacobs, Christopher. (2018) *The Jacob Surname YDNA Project: Descendants of John Jacob, Sr. of South River Hundred, Maryland Province*. https://www.familytreedna.com/groups/jacobs/about/background

Kane, James. (2017) WGS über Alles? *Irish Type 2 – Kane*. July 15. http://www.it2kane.org/category/snp-testing/

Larkin, Leah. (2019) DNA tests. *The DNA Geek*. http://thednageek.com/dna-tests/

Li, Runsheng, Hsieh, Chia-Ling, Young, Amanda, et al. (2015) Illumina synthetic long read sequencing allows recovery of missing sequences even in the "finished" C. elegans genome. *Nature. Scientific reports*. 5, article no. 10814. https://www.nature.com/articles/srep10814

Skaletsky, Helen, Kuroda-Kawaguchi, Tomoko, Minx, Patrick J., et al. (2003) The male-specific region of the human Y chromosome is a mosaic of discrete sequence classes. *Nature*. 423 (6942). pp. 825–837. http://www.nature.com/nature/journal/v423/n6942/full/nature01722.html

University of Strathclyde. Genealogical Studies Postgraduate Programme. (2014) *Bannockburn Genetic Genealogy Project*. https://www.stewartsociety.org/bannockburn-genetic-genealogy-project.cfm

Y Chromosome Consortium. (2002) A nomenclature system for the tree of human Y-chromosomal binary haplogroups. *Genome research*. 12 (2). pp. 339–348. http://genome.cshlp.org/content/12/2/339.short

Chapter 6

Russell, Judy G. (2017) The myth of the GD0. *The legal genealogist*. https://www.legalgenealogist.com/2017/11/26/the-myth-of-the-gd0/

Chapter 8

Pomery, Chris. (2009) The advantages of a dual DNA/documentary approach to reconstruct the family trees of a surname. *Journal of genetic genealogy*. 5 (2). pp. 86–95.
http://www.jogg.info/52/files/Pomery.htm
Pomery, Chris. (2010) Defining a methodology to reconstruct the family trees of a surname within a DNA/documentary dual approach project. *Journal of genetic genealogy*. 6 (1).
http://www.jogg.info/62/files/Pomery.pdf

Chapter 9

Bettinger, Blaine and Perl, Jonny. (2018) The Shared cM Project – Version 4.0. *DNAPainter*. https://dnapainter.com/tools/sharedcmv4
DNAPainter Probability Test Tool: https://dnapainter.com/tools/prob2
GEDmatch: https://www.gedmatch.com
Larkin, Leah. (2018) Science the heck out of your DNA (Parts 1-7). *The DNA Geek*. http://thednageek.com/science-the-heck-out-of-your-dna-part-1/
Perl, Jonny, Larkin, Leah and Millard, Andrew. (2018) Probability Test Tool v.0.2. *DNAPainter*. https://dnapainter.com/tools/prob2

Chapter 10

Advisory Panel on the Archaeology of Burials in England. (2013) *Science and the dead: a guideline for the destructive sampling of archaeological human remains for scientific analysis*. Swindon: English Heritage.
http://www.archaeologyuk.org/apabe/pdf/Science_and_the_Dead.pdf
Ashdown-Hill, John. (2006) Alive and well in Canada: the Mitochondrial DNA of Richard III. *The Ricardian*. 16. pp. 1–14.
http://www.richardiii.net/downloads/Ricardian/2006_vol16_ashdown_hill_alive_canada.pdf
Ashdown-Hill, John. (2017) The problems of Richard III's Y chromosome; the problems relating to the burials at Clare Priory, and the problems of working with Historic England. *Nerdalicious*.
http://nerdalicious.com.au/history/the-problems-of-richard-iiis-y-chromosome-the-problems-relating-to-the-burials-at-clare-priory-and-the-problems-of-working-with-historic-england/

Augenstein, Seth. (2018) 'Buck Skin Girl' case break is success of new DNA Doe Project. *Forensic magazine*. 04/16/2018. https://www.forensicmag.com/news/2018/04/buck-skin-girl-case-break-success-new-dna-doe-project

Bates, Clare. (2018) Who were my parents – and why was I left on a hillside to die? *BBC News. Stories*. 19 March. http://www.bbc.co.uk/news/stories-43420678

Cassidy, Lara M., Martiniano, Rui, Murphy, Eileen M., et al. (2016) Neolithic and Bronze Age migration to Ireland and establishment of the insular Atlantic genome. *Proceedings of the National Academy of Sciences of the United States of America*. 113 (2). pp. 368–373. http://www.pnas.org/content/113/2/368

Cooper, Alan and Poinar, Hendrik N. (2000) Ancient DNA: do it right or not at all. *Science*. 289 (5482). p. 1139. http://www.academia.edu/861833/Ancient_DNA_do_it_right_or_no t_at_all

Cox, Margaret & Jones, Peter. (2014) Ethical considerations in the use of DNA as a contribution toward the determination of identification in historic cases: considerations from the Western front. *New genetics and society*. 33 (3). pp. 295–312. http://dx.doi.org/10.1080/14636778.2014.946987

Defence Connect. *Australian soldiers identified from Battle of Fromelles*. https://www.defenceconnect.com.au/key-enablers/2126-australian-soldiers-identified-from-battle-of-fromelles

Englezos, Lambis. (2008) *My quest to find the missing*. Wartime magazine. 44. https://www.awm.gov.au/wartime/44/page16_englezos

Ermini, Luca, Olivieri, Cristina, Rizzi, Ermanno, et al. (2008) Complete mitochondrial genome sequence of the Tyrolean Iceman. *Current biology*. 18 (21). pp. 1687–1693. http://www.sciencedirect.com/science/article/pii/S0960982208012542

Green, Richard E., Krause, Johannes, Briggs, Adrian W., et al. (2010) A draft sequence of the Neandertal genome. *Science*. 328, issue 5979. pp. 710–722. http://science.sciencemag.org/content/328/5979/710

Jones, Martin. (2016) *Unlocking the past: how archaeologists are rewriting human history with ancient DNA*. Revised & updated edition. New York: Arcade Publishing.

Kennedy, Maev and Foxhall, Lin. (2015) The *bones of a King: Richard III rediscovered*. Chichester: John Wiley & Sons Inc.

King, Turi E., Fortes, Gloria Gonzalez, Balaresque, Patricia, et al. (2014) Identification of the remains of King Richard III. *Nature communications*. 5. p. 5631.
http://www.nature.com/ncomms/2014/141202/ncomms6631/full/nc omms6631.html

Levenick, Denise May. (2018) How to preserve and test old letters for Grandma's DNA. *The Family Curator*. April 19.
https://thefamilycurator.com/how-to-preserve-and-test-old-letters-for-grandmas-dna/

Manco, Jean. (2015) *Ancestral journeys: the peopling of Europe from the first venturers to the Vikings*. 2nd ed. London: Thames and Hudson.

Marciniak, Stephanie, Klunk, Jennifer, Devault, Alison, et al. (2015) Ancient human genomics: the methodology behind reconstructing evolutionary pathways. *Journal of human evolution*. 79, Special issue: Ancient DNA and Human Evolution. pp. 21–34.
http://www.sciencedirect.com/science/article/pii/S0047248414002693

Mulligan, Connie J. (2005) Isolation and analysis of DNA from archaeological, clinical, and natural history specimens. *Methods in enzymology*. 395 pp. 87–103.
http://www.sciencedirect.com/science/article/pii/S0076687905950076

Noonan, James P., Hofreiter, Michael, Smith, Doug, et al. (2005) Genomic sequencing of pleistocene cave bears. *Science*. 309, issue 5734. pp. 597–599.
http://science.sciencemag.org/content/309/5734/597

Olalde, Iñigo, Brace, Selina, Allentoft, Morten E., et al. (2017) The Beaker phenomenon and the genomic transformation of Northwest Europe. *bioRxiv*. p. 135962.
http://biorxiv.org/content/early/2017/05/09/135962

Oxford Archaeology. *Fromelles First World War mass graves*.
https://oxfordarchaeology.com/archaeology-case-studies/425-fromelles-first-world-war-mass-graves

Pääbo, Svante. (2014) *Neanderthal man: in search of lost genomes*. Philadelphia: Basic Books.

Poinar, Hendrik N., Schwarz, Carsten, Qi, Ji, et al. (2005) Metagenomics to paleogenomics: large-scale sequencing of mammoth DNA. *Science*. 311, issue 5759. pp. 392-394. http://science.sciencemag.org/content/early/2005/12/20/science.112 3360

Reich, David. (2018) *Who we are and how we got here: ancient DNA and the new science of the human past.* Oxford: Oxford University Press.

Reich, David, Green, Richard E., Kircher, Martin, et al. (2010) Genetic history of an archaic hominin group from Denisova Cave in Siberia. *Nature*. 468 (7327). pp. 1053–1060. https://www.nature.com/nature/journal/v468/n7327/full/nature0971 0.html

Richard III Society. Looking for Richard. http://www.richardiii.net/leicester_dig.php

Rincon, Paul. (2015) DNA sheds light on Irish origins. *BBC News. Science & Environment*. 28 December. http://www.bbc.co.uk/news/science-environment-35179269

Index